RENAULT 8, 10, 1100, 1962-72 AUTOBOOK

Workshop Manual for
Renault R8 1962-65
Renault 8 1965-72
Renault 8S 1968-72
Renault 1100 1964-69
Renaul R10 1967-69
Renault 10 1969-72

by

Kenneth Ball G I Mech E

and the

Autopress team of Technical Writers

AUTOPRESS LTD   GOLDEN LANE   BRIGHTON   BN1 2QJ   ENGLAND

The AUTOBOOK series of Workshop Manuals covers the majority of British and Continental motor cars.

For a full list see the back of this manual.

CONTENTS

Introduction

Acknowledgement

ISBN 0 85147 319 9

First Edition   1970

Second Edition, fully revised   1971

Third Edition, fully revised   1972

Fourth Edition, fully revised   1972

© Autopress Ltd 1972

Printed in Brighton England for Autopress Ltd by G Beard & Son Ltd

ACKNOWLEDGEMENT

My thanks are due to Renault Ltd for their unstinted co-operation and also for supplying data and illustrations.

I am also grateful to a considerable number of owners who have discussed their cars at length and many of whose suggestions have been included in this manual.

Kenneth Ball G I Mech E
Associate Member Guild of Motoring Writers

Ditchling Sussex England.

INTRODUCTION

This do-it-yourself Workshop Manual has been specially written for the owner who wishes to maintain his car in first class condition and to carry out his own servicing and repairs. Considerable savings on garage charges can be made, and one can drive in safety and confidence knowing the work has been done properly.

Comprehensive step-by-step instructions and illustrations are given on all dismantling, overhauling and assembling operations. Certain assemblies require the use of expensive special tools, the purchase of which would be unjustified. In these cases information is included but the reader is recommended to hand the unit to the agent for attention.

Throughout the Manual hints and tips are included which will be found invaluable, and there is an easy to follow fault diagnosis at the end of each chapter.

Whilst every care has been taken to ensure correctness of information it is obviously not possible to guarantee complete freedom from errors or to accept liability arising from such errors or omissions.

Instructions may refer to the righthand or lefthand sides of the vehicle or the components. These are the same as the righthand or lefthand of an observer standing behind the car and looking forward.

CHAPTER 1

THE ENGINE

1:1 Description

Full details of bore, stroke and capacity of the various engines covered by this manual are given in **Technical Data**, together with a great deal of further information. The engine is installed in the rear of the car directly behind the transmission, with the block running in line with the car.

Though the capacities vary the engine constructional details are very similar on all the models covered by this manual. The design follows the usual Renault principles and extensive use is made of light-alloy castings. An external view of the type 810 engine (1289 cc) is shown in **FIG 1:1** and sectioned views of the 689 engine are shown in **FIG 1:2**.

The crankshaft runs in five main bearings, using renewable steel-backed shells. Thrust and end float are controlled by renewable thrust washers. Note that the cylinder and main bearing nearest the flywheel is counted as number 1. The four connecting rods rotate about the crankshaft crankpins using renewable steel-backed bearing shells. Oil seals are fitted at either end of the crankshaft to prevent oil from leaking past. The rear oil seal is in the timing cover and the front oil seal is only

accessible after the clutch and flywheel have been removed. The flywheel is mounted on the front end of the crankshaft whilst at the very rear end is mounted the pulley that drives the water pump and generator.

A timing chain and timing sprocket inside the timing cover at the rear end of the engine transfer the drive from the crankshaft to the camshaft so that the camshaft runs at half engine speed. The valves are then operated from the camshaft through a system of cam followers, push-rods and rocker arms. The camshaft is mounted fully in the crankcase in four bearings and the cam followers also operate in bores in the crankcase.

Gears on the camshaft supply the drive for the distributor and oil pump. The fuel pump, mounted on the side of the crankcase, is also driven from the camshaft.

The pistons slide in renewable wet liners fitted into the cylinder block. The gudgeon pins, which connect the pistons to the little-ends of the connecting rods, are a free fit in the piston but an interference fit in the connecting rod.

All the bearings are lubricated by pressure from the oil pump, the oil being led through internal passages, and a metered supply is fed to the rocker shaft assembly. The

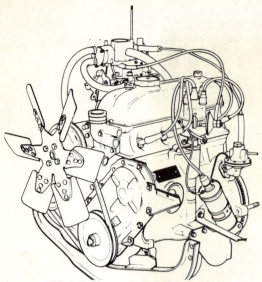

FIG 1:1 External view of the engine

oil from the rocker shaft lubricates the rocker arms and then flows back down to the sump, lubricating the cam followers on the way.

It should be noted that special versions are made for the North American market where emission must be strictly within the limits set by law.

Torque settings and thread repairs:

Various special tools are required for servicing and repairing the engine but the tool that will be required most is a torque spanner. Hire or borrow one, as in the long run it will save a great deal of frustration and possible damage.

Aluminium alloy is used extensively in the construction of the engine and being much softer than steel the threads will strip out very easily. The danger then is that the attachments are not securely tightened, to avoid any danger of overtightening, and they quickly work loose, causing oil leaks or damage.

The torque wrench settings are given for the various attachments in the relevant sections and also in **Technical Data**. All nuts and bolts must have clean threads before they are tightened otherwise dirt will cause the bolt to stick and give a false reading. Usually the bolts are refitted dry, as oil would make the bolt easy to turn and leave it at too high a setting, but in some cases—usually bolts that operate in oil—they are oiled before reassembly. Swill parts in clean fuel to remove dirt and oil and if necessary clean threads with a wire brush.

If the worst does happen and a thread strips, crossthreads, or wears out then the casting can be recovered by fitting Heli-Coil inserts into the damaged thread. This is a specialist operation and may be fairly expensive but at least it will be cheaper than a new casting.

1:2 Removing the engine

The engine can be removed separately, leaving the transmission fitted to the car, or the transmission can be removed leaving the engine in place. Even with the engine

fitted the cylinder head, sump, and timing cover can still be removed. This means that the majority of operations on the engine can be carried out with the engine still fitted. However, to remove the crankshaft or to carry out major repairs the engine should be removed from the car.

If the operator is not a skilled automobile engineer it is suggested that he will find much useful information in the **Hints on Maintenance and Overhaul** section in the **Appendix** at the rear of the manual, and it is advised that he reads it before starting work.

Whenever the car is raised off its wheel make sure that all supports are firm and secure. Serious injury or damage can result if the car falls, so use suitable stands whenever possible.

1 Disconnect the battery before doing anything else. Drain the cooling system (keeping the coolant for re-use if it is fresh), disconnect the hoses, and remove the radiator (see **Chapter 4**). Free the heater hose clips.

2 Disconnect the hose to the air filter and remove the air filter from the carburetter. Disconnect the throttle cable from the bellcrank on the manifolds. Disconnect the fuel pipe at the fuel pump inlet.

3 Disconnect the electrical leads at the starter motor, generator, ignition coil and temperature switch. Label the leads if the colours have faded or if there is any danger of forgetting their correct connections. Take out the three nuts and bolts that secure the starter motor in place and ease out the motor.

4 Disconnect the clamp that secures the silencer (muffler) to the exhaust manifold and remove the silencer. Remove the clutch protecting plate, stiffening bar (if fitted) and then take out the engine floor trays. The attachments of the floor trays with a 689 engine are shown in **FIG 1:3**. Unscrew the bolts that secure the engine to the clutch housing, noting that on some models the upper bolts cannot be pulled out.

5 **Check that the only connections between car and engine now are the engine mountings.** Remove the rocker cover and attach the sling Mot.130, as shown in **FIG 1:4**, and support the weight of the engine with a hoist or tackle. Remove the four bolts that secure the rear crossmember to the mounting pads. Pull the engine rearwards until the gearbox input shaft is clear of the clutch and then lift the engine out of the car.

Refitting:

The engine is refitted in the reverse order of removal. Make sure that the cooling system is filled and bled correctly (see **Chapter 4**) and also make sure that all lubricant levels are correct.

Power unit removal:

The complete power unit, including the engine, transmission and rear suspensions, can be removed as one complete assembly. The assembly comes out from underneath so the car must be raised considerably off the ground.

Carry out the operations 1 to 4 inclusive for removing the engine but do not take out the starter motor bolts or the bolts that secure the engine to the clutch housing.

Raise the rear of the car on suitable stands. Disconnect the clutch cable, gearshift link, speedometer drive cable,

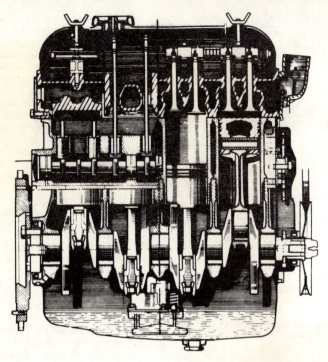

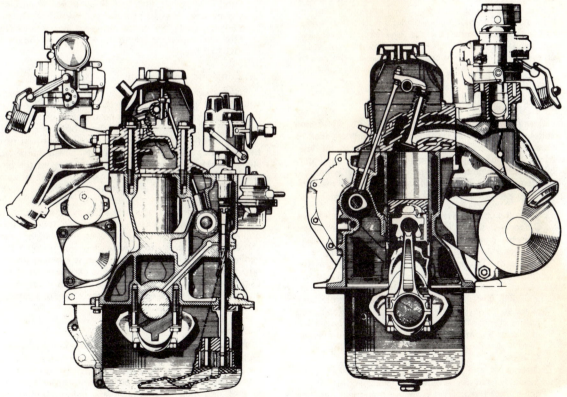

FIG 1:2   Sectioned views of the engine

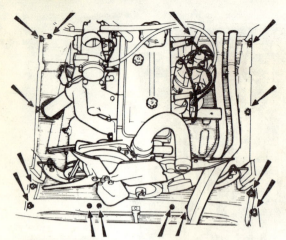

FIG 1:3 The engine compartment floor panels

hydraulic pipe to the brake limiter valve, handbrake cables, suspension tie bar, accelerator cable and the battery cable from its clip.

Support the assembly from underneath. Remove the bolts that secure the suspension front crossmember to the frame side members as well as the bolts that secure the engine crossmember to the mounting pads. Disconnect the mounting at the front of the transmission. Lower the complete assembly down and out of the car, after making sure that there are no connections to hold it.

The assembly is refitted in the reverse order of removal. All adjustments that have been disturbed must be correctly set and coolant and lubricant levels should also be checked. The braking system must be refilled and bled (see **Chapter 11**).

1:3 Removing the cylinder head

The cylinder head can be removed with the engine still fitted in the car. Whenever the cylinder head is removed it is advisable to check the wear in the liner bores. Special gauges are required to do this accurately but a good estimate of the wear can be made by judging the depth of the unworn ridge around the top of the bore.

Removal:

1 Drain the cooling system and disconnect the battery. Disconnect the radiator hoses and the heater hoses from the water pump. Slacken the bolts that secure the generator and press it towards the engine to loosen the fan belt. Remove the fan belt and the cooling fan. On the models fitted with a radiator screen it will be necessary to free the attachments, including electrical lead, and tilt the assembly back as far as it will go. The water pump can be removed before lifting off the cylinder head or it can be left in place so that it remains attached to the cylinder head. Fuller details for this operation are all given in **Chapter 4**.

2 Disconnect the hose and remove the air cleaner assembly from the carburetter. Disconnect the throttle cable from the bellcrank on the manifolds and free the clip that secures the silencer to the exhaust manifold. Disconnect the fuel line at the carburetter float chamber. If desired remove the carburetter and manifolds, though they can be left in place and removed with the head.

3 Disconnect the sparking plug HT leads, after labelling them for order, and remove the distributor. Disconnect the electrical lead from the temperature switch. Remove the rocker cover.

4 It is best, though not essential, to take out the bolts that secure the rocker assembly and then lift it off complete. The pushrods should then be lifted out and stored in the correct order for reassembly. If the rocker assembly is not removed then the pushrods must be collected after the cylinder head has been freed.

5 To avoid danger of distortion, progressively and evenly slacken the cylinder head bolts in the same order as they are tightened, see **FIG 1:5**. After 1967 a 'Reinz Super Special' head gasket is fitted to most models. **This gasket sticks very firmly to the cylinder head liners and if the cylinder head is lifted directly off the liners may be partially withdrawn to the detriment of their bottom seals.** The method of overcoming this is to leave the bolt marked with a cross in **FIG 1:6** loosely in place and use a plastic mallet to tap the head so that it pivots about the bolt as shown and the gasket frees. Lift off the cylinder head.

6 **The liners must not be allowed to move once the cylinder head has been removed.** On the majority of engines special washers Mot.124 are fitted as shown in **FIG 1:7**. Suitable penny washers can be used instead of the special washers. On the 810 engine (1289 cc) a different special tool No. Mot.484 is used instead of the washers, as shown in **FIG 1:8**.

Cleaning and examination:

Full servicing and decarbonizing of the cylinder head will be dealt with in the next section. It is important that the mating faces of the cylinder head and block are clean, free from old gasket and flat without bow or damage. **As the faces are aluminium alloy they must not be scraped with sharp metal tools.** Use a sharpened stick of solder or hardwood to remove most of the dirt and then soak the remainder with a suitable solvent, such as trichlorethylene, so that it softens and can all be wiped and scraped off.

Lay a steel straightedge across the cylinder head and use feeler gauges to measure the distortion. If the distortion exceeds .05 mm (.002 inch) then the cylinder head should be sent away for specialist grinding but if the minimum height of the cylinder head is reached then a new head must be fitted. High spots can be checked for using engineer's blue on a surface table or plate glass and they can be removed by very careful use of a scraper or smooth file.

Reassembly:

The parts are refitted in the reverse order of removal. The new gasket is fitted with its crimped edges downwards. **Do not use grease or jointing compound.** If the rocker assembly is in place the pushrods must be refitted, into their original positions, before refitting the cylinder head and care must then be taken to ensure that the pushrods are correctly located in the cam followers.

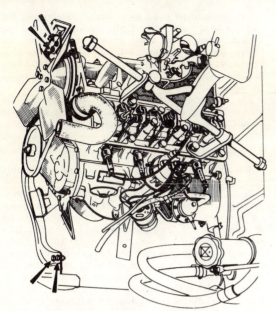

FIG 1:4   Lifting out the engine

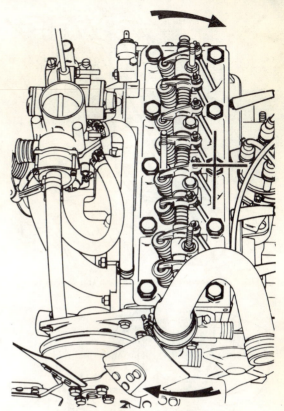

FIG 1:6   Freeing the cylinder head

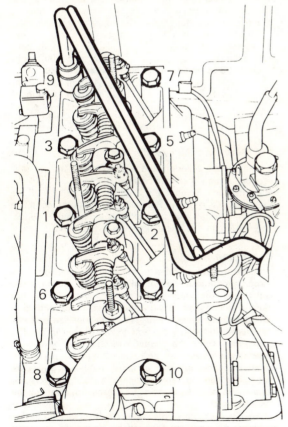

FIG 1:5   The sequence for tightening the cylinder head bolts

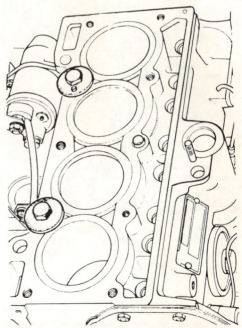

FIG 1:7   Securing the liners with special washers

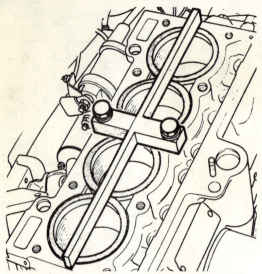

FIG 1:8 Securing the liners with the special tool

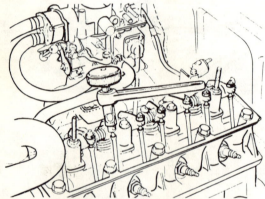

FIG 1:9 Adjusting the valve clearances with the special wrench

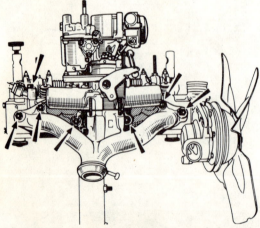

FIG 1:10 The manifold and temperature switch attachments

Lay the cylinder head back into place and refit the cylinder head bolts finger tight, making sure that the threads are perfectly clean. Progressively tighten the bolts in the order shown in **FIG 1:5** until they are all at the correct load of 6 kg m (45 lb ft). If the rocker assembly has been removed it should be refitted after the pushrods have been refitted.

The remainder of the parts are then refitted in the reverse order of removal but before refitting the rocker cover set the correct valve clearances.

Setting valve clearances:

A special wrench is made for this purpose and the tool is used as shown in **FIG 1:9**.

Turn the engine using the starting handle, noting that the engine will be easier to turn if all four sparking plugs are removed. Turn the engine until the cylinder to be adjusted is at the firing position with both valves fully closed. Slacken the locknut on the rocker arm and then screw the adjuster until the correct thickness feeler gauge can be inserted between the end of the rocker arm and valve stem. Press firmly down on the adjuster to take up any clearances and to break the oil film, while tightening the adjuster until the feeler gauge is just lightly nipped and drag is felt on it as it is moved. Hold the adjuster firmly with one hand to prevent it from rotating and tighten the locknut. Check that the clearance has not altered. The special tool contains a female key concentric with the spanner and therefore makes the adjustment easier.

On 956 cc engines the correct clearances are:

Inlet	..	..	.15 mm (.006 inch)
Exhaust	..	..	.20 mm (.008 inch)

On 1108 cc engines the correct clearances are:

Inlet	..	..	.18 mm (.007 inch)
Exhaust	..	..	.25 mm (.010 inch)

1:4 Servicing the cylinder head

Remove the cylinder head as described in the previous section, noting that clamps must be fitted to hold the liners in place. Remove the water pump and take off the rocker shaft assembly. Remove the manifolds complete with carburetter and take off the temperature switch. The manifold attachment is shown in **FIG 1:10**.

Decarbonizing:

Leave the valves fitted in the cylinder head until the carbon and deposits have been cleaned out, as the valves will protect the seats in the cylinder head. Scrape out most of the deposits using a stick of solder or hardwood sharpened to a chisel point. The remainder can be carefully removed using worn emerycloth dipped in paraffin (kerosene). Once the combustion chambers have been cleaned the valves can be removed and the ports very carefully cleaned in a similar manner but taking great care not to damage the valve guides or seats. Metal tools or rotary wire brushes must not be used for cleaning the cylinder head.

Special wire rotary brushes are made for cleaning valve guides but if these are not available then clean the bores of the valve guides by pulling through with piece of rag.

Smear the tops of the bores of the liners with grease, to trap dirt, and plug the waterways with pieces of rag. Turn the engine until a pair of pistons is nearly at TDC and spring old piston rings into the bores above them. The old rings will protect the ring of carbon around the periphery of the piston, which acts as a heat shield for the top ring as well as acting as an additional oil seal. Remove the deposits from the piston crown with a stick of hardwood or solder only. **Do not use emerycloth as the particles cannot all be cleaned away afterwards.** When one pair of piston crowns has been cleaned turn the engine to the position for cleaning the other pair. Blow away loose dirt and then wipe the tops of the bores to remove the grease and dirt stuck there. Make sure that all the pieces of rag have been removed before the cylinder head is refitted.

Cam followers:

Withdraw the cam followers from their recesses in the cylinder block and store them in the correct order for reassembly. Use a strong magnet to lift them out.

Wash each follower and check that it is a free fit in its bore. Renew cam followers that stick or show signs of wear or chipping.

Pushrods:

Check that the ends are not worn or damaged and use a steel straightedge to make sure that the pushrods are straight and true. Renew any that are defective or bowed.

Valve removal:

Once the rocker shaft assembly has been removed the valves can be taken out. Compress the valve springs with a suitable compresser and lift out the split collets securing the valve. Release the tool slowly and once it is free lift off the cap and spring and then withdraw the valve out through the combustion chamber.

After servicing the valves are refitted in the reverse order of removal. Note that the split collets are different for the valves and **FIG 1:11** shows these differences, **A** being those for inlet valves and **B** those for exhaust valves. Valves must be refitted into their original positions.

Valve examination:

Remove deposits from the head using a metal scraping tool or emerycloth. If a suitable drill is available mount the valve in the chuck and remove the deposits as the valve spins. **Take care not to score or damage the ground portion of the stem** and deposits on this can be washed off with a suitable solvent. **Similarly take care not to damage the seat face.**

On old valves after several regrindings the seat face becomes wider and wider. A valve should be renewed before the seat face makes a sharp edge with the face in the combustion chamber. Check the stems for wear or signs of picking-up and renew defective valves. Check the stems with a straightedge and renew any valves that have bent stems.

Valve springs:

It should be noted that by using a special tool that fits into the combustion chamber through the sparking plug hole to hold the valve head it is possible to renew

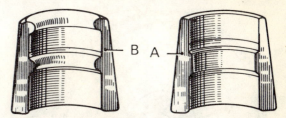

FIG 1:11 **A** is the split collet for inlet valves and **B** for exhaust valves

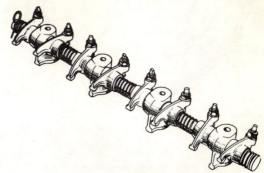

FIG 1:12 The rocker shaft assembly

the valve spring without having to remove the cylinder head from the engine.

Special rings are made for testing valve springs but a check can be carried out using a spring balance to apply the measured load and then measuring the extension with a steel ruler. The simplest method, and least accurate, is to mount the old spring end on to a new one and then compress the pair between the jaws of a vice. If the old spring is appreciably shorter than the new one then it is weak and should be renewed.

FIG 1:13 The clutch attachments

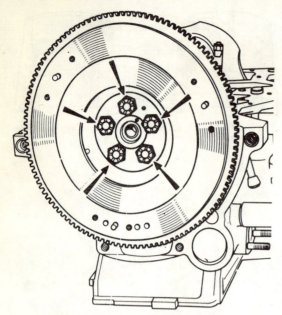

FIG 1:14   The flywheel attachments

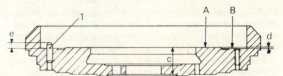

FIG 1:15   Sectioned view of the recessed-type flywheel

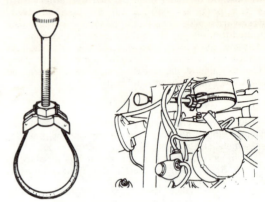

FIG 1:16   Renewing the oil filter

Valve guides:

Worn guides should be renewed otherwise they will increase the oil consumption by allowing oil to run down into the combustion chamber.

Special tools are really required for renewing the valve guides and as the seats in the head must be recut after new guides have been fitted, to ensure concentricity, the operation is best left to an agent.

The old guides are pressed out with a special drift and press. Two repair stages are supplied and once the old guide has been pressed out the bore in the cylinder head must be reamed out to accept the next oversize. The new guide is then pressed back into place with a special sleeve setting the protrusion at the correct dimension. Once the guide is in place it must be reamed out to 7 mm internal diameter and the valve seat then recut using garage equipment. The tools for removing and refitting guides are No. Mot.148 and the set of reamers are No. Mot.132. The head should be supported on plate No. Mot.121.

Grinding-in valves:

If the valves or seats are excessively pitted they should be recut or ground using garage equipment in order to prevent removing excess metal from the mating sealing face.

Fit the valve back into its original position with a light spring between it and the cylinder head. Smear a little grinding paste evenly around the face. Use medium-grade paste initially unless the seats are in good condition in which case fine-grade paste may be used from the start.

Press the valve down with a suction cup tool and grind with a semi-rotary motion. Allow the valve to rise up at frequent intervals and turn it through a quarter-turn before pressing it down and continuing grinding. When the

majority of pits have been removed take out the valve and clean off all old paste. Change to fine-grade and carry on grinding until both seats are matt-grey, smooth with no pits. Once all the valves have been ground in the parts should be thoroughly washed with fuel to remove all traces of abrasive from the valves, seats and ports.

Valve seats:

Steel insert seats are fitted into the aluminium alloy of the cylinder head. Once the valves have been ground in the width of the sealing face in the inserts should be checked. A broad sealing face is not as effective as a narrow one and it also limits the gas flow past the valve. A very narrow seat is fine for racing but for normal use where reliability over long periods is required, without having to remove the cylinder head often, a compromise must be reached. For exhaust valves, which need a slightly wider seat for heat transfer, the width of the seating faces in the inserts should be approximately 2 mm ($\frac{3}{32}$ inch) while for inlet valves it should be 1.6 mm ($\frac{1}{16}$ inch). If the seats are too wide they should be reduced using cutters. A large angle cutter will recess the seat into the cylinder head while a small angle one will raise it out, so use cutters to ensure that the seat meets the valve in the middle of its seating face.

If the seats are so worn that the valve sinks into the head then new steel inserts should be fitted by an agent.

Rocker assembly:

The complete assembly is shown in **FIG 1:12**. To dismantle the parts take off the clips and slide the parts off the shaft, keeping them stored in order. **The plugs in the end of the shaft are pressed in and cannot be removed.**

Wash the parts in clean fuel and examine them for wear. If the faces on the rocker arms are lightly worn or scored they can be smoothed down with an oil stone but if the damage is deep then new arms should be fitted. Worn arms make it difficult to set the valve clearances correctly. Check the shaft and renew it if it is worn or scored.

The parts are reassembled in the reverse order of dismantling. The bearing securing holes must be aligned with the notches in the shaft.

Reassembly:

The parts are reassembled in the reverse order of dismantling. New gaskets and seals should be used throughout, available as a de-coke kit, and all bearing surfaces should be liberally lubricated with clean engine oil.

Note that if the cylinder liners have shifted or been removed they must be refitted, using new bottom seals, so that the liner protrusion above the cylinder block is correct.

1:5 The clutch and flywheel

This section only deals with removing and refitting the clutch and full details of servicing the clutch and its mechanism are given in **Chapter 5**.

If the engine is still fitted in the car it will be necessary to remove the transmission unit (see **Chapter 6**) in order to gain access.

Removal:

The attachments are shown in **FIG 1:13**. The mandrel through the centre is fitted for centralizing the driven plate assembly. Lightly mark the clutch cover and flywheel as shown so that the clutch will be refitted into its original position on reassembly and the balance will therefore not be lost. The mandrel can also be fitted as it will prevent the driven plate from dropping. Progressively and evenly slacken the bolts that secure the cover, using a diagonal sequence. **If the bolts are not slackened progressively the pressure of the spring can distort the clutch cover.** Lift off the cover when all the bolts are free and take out the driven plate assembly.

Mark the position of the flywheel with reference to the flywheel, as shown in **FIG 1:14**. Take out and discard the bolts that secure the flywheel and then pull the flywheel off the crankshaft.

Flywheel:

Two types of flywheel are fitted. On the 956 cc engines the flywheel is flat but on other models the flywheel is recessed as shown in **FIG 1:15**. Apart from this recessing the flywheels can be treated in the same manner. Check the friction face **A** for damage such as scoring or burn marks. If the face is damaged then it can be refaced either by specialist grinding or turning. Both faces **A** and **B** must be machined by the same amount to preserve the dimension **D** at the correct amount of $.5\pm.1$ mm (.016 to .024 inch). If the dimension **C** is less than $27\pm.1$ mm (1.059 to 1.067 inch) for the recessed flywheel shown— $22.5\pm.1$ mm (.882 inch) for flat flywheels—after machining then a new flywheel must be fitted. When machining the face the dowels 1 should be removed. Fit new dowels after machining and set the protrusion **E** to $7\pm.25$ mm (.226 to .286 inch).

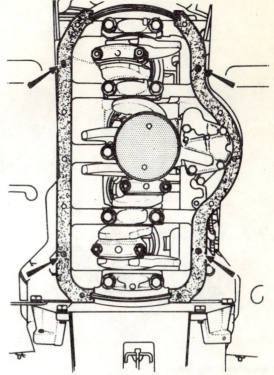

FIG 1:17 The sump gaskets

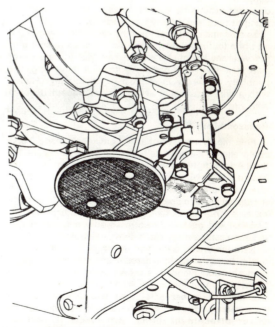

FIG 1:18 The oil pump attachments

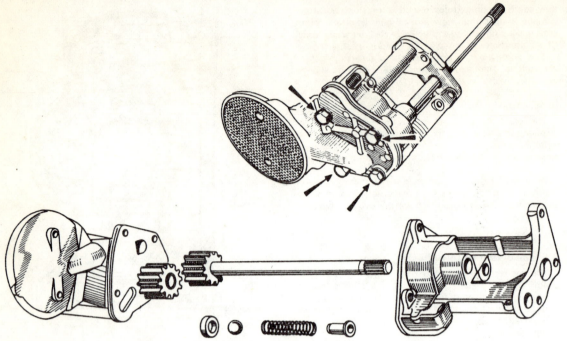

FIG 1:19   The oil pump components

Flywheel ring-gear:

The ring fitted around the flywheel is a shrink fit and can therefore be renewed if the teeth are worn. It is advisable to take the flywheel to an agent for fitting a new ring as the ring must be heated to the correct temperature. Too little heating will mean that the ring does not expand far enough to slip into place and too much heating will destroy the temper of the metal.

The old ring can be removed by carefully drilling at the root of a tooth and then using a cold chisel to split it at the weakened spot. Take great care not to damage or mark the flywheel. Before refitting a new ring the periphery of the flywheel must be thoroughly cleaned with a wire brush and all high spots smoothed down with emerycloth.

Reassembly:

Refit the flywheel so that the previously made marks again align. Use new self-locking bolts to secure the flywheel and tighten them to a torque of 5 kg m (35 lb ft). Mount a DTI (Dial Test Indicator) on the crankcase and check that the flywheel runout near to the outer edge of the operating face does not exceed .06 mm (.003 inch). Excessive runout can be caused by dirt between the flywheel and crankshaft, so make sure that the mating faces are scrupulously clean before reassembly.

Refit the driven plate with its longer side of the boss facing towards the transmission and locate it in place with a suitable mandrel as shown. Refit the clutch cover assembly so that the previously made marks are again in alignment. **It is essential that the driven plate is centralized using a mandrel when tightening the cover attachment bolts, otherwise it will be impossible to pass the gearbox input shaft** through the clutch into the crankshaft bearing when refitting the engine or gearbox. Tighten the bolts progressively in a diagonal sequence to prevent the pressure of the spring from distorting the cover.

1:6 The sump, oil pump and oil filter

Oil changes should also be carried out at regular intervals and the filter should also be renewed at regular intervals. If this is not carried out the oil will become dirtier and dirtier with both particles and acids which will cause excessive wear. The filter is fitted with a bypass valve so that if the element does choke then the engine will still receive a supply of oil but the oil will be completely unfiltered.

Drain the oil into a suitable container by removing the drain plug on the sump. It is best to drain the engine immediately after a long run as the oil will be hot and flow easier while dirt will be held in suspension and flushed out with the old oil. On the models where the complete filter is contained in a renewable canister use a strap spanner, as shown in **FIG 1:16**, to remove and fit it. Unscrew the old canister and discard it. Check the rubber seal on the new canister and smear it lightly with a little engine oil. Screw the new filter back into position until the seal just touches the crankcase and tighten the filter by a quarter-turn. Unscrew the filter again until the seal is free and then screw it in until the filter seal touches once more. Tighten the filter by a further $\frac{1}{2}$ to $\frac{3}{4}$ turn and check for oil leaks once the engine has been started.

Refit the sump drain plug and fill the engine up to the upper mark on the dipstick with fresh oil. At this stage a small amount of overfilling is not harmful as the surplus will be drawn into the filter and oil passages.

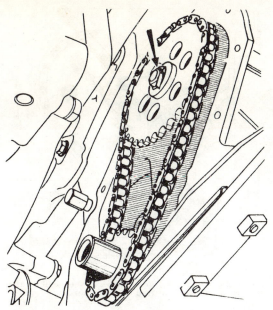

FIG 1:20   The bolt securing the camshaft sprocket

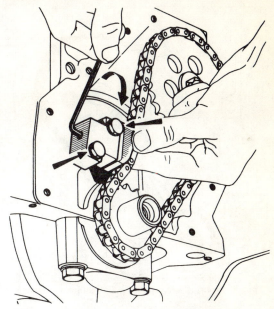

FIG 1:21   The timing chain tensioner

Start the engine and leave it to run for a few minutes. Switch off and leave for a minimum of five minutes to allow the level to settle before checking. Top up as required but do not overfill. Running with an over-full engine will raise the oil consumption because the extra oil tends to burn or leak away and it is also not satisfactory because the big-ends will dip into the oil and cause excessive frothing.

Sump:

The sump can be removed with the engine still fitted to the car but it will be necessary to raise the rear of the car in order to get access room. **Make sure that all supports are strong enough and firmly based.**

Drain out the oil, leaving it for as long as possible so that all the oil is out when the time comes to remove the sump, as this saves drips. On the models fitted with a stiffener bar across the clutch housing remove this bar by taking out its two attachment bolts. Unscrew all the bolts that secure the sump in place and lower it down to remove it. Discard the rubber seals over the front and main bearing caps as well as the cork side gaskets.

Fit new rubber seals onto the main bearing caps, using a little jointing compound. Smear the side gaskets lightly with grease or jointing compound and fit them back into place onto the four dowels, arrowed in **FIG 1:17**, making sure that they overlap on the ends of the rubber seals. Lift the sump back into position, taking great care not to move the gaskets, and secure it with the bolts. Refill the engine with oil and check the level after the engine has been run and then stood for at least five minutes.

Whenever the sump is removed check the strainer on the oil pump inlet for blocking or damage. Clean or renew the strainer as required. At the same time wash out the inside of the sump.

Oil pump:

The oil pump fitted to the engine is shown in **FIG 1:18**. Remove the sump to gain access and then take out the three bolts that secure the pump to the crankcase so that the pump can be withdrawn and removed.

The components of the pump are shown in **FIG 1:19** and the pump can be dismantled by taking out the four bolts arrowed. Check the parts for wear or damage. Renew the relief valve seat and ball if they are pitted or damaged and renew the relief valve spring if it is weak and causing low oil pressure. Use feeler gauges to check the clearance between the gearteeth and side of the pump and renew the gearwheels if the clearance is greater than .2 mm (.008 inch). If the end cover is scored it may be refaced by lapping with fine-grade grinding paste spread on plate glass.

The pump is reassembled and refitted in the reverse order of removal. It is advisable to lubricate the pump well with engine oil as it is being reassembled. On the models where the inlet filter gauze is held on by screws use Locktite on the threads of these screws to lock and seal them in use.

Oil pressure:

If the oil pressure requires checking it will be necessary to remove the switch for the oil pressure warning light and fit a pressure gauge and adaptor into its place. The minimum oil pressure at 600 rev/min should be .7 kg/sq cm (10 lb/sq in) and at 4000 rev/min the minimum should be 3.5 kg/sq cm (50 lb/sq in).

1:7 Valve timing and camshaft

The timing gear can be removed with the engine still fitted to the engine but if the camshaft is to be removed it is advisable to take the engine out of the car.

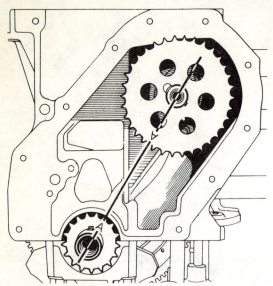

FIG 1:22 The valve timing marks aligned correctly

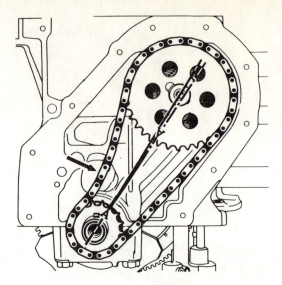

FIG 1:23 The valve timing marks as they will be after the chain has been refitted and tensioned

Timing chain with engine fitted in car:

Jack up the rear of the car and remove the sump as described in the previous section.

1 Slacken off the generator attachments so that the fan belt can be removed from the crankshaft pulley. Unscrew the starter dog, noting that it may be very tight and that it may be necessary to engage a gear and apply the handbrake in order to prevent the engine from turning. Remove the crankshaft pulley and take out the securing bolts so that the timing cover can be removed.

2 Take out the bolt in the end of the timing chain tensioner and pass a 3 mm (.118 inch) Allen key in through the hole where the bolt fitted, as shown in **FIG 1:20**. Turn the Allen key in a clockwise direction until the pressure of the slipper pad on the chain is relieved. **The Allen key must always be turned clockwise when slackening or adjusting the tensioner and no attempt must be made to force the slipper back into the body.** When the tension is free remove the tensioner by taking out its two securing bolts, carefully collecting any shims and the filter.

3 Unlock the bolt that secures the camshaft sprocket, arrowed in **FIG 1:21** and remove the sprocket and chain. The crankshaft sprocket can be levered off using two screwdrivers.

4 Check the timing chain and sprockets for wear. If the chain is worn it is best to renew the sprockets as well, as their teeth wear and will quickly tear a new chain.

5 Turn the crankshaft until the key is upwards and refit the crankshaft sprocket. Refit the camshaft sprocket and turn the camshaft until the two engraved V marks are exactly in line, as shown in **FIG 1:22**. Remove the camshaft sprocket and encircle both sprockets with the timing chain and then refit the camshaft sprocket with a new lockwasher and its bolt. Check that the timing marks are still exactly in line **with the chain**

hanging freely. Note that when pressure is applied to the chain so that it is taut, the timing marks will lie on the lines shown in **FIG 1:23**. Tighten the bolt for the camshaft sprocket to a torque of 2 kg m (15 lb ft).

6 Refit the timing cover. Ideally it should be located with the special tool No. Mot.128, which fits into the oil seal and centralizes the cover on the crankshaft.

7 The remainder of the parts are then refitted in the reverse order of removal.

Front oil seal:

This is fitted into the timing cover. The seal is delicate and must not be mishandled. If the cover has been removed the old seal can be peeled out and a new seal pressed back into place using the special mandrel Mot.131-02. It will help to offset the seal by 3 mm ($\frac{1}{8}$ inch) out from its original position so that it does not operate on the same portion of the crankshaft, which might be slightly worn from the original seal.

Special tools No. Mot.457 are made for removing and refitting the seal while the cover is still fitted to the engine. The extractor has a chamfered edge which passes through the oil seal and the lipped edge then draws out the old oil seal. A mandrel acting along a stud screwed into the crankshaft pulls the new seal back into position.

Camshaft:

Before removing the camshaft it will be necessary to remove the timing gear as described earlier. Remove the cylinder head (see **Section 1:3**) and remove the cam followers from their bores. Remove the fuel pump. Remove the oil pump and distributor drive gear. The distributor drive gear can be withdrawn using a 12 mm 175 pitch bolt or it can be withdrawn on a suitable piece jammed into it. Take out the two bolts securing the camshaft flange, arrowed in **FIG 1:24**, and carefully withdraw the camshaft.

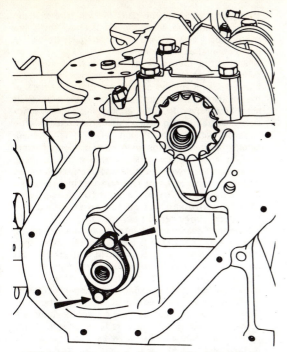

FIG 1:24   The camshaft flange attachment bolts

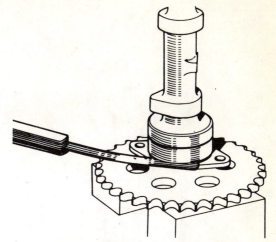

FIG 1:25   Checking the camshaft end float

Refit the sprocket to the camshaft, tightening the bolt to a torque of 2 kg m (15 lb ft), and use feeler gauges to check the end float as shown in **FIG 1:25**. If the end float is not correct within the limits of .06 to .11 mm (.002 to .005 inch) then the flange and spacer must be removed and a new flange fitted. When the new flange has been fitted press on the spacer using a piece of tube until the spacer comes into contact with the shoulder.

The camshaft is refitted in the reverse order of removal but note that the distributor drive gear must be correctly refitted.

Distributor drive:

When it comes to refitting the distributor drive turn the engine until it is at TDC of the firing position for No. 1 (nearest flywheel) cylinder. This position is found by turning the engine until the cams of No. 4 (nearest timing chain) cylinder are at the point of balance. Use a suitable bolt or piece of wood to lower the drive back into position so that, allowing for the turning on meshing, the drive slot in the gear is at right angles to the engine axis and the larger offset is towards the clutch, as shown in **FIG 1:26**, when the drive has been fully meshed. Once the drive is in place the oil pump can be refitted.

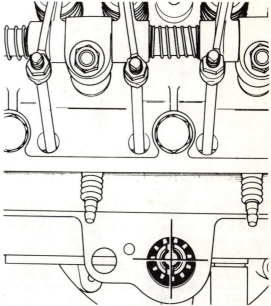

FIG 1:26   The distributor drive correctly refitted

1:8 The pistons, connecting rods and liners

The complete assemblies should be removed from the car for servicing or examination. It is not necessary to remove the engine, though the task will be easier with the engine out, as both the sump and cylinder head can be removed while the engine is fitted.

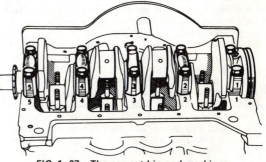

FIG 1:27   The correct big-end markings

FIG 1:28   Refitting the piston to the liner

Big-end bearings:

These can be attended to after the sump has been removed. If, after dismantling, the crankpins are found to be worn or scored then the engine must be removed from the car in order to take out the crankshaft and send it away for specialist regrinding.

If the cylinder head has been removed for servicing but it is intended to leave the pistons and liners in place then it is essential to fit the special washers or tool that hold the linings in place and prevent them from moving (see **FIGS 1:7** and **1:8**).

1 Remove the sump as described in **Section 1:6**. Check that the reference numbers are stamped on both the caps and connecting rods, as shown in **FIG 1:27**, with No. 1 nearest to the clutch end. If the numbers are not present then mark the parts with a code of light punch dots.

2 Turn the crankshaft to a convenient position for working and then slacken all the nuts that secure the bearing cups. Remove the nuts and pull off the caps. Press the connecting rods down the bores of the cylinders until the big-ends are clear from the crankpins. **When turning the engine take great care not to trap the end of the connecting rod between the throw and side of the crankcase.**

3 Slide out the shell bearings from the connecting rods and bearing caps and store all the parts in the correct order for reassembly.

4 Thoroughly clean all the parts making sure that the crankpins and the seats for the bearing shells are scrupulously clean. Wipe the bearing shells with a piece of lint-free cloth or leather.

5 Measure the crankpins at several points using a micrometer gauge. If the crankpins are worn oval, tapered, barrel shaped or with an hour glass neck in the middle or if they are scored then the crankshaft must be removed from the engine and sent away for specialist regrinding. New shell bearings will be supplied with the crankshaft when it is returned. Check the shell bearings for signs of cracking, flaking, scoring or shiny finish denoting a metal to metal contact and renew the complete set if any shell shows any defect. **Do not file the connecting rod, cap or bearing shells in an attempt to take up wear as this will make the parts non-standard and also cause very rapid bearing failure.**

6 Fit the shell bearings back into their correct locations, making sure that the tags locate securely. New shell bearings are fitted as received, apart from cleaning off any protective, and do not require scraping or boring. Pull the connecting rods down into contact with the crankpins and refit the bearing caps. Liberally lubricate the bearings with fresh engine oil before refitting them. Refit the bearing caps into their correct locations and make sure that all the numbers face correctly. If the engine was fitted with lockwashers then fit new ones in their place. Refit the nuts and tighten them to a torque of 3.5 kg m (25 lb ft) and then lock them with the lockwashers. Refit the sump and fill the engine with oil.

Removing parts:

Remove the sump and cylinder head. Disconnect the big-ends as just described and carefully drive the liners up and out through the top of the block. Before removing the liners lightly mark them in order with the marks facing the clutch end of the engine.

The piston and connecting rod assemblies can then be withdrawn out through the bottom of the liners.

The gudgeon pins are an interference fit in the connecting rod so they should not be removed unnecessarily.

Gudgeon pins:

A press and special tools (No. Mot.122) are needed for removing the piston from the connecting rod which must be heated to a temperature of 250°C in an oven before the gudgeon pin is pressed back into place using the special tools and a pressure of 1200 kg (2650 lb). For these reasons gudgeon pin removal and refitting should be left to an agent.

Piston rings:

The best method of removing and refitting piston rings is to use a ring spreader which grips the ring by the ends and then gently parts them. If the correct spreader is not available three shims, such as discarded feeler gauges, can be used instead. Lift out one end of the ring and slide a shim under it. Work the shim around under the ring lifting the ring as it comes free onto the piston land above it, **taking great care not to force the ring or it will snap.** When all the ring is on the land slide the other two shims under the ring so that all three shims are equally spaced and then slide the ring up off the piston on the shims. Part the ends of the ring slightly with the thumb nails and make sure that the back of the ring does not score the piston.

Rings are refitted in the reverse order of removal. New piston rings are fitted as received as they have been set to the correct end gap at the factory.

Pistons:

Once the piston rings have been removed clean the ring grooves with an old broken ring. Remove all the carbon but take care not to scrape away any metal otherwise the oil consumption will be increased. Clean the return holes behind the lower ring with a piece of blunt-ended wire.

The crowns can be lightly polished with worn emery-cloth dipped in paraffin as all abrasive particles can be washed off afterwards. **No abrasive may be used on the piston sides** and any lacquering should be washed off with a strong solvent such as trichlorethylene.

If the pistons are scored or the ring grooves excessively worn then new pistons should be fitted.

Connecting rods:

These should be checked by the agent for bend and twist after the pistons and gudgeon pins have been removed from the little ends.

Liner bores:

Whenever the cylinder head is removed the bores should be examined for wear or scoring. A guide to the wear is given by the depth of the unworn ridge around the top of the bore but for accurate results measurements must be taken at several points in each bore, using a special form of gauge. If the bores are excessively worn, scored, tapered or out of round then new pistons and liners should be fitted.

If wear is not sufficient to warrant new pistons and liners but the oil consumption is high enough to require new rings to cure it, the unworn ridge around the top of the bore should be removed using garage equipment. If the ridge is left then the new ring will hit it on every stroke and may quickly fracture.

Fitting liners:

The correct protrusion of the liner above the cylinder block is vital as it ensures that the liner is correctly sealed both at the top and at the bottom.

The correct protrusion is best checked using a DTI and block though it can be checked by laying a steel straight-edge across the top of the liner and measuring the gap to the block with feeler gauges. On all models the correct protrusion is .05 to .12 mm (.002 to .005 inch) and it is set by the thickness of the seal between the liner and crankcase. Before fitting the liner thoroughly clean the base of the liner with a wire brush but use less drastic methods on the seat in the crankcase as this is aluminium alloy.

Seals are available in three thicknesses:
.07 mm (.003 inch) coloured blue
.10 mm (.004 inch) coloured red
.13 mm (.005 inch) coloured green

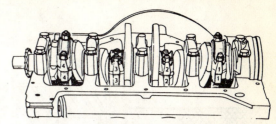

FIG 1:29   The correct main bearing markings

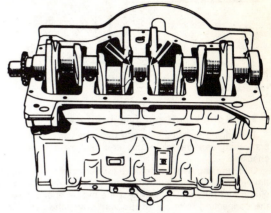

FIG 1:30   The crankshaft thrust washers

Fit the thinnest blue seal onto the liner and slide the liner back into position. Press the liner down by hand and measure the protrusion, fitting thicker seals if required. If this varies by more than .02 mm (.001 inch) on either side then try turning the liner through 180 degrees and try again. When the correct seals have been fitted remove the liners again, making sure that they are marked for order and position.

Reassembly:

Turn the piston rings around in the piston until their gaps are evenly spaced and no gap is in line with the gudgeon pin. Lightly oil the rings.

Invert the liner and slide the piston into the special sleeve shown in **FIG 1:28**. The three different sleeves for the different bores are Mot.123, Mot.218 and Mot.459 the larger the number indicating the larger the bore. A large worm-driven hose clip can be used if the special sleeve or standard piston ring clamp is not available though more care is required.

Insert the crown of the piston into the liner, making sure that the arrow will point to the clutch end of the engine when the liner is correctly fitted, and gently press it in allowing the rings to slide into the liner. Do not force the rings or allow them to escape from the tool before they are in the liner otherwise they will most likely snap.

When the piston is fully in the liner refit the assembly to the crankcase and secure the liners with the washers or special tool to prevent them from moving. Reconnect the big-ends as described earlier and reassemble the engine in the reverse order of dismantling.

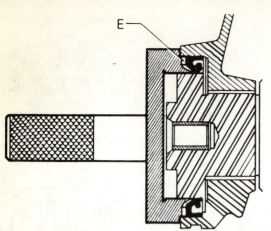

FIG 1:31 Refitting the oil seal to the flywheel end of the crankshaft

1:9 The crankshaft and main bearings

The engine must be removed from the car before the crankshaft can be taken out and the main bearings checked.

Once the engine is out remove the sump and oil pump, timing cover and chain with sprockets as well as the clutch and flywheel. Disconnect the big-ends and push the connecting rods out of the way down the cylinder bores.

Check that the bearing caps are numerically marked in order, as shown in **FIG 1:29** and if they are not mark them and the crankcase with an identifying code of light dot marks to ensure that they will be refitted in order and facing the correct way.

Slacken the bolts evenly and progressively and then remove them and the bearing caps. Lift out the crankshaft and slide the bearing shells out of crankcase and bearings caps, storing them in the correct order for reassembly. Collect the thrust washers.

Wash all the parts in clean fuel and blow through the oilways in the crankshaft with paraffin followed by air. Wipe the bearing shells with a piece of clean lint-free cloth or leather. Renew the complete set of bearing shells if any shell shows signs of defects.

Measure the journals at several points with a micrometer gauge and send it away for specialist regrinding if the journals are worn or scored. **Do not file the bearing caps in an attempt to take up wear in the bearings.**

Refit the shells into their positions, making sure that the tags are correctly located and noting that the shells with the oil holes are fitted into the crankcase. Oil the journals liberally and lay the crankshaft back into place. Fit the thrust washers on either side of the centre main bearing (arrowed in **FIG 1:30**) with the machined faces towards the crankshaft. Refit the bearing caps and progressively tighten the bolts to a torque of 6 kg m (45 lb ft). Check that the crankshaft rotates freely.

Mount a DTI onto the crankcase, or else use feeler gauges at a main bearing, and lever the crankshaft firmly backwards and forwards so that the end float can be measured. If the end float is outside the correct limits of .045 to .19 mm (.002 to .008 inch) then the crankshaft must be removed again and new or oversize thrust washers fitted to bring the end float within limits.

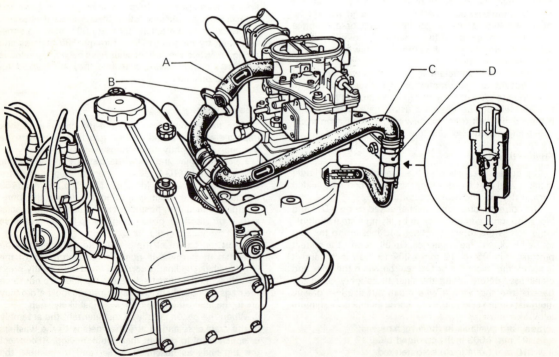

FIG 1:32 The emission control crankcase breathing system

When the crankshaft is in place refit the oil seal to the front main bearing. The seal is very delicate and should only be fitted using the special mandrel Mot.131 (which is in two parts) or Mot.131A the latter being shown in **FIG 1:31**. Press the seal into position until the mandrel touches the crankcase. Remove the mandrel and fit a 3 mm ($\frac{1}{8}$ inch) spacer **E** as shown and then press the mandrel in until it again touches the crankcase. If the original crankshaft is being used the spacer can be omitted as this ensures that the seal is 3 mm further out and working on an unworn portion of the crankshaft. A suitable spacer **E** is an old piston ring from a 668 engine (85 mm bore).

Once the seal is in place the remainder of the engine can be reassembled in the reverse order of dismantling.

Spigot bearing:

A bush is pressed into the flywheel end of the crankshaft for the spigot on the gearbox input shaft to run in. If the bush is worn or shows chatter marks it should be removed and a new bush fitted. The bush can be removed by tapping a thread in it and screwing in a bolt so that the bush is withdrawn using the bolt. Another method is to find or turn a piece of rod that is a snug sliding fit in the bush. Pack the bush fully with grease, leaving no air bubbles, and press the rod into the end of the bush. A few hammer blows on the end of the rod will drive the bush out of the crankshaft by hydraulic action.

1:10 Emission control

Engines destined for the North American market are built to close tolerances and are also fitted with emission control systems. At certain speeds the mechanism opens the throttle butterfly slightly to ensure that the engine idles at a high speed on deceleration. A different cylinder head with individual ports to each cylinder is fitted and the pistons have a reduced crown clearance.

The gases from the crankcase are drawn in with the mixture and burnt in the cylinders by the system shown in **FIG 1:32**. The gases pass out from the rocker through a T-piece. One hose **A** leads directly to the carburetter through the flame trap capsule **B**. The flame trap prevents backfires from igniting the oil air vapour in the crankcase. The other hose **C** leads to the inlet manifold through the valve **D**. At high vacuum in the manifold the valve **D** closes and prevents the fumes from being drawn directly into the manifold, where they would be sufficient to alter the mixture strength. Instead they are drawn in with the air into the inlet in the carburetter.

At regular intervals the hose connections should be checked and the valve **D** cleaned. Methylated spirits is usually sufficient for removing deposits but if they are obstinate boil the metal parts in water to soften them.

1:11 Reassembling a stripped engine

All the operations have been dealt with in the relevant sections so it is only a question of tackling the tasks in the best order.

Make sure that all the parts are scrupulously clean before reassembling them. Soften all old gaskets and seals so that they can be scraped off with hardwood. Discard all seals and gaskets that have been removed and use new ones on reassembly.

Lubricate all bearing surfaces liberally with fresh oil as the parts are refitted.

Fit the crankshaft first followed by the flywheel and clutch. Check that the crankshaft rotates freely and then fit the piston, liner and connecting rod assemblies, again checking that the crankshaft rotates freely after the liners have been clamped down. When these parts are in place the camshaft and timing gear, including cover, can then be fitted. Refit the cylinder head complete with rocker gear and set the valve clearances. Align the distributor drive correctly and then refit the oil pump and sump. Leave external accessories until last as they are less likely to be damaged.

1:12 Fault diagnosis

(a) Engine will not start

1 Defective ignition coil
2 Faulty distributor capacitor
3 Dirty, pitted or incorrectly set ignition points
4 Ignition wires loose or insulation faulty
5 Water on sparking plug leads
6 Battery discharged, terminals corroded
7 Faulty or jammed starter motor
8 Sparking plug HT leads incorrectly connected
9 Vapour locks in fuel line
10 Defective fuel pump
11 Overchoking or underchoking
12 Blocked fuel filter or jammed float chamber needle valves
13 Leaking valves
14 Sticking valves
15 Valve timing incorrect
16 Ignition timing incorrect

(b) Engine stalls

1 Check 1, 2, 3, 4, 5, 10, 11, 12, 13 and 14 in (a)
2 Sparking plugs defective or gaps incorrect
3 Retarded ignition
4 Mixture too weak
5 Water in fuel system
6 Petrol tank vent blocked
7 Incorrect valve clearances

(c) Engine idles badly

1 Check 2 and 7 in (b)
2 Air leaks at manifold joints
3 Worn piston rings
4 Worn valve stems or guides
5 Weak exhaust valve springs

(d) Engine misfires

1 Check 1, 2, 3, 4, 5, 10, 12, 13, 14, 15 and 16 in (a) and also check 2, 3, 4 and 7 in (b)
2 Weak or broken valve springs
3 Defective HT lead

(e) Engine overheats (see **Chapter 4**)

(f) Compression low

1 Check 14 and 15 in (a); 3 and 4 in (c) and 2 in (d)
2 Worn piston ring grooves
3 Scored or worn cylinder bores

(g) Engine lacks power

1 Check 3, 10, 11, 13, 14, 15, 16 and 17 in (a); 1, 2, 3 and 6 in (b); 3 and 4 in (c) and 2 in (d). Also check (e) and (f)
2 Leaking cylinder head gasket
3 Fouled or worn out sparking plugs
4 Automatic advance not operating

(h) Burnt valves or seats

1 Check 14 and 15 in (a); 7 in (b) and 2 in (d). Also check (e)
2 Excessive carbon around valve seat and cylinder head

(j) Sticking valves

1 Check 2 in (d)
2 Bent valve stem
3 Scored valve stem and guide
4 Incorrect valve clearance
5 Gummy deposits on valve stem

(k) Excessive cylinder wear

1 Check 11 in (a) and also check (e)
2 Lack of oil
3 Dirty oil
4 Piston rings gummed up or broken
5 Connecting rods bent

(l) Excessive oil consumption

1 Check 4 in (k) and also check (f)
2 Oil return holes in pistons choked with carbon
3 Oil level too high
4 External oil leaks

(m) Crankshaft or connecting rod bearing failure

1 Check 2 and 3 in (k)
2 Restricted oilways
3 Worn journals or crankpins
4 Loose bearing caps
5 Bent connecting rod
6 Extremely low oil pressure

(n) Low oil pressure

1 Check 2 and 3 in (k) and 2, 3 and 4 in (m)
2 Choked oil filter
3 Weak relief valve spring or dirt under seat
4 Faulty gauge, switch or connections

(o) Internal coolant leakage (see Chapter 4)

(p) Poor coolant circulation (see Chapter 4)

(q) Corrosion (see Chapter 4)

(r) High fuel consumption (see Chapter 2)

CHAPTER 2

THE FUEL SYSTEM

2:1 Description

All the models are fitted with a single carburetter and a mechanically operated fuel pump. The fuel pump is mounted on the side of the engine crankcase and driven from the camshaft. Fuel is stored in a tank in front of the engine and it should be noted that the engine must be removed before the fuel tank can be taken out.

Models destined for the North American market are fitted with Solex DIDTA.5 carburetters. These carburetters are of the twin-barrel type with the first barrel operating directly from the throttle linkage, but the second is operated by a special progressive linkage. This type of carburetter is made to specially high standards and the amount of work that can be carried out on it is strictly limited. A fast-idle mechanism is fitted to raise the engine idling speed on deceleration and thus limit the emissions when decelerating.

A filter gauze is fitted to the fuel pump and most models also have a strainer at the inlet to the carburetter float chamber, to ensure that the fuel reaching the jets is clean.

An air cleaner is fitted to filter the incoming air for the carburetter. The cleaner also serves the purpose of silencing the carburetter intake.

2:2 Maintenance

The carburetter itself should require little maintenance. Regularly check that the throttle linkage operates fully and freely, lubricating pivot points lightly with oil.

At longer intervals clean out the fuel pump sediment chamber and filter. The two different types of pump, and their attachments, are shown in **FIGS 2:1** and **2:2**. It is advisable to disconnect the inlet pipe to the pump and either clamp it or block it off with a suitable bolt otherwise fuel may syphon through out of the tank. On the models with a cover this is taken off after the small central bolt has been removed while on the other models the gauze is under the bolt. The filter should be washed in clean fuel and renewed if it is torn or defective. Refit the filter in the reverse order of removal. Make sure that the seals are in good condition and squarely refitted. It is advisable to check for leaks after the engine has been started. If the filter is dirty check the filter gauze at the carburetter float chamber inlet as well. If the filters often become dirty try syphoning the fuel out of the tank and refilling with clean fuel, but if this fails then the tank must be removed for swilling out or renewal. On all models do not forget to take out the front bolt above the transmission case when removing the tank, as well as

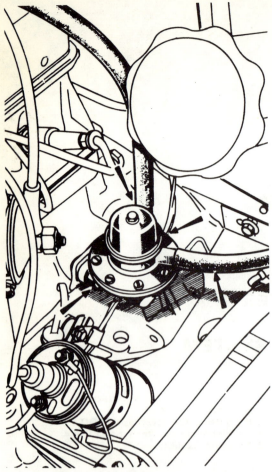

FIG 2:1 The fuel pump attachments

disconnecting leads, pipes and filler tube. On the later versions of R1130 models it will be necessary to remove the four bolts which secure the suspension crossmember to the side frames, and then to raise the car on slings so that the crossmember clears the sidemembers by approximately 4 cm (1½ inch). Remember that on all models the engine must be removed before the tank can be taken out.

At regular intervals, depending on the conditions that the car is driven in, check the air cleaner element. On models fitted with a paper element tap the element onto a firm hard surface to dislodge surface dirt and fit a new element when the old one becomes choked. **Under no circumstances may paper elements be washed in any solvent, including water.** If a gauze element is fitted wash the element in clean fuel or paraffin and when it is dry soak it with engine oil. Allow the surplus oil to drain away before refitting the element.

2:3 The fuel pump

The components of a typical fuel pump are shown in **FIG 2:3**. The rocker arm 19 pivots about the post 18 under the action of the cam on the camshaft. The arm is

designed so that it will only pull the rod of the diaphragm 12 downwards but the arm cannot push the rod back up. When the diaphragm is pulled down a suction is set up above it and this draws fuel from the tank, through the filter 6 and inlet valve 9 with its spring 10. When the rocker arm releases the diaphragm the return spring 13 presses the diaphragm back up and the fuel is forced out through the outlet valve to the carburetter float chamber. When the float chamber is full its needle valve shuts off and prevents further fuel from entering. The fuel pressure then holds the diaphragm down against the action of its return spring and the drive linkage of the pump freewheels until such time as more fuel is required by the carburetter float chamber and the diaphragm can rise again. Except when filling the float chamber the pump does not operate in a sequence of strokes and therefore the return spring 13 controls the actual fuel pressure in the system. High fuel pressure will only be caused by too strong a return spring or a stiff diaphragm. Low fuel pressure can be caused by the spring weakening, defective diaphragm, leaking valves, blocked pipes or just general wear in the pump.

As a rough test on the pump operation, disconnect the fuel line at the carburetter inlet and point it into a suitable container. Crank the engine either on the starter motor or starting handle and at every other revolution (camshaft is driven at half engine speed) there should be a good spurt of fuel out of the pipe.

Servicing:

Remove the pump by disconnecting the lines and taking out the two bolts that secure it to the engine. Plug the feed pipe to prevent fuel from syphoning through.

Clean the outside of the pump and then lightly make a file mark across the flanges of the upper body 2 and lower body 21, as these will assist in aligning the parts on reassembly. In a diagonal sequence progressively slacken and unscrew the screws 1 that hold the pump together. Part the upper from the lower body.

Check the valves 9 with their springs 10 by blowing and sucking through them. If necessary remove the valves but **note that they must be correctly refitted facing in their original directions otherwise the pump will not operate correctly.**

Lightly press down the diaphragm and unhook its rod from the rocker arm so that the diaphragm can be removed. Check both the diaphragm and its spring for any sign of defect and renew them if necessary. The oil seal 15 and its retainer 14 should only be renewed if they are defective.

The rocker arm 19 and its pivot 18 can be renewed but if they are worn it is likely that the pump has seen long service and consideration should therefore be given to fitting an exchange or new unit.

Clean out all sediment and dirt and reassemble the pump in the reverse order of dismantling. Hold the rocker arm so that the diaphragm is level while tightening the screws 1 fingertight, and exercise the pump for a few full strokes before fully tightening them in a diagonal sequence.

Check the operation by first blocking the inlet pipe and seeing that there is a suction when the pump is operated by hand. Similarly check that there is a pressure build up at the outlet pipe.

2:4 Carburetter operation

A schematic sectioned view of a Solex 32.PDIST carburetter is shown in **FIG 2:4**.

Fuel enters through the inlet pipe on the left of the figure and fills the float chamber. As the chamber fills the float rises until when the level is correct, the float closes the needle valve so that no more can enter. As fuel is used the level drops slightly and the needle valve opens to keep the level constant within small limits.

When an airflow is speeded up by passing through a constriction, the static pressure drops. A choke tube (venturi) **K** is fitted to speed up the airflow in the carburetter. At slow running speeds there is insufficient airflow to draw fuel from the main jets but there is a constriction at the side of the throttle butterfly valve which is nearly closed. Fuel for slow-running is drawn through the slow-running jet '**g**' and enters just beside the throttle valve. Extra outlets are fitted higher up to give a smooth transition from the slow-running jet to the main jet.

When the throttle valve is open, the suction in the neck of the choke tube draws the fuel through the main jet **Gg**. An emulsifier tube and air jet '**a**' are fitted to correct the mixture strength at high engine speeds.

An extra rich mixture is required for acceleration and the excess fuel is supplied by an accelerator pump connected to the throttle linkage. The pump draws fuel from the float chamber as it returns and when the throttle is opened the fuel in the pump is injected into the airstream in the carburetter inlet.

An econostat device is fitted to ensure economy at reasonable speeds. At full throttle the diaphragm allows extra fuel to flow into the airstream from the float chamber.

A very rich mixture is required to ensure that the engine fires when cold and a rich mixture is then required to keep it running until it has warmed up sufficiently to allow efficient atomization of the fuel. The choke valve at the inlet is controlled by a bi-metallic spring. When the engine is cold the bi-metallic spring exercises a strong closing force on the choke valve. The valve stays closed and ensures that the increased suction in the carburetter draws fuel through the jets. As soon as the engine fires the airflow over the offset valve tends to open it against the action of the bi-metallic spring, so that the mixture strength is slightly reduced. Coolant passes around the housing for the bi-metallic spring which, as it heats, weakens and allows the valve to open further. A vacuum assisted piston also assists the valve until when the engine is at its normal operating temperature the valve is fully open.

The coolant for the choke housing also passes through a housing at the base of the carburetter. By heating the mixture slightly as it passes through efficient atomization is ensured, thus reducing emission, and icing in the carburetter is also prevented.

2:5 Carburetter faults

The most likely cause of trouble is dirt in the system. Dirt trapped under the needle valve will cause flooding, and dirt in the jets will cause rough or erratic running.

The most likely points of wear are the throttle spindle and its bushing points in the body. The carburetter must be dismantled to renew the spindle. If fitting a new spindle does not cure the play then a new carburetter

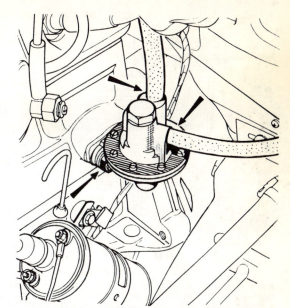

FIG 2:2 The fuel pump attachments

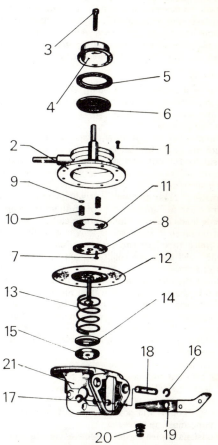

FIG 2:3 The fuel pump components

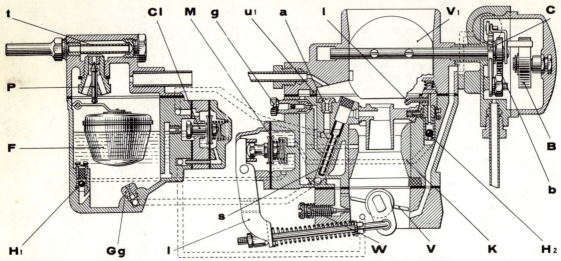

FIG 2:4 Sectional view of Solex carburetter type 32.PDIST

Key to Fig 2:4 **a** Correction jet **B** Bi-metal coil **b** Small bi-metal coil **C** Cam **C1** Enrichment device valve **F** Float
Gg Main jet **g** Pilot jet **H1/H2** Pump check valves **i** Injector **K** Choke tube **l** Pump lever **M** Diaphragm **P** Needle valve
s Emulsion tube **t** Filter **U1** Idle orifice **V** Throttle **V1** Choke plate **W** Volume control screw

must be fitted. Note that the butterfly valve must be removed to take out the spindle and when refitting the valve take care to position it so that it does not foul in the bore as it opens and closes. When the butterfly valve is in place make sure that the screws that secure it to the spindle are locked by peening or with Locktite.

Cleaning:

This will cover both flooding and starvation in the carburetter. If flooding is occurring make sure that it is genuine and not caused by loose attachments or defective gaskets.

Remove the air cleaner and take out the screws that secure the float chamber cover. Pivot the cover over to one side and lift out the float. The jet positions on standard carburetters are shown in **FIG 2:5**. Make sure that well-fitting screwdrivers are used to remove the jets, as they are made of brass and will be easily damaged. Wash the jets in clean fuel and blow through them to clean them. Special fluids are made for cleaning carburetters but care must be taken in their use as they can be injurious. **Do not poke through the jets to clean them.** Poking through will wear the calibrated orifices and alter their flow characteristics.

Check the float before refitting it. If fuel is heard inside it as it is shaken then a new float must be fitted. Leaks can be found by immersing the jet in hot water, when the fuel evaporating (or the air expanding) will then show as a stream of bubbles. Do not attempt to repair the float by soldering as this will alter its weight and therefore also alter the fuel level.

Blow through the needle valve to dislodge dirt or else crank over the engine so that the petrol flushes through it. Check the valve by holding it gently closed with a finger and trying to blow through it. If the valve leaks and flushing through will not dislodge dirt, then the valve is worn and must be renewed.

If gaskets are leaking or defective, service lists of new parts are available.

Choke:

If the bi-metallic spring is defective or the housing damaged, the parts cannot be dismantled and a new housing assembly must be fitted.

When removing the assembly the coolant hoses require to be disconnected, so they should either be clamped to prevent the loss of coolant or the cooling system should be partially drained. Once the hoses have been reconnected the cooling system must be bled (see **Chapter 4**).

Once the hoses have been disconnected the assembly can be removed after taking out the three screws that secure it. Before removing it make sure that the alignment marks are visible.

Refit the choke assembly in the reverse order of removal. Make sure that the eye of the bi-metallic spring fits over the lever and then turn the housing clockwise to align the marks shown in **FIG 2:6**.

Difficulty in adjusting slow-running:

The volume control screw has a taper on the end which operates in an orifice. **The screw must never be tightened hard onto its seating otherwise the taper will wear to a step.** After long use a step may wear in the taper, so if the slow-running adjustment seems very erratic and the mixture cannot be set with accuracy stop the engine and take out the volume control screw. If the taper is stepped, discard the screw and fit a new one.

2:6 Adjusting standard carburetter

Before trying to set the carburetter make sure that the ignition system is functioning correctly and properly set (see **Chapter 3**).

A vacuum gauge and tachometer will be most useful and will make the setting more accurate, though they are not essential. If the instruments are available connect the tachometer as instructed by the maker and connect the vacuum gauge to the inlet manifold (similarly to a tapping for a brake servo).

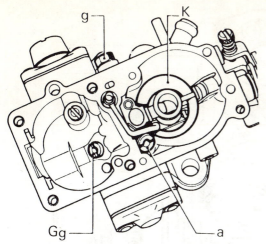

FIG 2:5   The jet positions in a standard carburetter

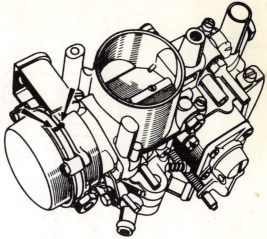

FIG 2:6   Refitting the automatic choke

Start the engine and run it until it has reached its normal operating temperature with the choke valve fully open. Set the correct idling speed of 600 to 650 rev/min using the stop screw on the throttle linkage. Adjust the volume control screw until the idling speed has increased as much as possible with the engine running smoothly. If a vacuum gauge is used adjust for the highest vacuum. Reset the idling speed and carry out further small adjustments to the volume screw to make the exhaust beat even and if necessary readjust the idling speed once more.

2:7 Emission control carburetters

Most of the adjustments on the Solex 26-32 DIDTA.5 carburetter are made at the factory, and by the factory only. The screws 1, 2 and 3 shown in FIG 2:7 are set with extreme accuracy and must under no circumstances be altered.

The operations that can be carried out are limited to the following:

Removing float chamber top (for renewing jets, needle valve, float, accelerator pump piston or gasket)

Renewing 'lung' (vacuum capsule for progressive linkage)

Renewing choke assembly

Renewing solenoid operated idling valve (damper)

Operation:

Each barrel of the carburetter operates on very similar principles to the standard carburetter described earlier. The throttle valve of the first barrel is operated directly from the throttle linkage while the second throttle valve for the other barrel is opened by a 'lung' vacuum capsule which takes its suction from both barrels of the carburetter. The progressive linkage, shown in FIG 2:8, ensures that

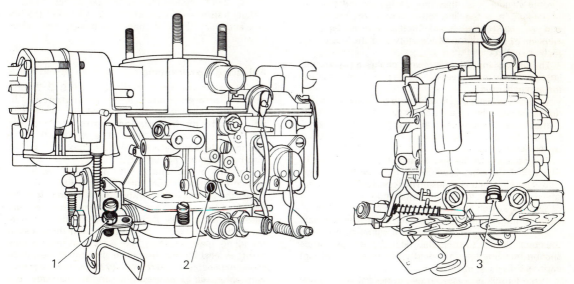

FIG 2:7   These three screws must under no circumstances be adjusted or altered

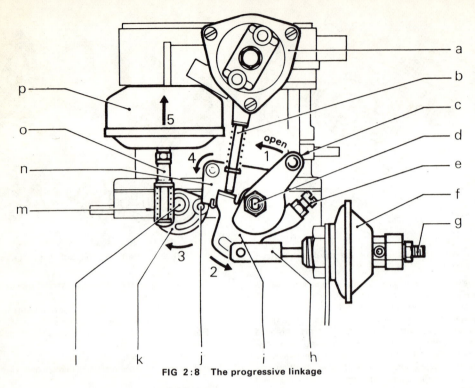

FIG 2:8 The progressive linkage

the opening of the first throttle valve controls the amount of movement available to the second throttle valve.

The lever 'd' is connected directly to the throttle linkage and rotates the spindle of the first butterfly throttle valve. When the throttle opens it moves in the direction 1 and pushes the plate 'n' in the direction 4, and this movement allows the stop peg 'j' to move down the slot in the triangle 'k'. 'k' is attached to the second throttle spindle 'l' so they move together and the pull of the lung 'p' in the direction 5, through the linkage 'o' and 'm', opens the second throttle valve as far as is allowed by the position of the stop 'j' in the slot of the plate 'k' in the direction 3.

The link 'b' from the automatic choke 'a' opens the linkage slightly to increase the slow-running speed when the engine is cold.

The vacuum capsule 'f' is fitted to increase the slow-running speed when required by the system. When vacuum is applied the capsule draws the link 'h' in the direction 2 to open the throttle. The amount of increase is controlled by the screw 'g'.

The parts of the fast-idle system are shown fitted in FIG 2:9. A centrifugal switch 1 is fitted on the lefthand side of the radiator bulkhead and this operates from engine speed. On models fitted with automatic transmission no centrifugal switch is fitted as the electronic computer supplies the signal for the system. When the contacts in the centrifugal switch close, or a signal comes from the computer, the solenoid flap valve 2 closes and stops suction from the inlet manifold passing to the vacuum capsule 3 (item 'f' in FIG 2:8).

If the throttle is pressed down in neutral (on manual transmissions only) it is possible for the system to operate,

and because of the limits in the settings the engine will stick at fast-idle (in gear the car slowing-down automatically brings the speed of the engine below the point at which the system operates). To prevent this from happening a neutral switch, shown in FIG 2:10, is fitted to the gearbox. When the gearbox is in neutral the switch is operated and current passes to the flap so that normal slow-running is restored.

FIG 2:11 shows the centrifugal switch fitted to manual transmission cars and FIG 2:12 shows the fuse box and relay fitted to models with automatic transmission.

Adjusting slow-running:

Note that the screws shown in FIG 2:7 must not be altered under any circumstances. An accurate tachometer is essential for setting all adjustments on the emission-control carburetters, noting that if one is fitted to the car it will not be sufficiently accurate. An exhaust gas analyser will also be useful but not essential.

Start the engine and run it until it has reached its normal operating temperature. Refer to FIG 2:13 and adjust the air screw A until the engine is running at 700 rev/min (775 rev/min for models with automatic transmission). Now adjust the fuel screw B until the idling speed has increased to a maximum, and then readjust the idling speed on the screw A. Repeat these adjustments at least three or four times until the highest idling speed obtainable is 700 rev/min (775 rev/min for models with automatic transmission) when the fuel screw B is adjusted.

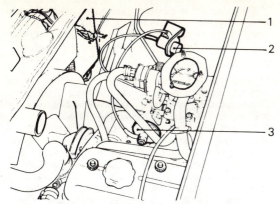

FIG 2:9   The fast-idle components

FIG 2:12   The components fitted with automatic transmission

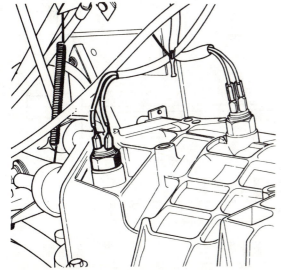

FIG 2:10   The neutral switch

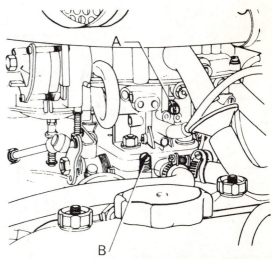

FIG 2:13   Adjusting the emission controlled carburetter

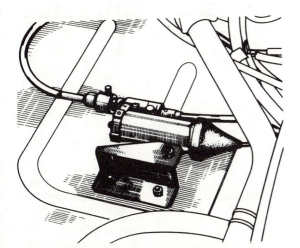

FIG 2:11   The centrifugal switch

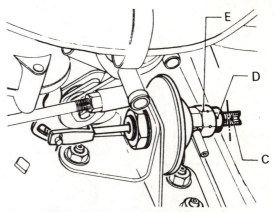

FIG 2:14   Setting the fast-idle speed

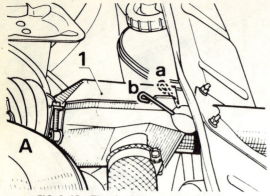

FIG 2:15   The air cleaner warm air valve

Once this point has been set adjust to the correct idling speed of 675 rev/min (750 rev/min for models fitted with automatic transmission) by turning the fuel screw **B** clockwise until the correct speed is reached.

Adjusting fast-idle:

Make sure that the slow-running is accurately set and that the engine is at its normal operating temperature. Disconnect the grey lead from the solenoid flap valve and start the engine, which will now run at fast-idle.

Refer to **FIG 2:14** and hold the nut **E** with a 16 mm spanner while slackening the locknut **D** with a 10 mm spanner. Use a 3 mm Allen key to turn the adjusting screw **C** until the fast-idle speed is correct at 1450 to 1530 rev/min. Hold both the nut **E** and the adjusting screw **C** while tightening the locknut **D**. Check that the adjustment has not altered when tightening the locknut.

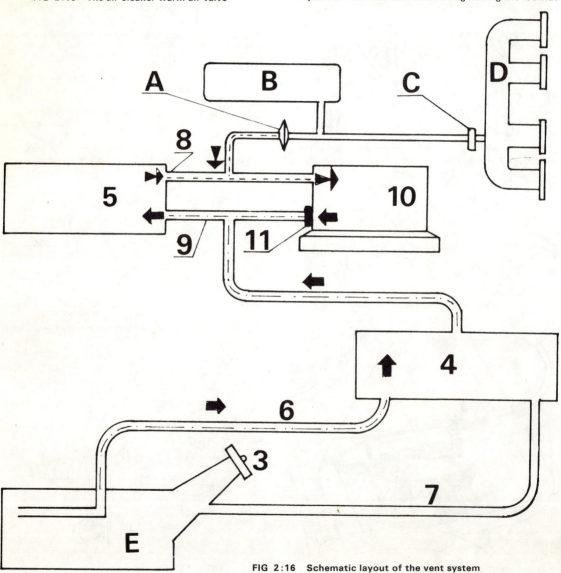

FIG 2:16   Schematic layout of the vent system

Snap the throttle open several times to make sure that the fast-idle returns to the correct speed, and does not vary, when the throttle closes. Stop the engine and reconnect the grey lead to the flap valve.

Idling jet:

The idling jet may be fitted with a solenoid-operated damper. When the ignition is switched on the solenoid is energized and a needle drawn out of the jet to allow the fuel to flow. As soon as the ignition is switched off the needle closes and prevents fuel being drawn through the jet as the engine runs to a halt. The solenoid is fitted with a screw that is normally used to adjust the jet so that it opens when the ignition is on but closes the jet as soon as the ignition is switched off. Check the adjustment, at slow-running, by disconnecting the lead from the solenoid and the engine should stop. This adjusting screw can also be used to hold the needle open in cases of solenoid failure, so that the car can be driven until a new jet can be fitted.

Check the operation of the solenoid by brushing the lead, with the ignition switched on, across the terminal of the solenoid and the needle should be heard to chatter.

Fast-idle circuit faults:

Make sure that all connections are clean and tight and that the vacuum pipes are connected correctly. Note that there should be a clearance of 1.6 mm ($\frac{1}{16}$ inch) between the end of the fork for the vacuum capsule and lever 'i' when at slow-running.

The solenoid flap valve can be checked by disconnecting its lead and other components should be checked by bridging past them. If any of the components are defective they cannot be repaired and they must be renewed instead.

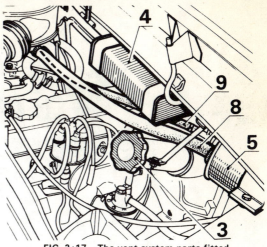

FIG 2:17 The vent system parts fitted

2:8 Emission control

Air cleaner:

The air cleaner is fitted with a valve that controls the air flow, shown in **FIG 2:15**. The valve should be put into the 'a' position when the air temperature is below 10°C (50°F) so that warmed air from the engine compartment is drawn in. At higher temperatures leave the valve in position 'b' so that cold air is drawn in.

Fuel tank vent:

On some later models a system is fitted which traps the fuel fumes from the tank. This system is shown schematically in **FIG 2:16**. The fuel tank **E** is fitted with a sealed filler cap 3 and the vent pipes 6 and 7 lead to an expansion chamber which collects any surplus liquid fuel and allows only fumes to pass through. When the engine

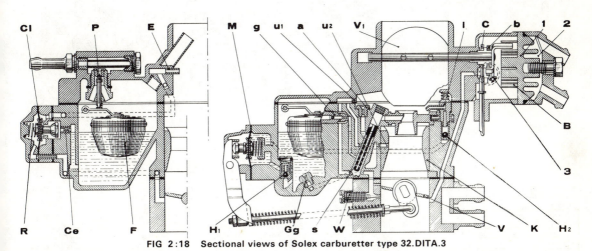

FIG 2:18 Sectional views of Solex carburetter type 32.DITA.3

Key to Fig 2:18 **a** Correction jet **B** Bi-metal coil **b** Small bi-metal coil **C** Cam **C1** Enrichment device valves **Ce** Calibrated orifice **E** Discharge tube **F** Float **Gg** Main jet **g** Pilot jet **H1/H2** Pump check valves **i** injector **K** Choke tube **l** Pump lever **M** Diaphragm **P** Needle valve **R** Spring **s** Emulsion tube **U1/U2** Idle orifices **V** Throttle **V1** Choke plate **W** Volume control screw **1** Body **2** Chamber **3** Lever

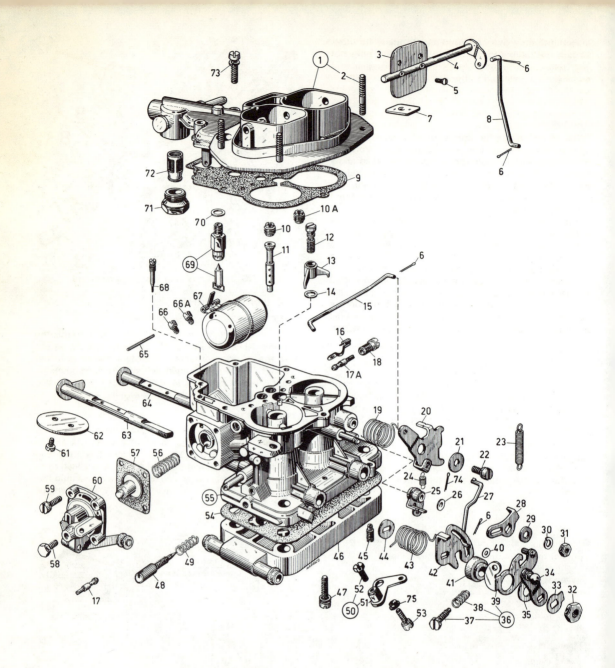

FIG 2:19   Components of Weber carburetter type 32.DIR.4

Key to Fig 2:19   1 Top cover   2 Studs   3 Choke plate   4 Spindle   5 Screw   6 Splitpin   7 Plate   8 Control rod   9 Gasket
10 and 10A Emulsion tube screws   11 Emulsion tubes   12 Pump jet valve union   13 Pump jet   14 Washer
15 Choke operating rod   16 Clip   17 Primary idle jet   17A Secondary idle jet   18 Jet holders   19 Spring
20 Choke operating lever   21 Washer   22 Screw   23 Spring   24 Spring   25 Choke operating lever   26 Washer
27 Fast-idle control rod   28 Secondary throttle operating lever   29 Washer   30 Spring washer   31 Nut   32 Nut   33 Lockwasher
34 Throttle operation lever   35 Washer   36 Primary relay lever assembly   40 Washer   41 Spacer   42 Fast-idle control lever
43 Spring   44 Washer   45 Secondary throttle adjusting screw   46 Water heating flange   47 Fixing screws
48 Idle mixture control screw   49 Spring   50 Choke control lever assembly   53 Pivot screw   54 Gasket   55 Carburetter body
56 Pump spring   57 Diaphragm   58 Cable securing screw   59 Cover securing screws   60 Pump cover   61 Grubscrews
62 Throttle plates   63 Primary throttle spindle   64 Secondary throttle spindle   65 Float pivot   66 Primary main jet
66A Secondary main jet   67 Float   68 Pump discharge control screw   69 Needle valve   70 Washer   71 Screw plug   72 Filter
73 Cover securing screw   74 Splitpin   75 Bush

is running, the valve 11 allows the fumes to be drawn directly into the carburetter 10. When the engine is stopped the fumes are absorbed by a charcoal granule canister 5. As soon as the engine starts purging, air passes through the canister and the fumes are swept out. The adsorption canister must be renewed regularly and it must also be renewed if the charcoal granules come into contact with liquid fuel. A vacuum reservoir **B** is fitted into the system to prevent running-on.

A yellow electronic unit as well as special decelerator adjustments are fitted to models with automatic transmission. The general layout of the parts is shown in **FIG 2:17**.

2:9 Solex carburetter type 32.DiTA.3

This type of carburetter is fitted to various models of the R10 with engines of either 1108 cc or 1289 cc capacity. It is very similar to the type 32.PDIST described earlier in this chapter, but has a slightly different type of water controlled mixture regulator.

Although the internal arrangements for the idle mixture supply have been changed, the method of adjustment remains the same, with the slow-running adjustment screw on the throttle lever controlling the idle speed and the volume control screw (**W** in **FIG 2:18**), adjusting the richness of the mixture.

2:10 Weber carburetter type 32.DIR.4

This is a double barrelled, downdraught carburetter, having a manually operated choke and a water heated body. The manufacturers stress that for reasons of both performance and reduction of pollution it is carefully adjusted at the works and that no further alterations to the settings should be made. An exploded view showing the individual components of the carburetter is given in **FIG 2:19**, and a diagram showing the main features and servicing points in **FIG 2:20**.

Removal:

Unscrew the four securing nuts and lift off the air cleaner assembly, then disconnect the fuel supply pipe.

First loosen the sheath retaining screw then the cable securing nut and remove the choke control cable. Disconnect the throttle operating rod from the ball joint on the throttle control lever.

Withdraw the connecting pipe for the vacuum advance and remove the heater flange connecting pipes.

Undo the four securing nuts and lift off the carburetter, not forgetting to cover the manifold induction port to prevent any foreign matter from falling in.

Filter:

This is removed by unscrewing the hexagonal plug which holds the cylindrical filter element on its seat in the cover and then carefully washed in petrol.

Note that there is no sealing washer and the plug depends on its conical seat for making a good joint seal when refitting.

Float level:

To gain access to the float and float chamber it is first necessary to remove the top cover which is held in place by five screws. The connecting rod and stop must also be removed. Take care not to damage the gasket if a replacement is not available.

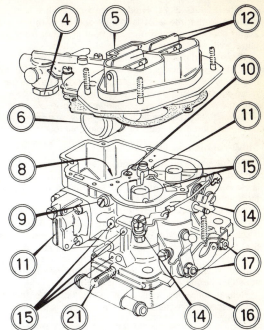

FIG 2:20 Showing main components of carburetter

Key to Fig 2:20   4 Filter   5 Top cover   6 Float 8 Main jets   9 Idle jets   10 Air correction jet and emulsion tubes   11 Acceleration pump   12 Chokes   14 Choke lever 15 Auxiliary venturi   16 Heater flange   17 Throttles 21 Idle mixture control screw

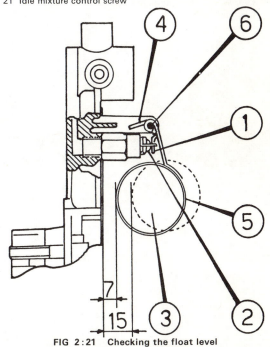

FIG 2:21 Checking the float level

Key to Fig 2:21   1 Tab   2 Needle valve and ball 3 Float in lower position   4 Stop tab   5 Float in high position   6 Pivot

Refer to **FIG 2:21**. Hold the top cover in a vertical position so that the tab 1 is in light contact with the ball 2 and check that the top of the float is 7 mm from the surface of the cover when the gasket is fitted.

When this dimension has been assured the total travel of the float must be checked. This should be 8 mm, and if necessary the position of the stop tab 4 should be adjusted, remembering that the tab 1 must always be in light contact with the needle valve and perpendicular to its axis.

Check finally that the float moves freely on its pivot and does not rub on the sides of the float chamber.

Slow-running adjustment

Before commencing this operation, unscrew the idle mixture adjustment screw and check that its tapered end is clean and that the orifice is not obstructed, by blowing through with compressed air.

Set the idle mixture screw to a starting position of one turn out from fully closed, then start the engine and when it has reached working temperature adjust the speed to 600 to 650 rev/min by means of the throttle stop screw.

Adjust the mixture screw to give the fastest possible engine speed and then bring it back to the correct idling speed by further use of the throttle screw.

Repeat these last two adjustments until the fastest engine speed, consistent with even running, is 600 to 650 rev/min.

2:11 Fault diagnosis

(a) Insufficient fuel delivery or fuel leakage

1 Fuel tank vent restricted or blocked
2 Petrol lines blocked
3 Air leaks at fuel pipe connections
4 Filters blocked

5 Defective fuel pump
6 Defective float in float chamber
7 Worn needle valve or valve held by dirt
8 Defective fuel pump

(b) Excessive fuel consumption

1 Choked air cleaner
2 Carburetter requires adjustment
3 Fuel leakage
4 Idling speed too high
5 Excessively worn carburetter
6 Excessive engine temperature
7 Brakes binding
8 Tyres underinflated
9 Car overloaded

(c) Idling speed too high

1 Rich fuel mixture
2 Carburetter controls sticking
3 Slow-running incorrectly adjusted
4 Worn butterfly valve
5 Fast-idle circuit defective (emission control only)

(d) Noisy fuel pump

1 Mountings loose
2 Air leak on suction side
3 Obstruction in fuel line

(e) No fuel delivery

1 Tank empty
2 Float needle valve stuck closed
3 Blocked fuel lines or filters
4 Defective fuel pump

CHAPTER 3

THE IGNITION SYSTEM

3:1 Description

A distributor is fitted to the engine and it is driven by gears from the engine camshaft at half engine speed. The components of a typical distributor are shown in **FIG 3:1**. An ignition coil generates the very high voltage required and the HT voltage is led through special heavily insulated leads. The HT voltage jumping across the electrodes of the sparking plug makes the spark that ignites the mixture in the cylinder at the appropriate instant.

The distributor shaft is fitted with a cam for operating the contacts and it also carries the rotor arm with it. The distributor and ignition coil are connected in series from the battery so that when the contacts are closed current flows through both of them. A magnetic field is set up around the primary windings of the ignition coil by this current. When the contacts open the current is sharply cut off, assisted by the action of the capacitor, and the collapse of the magnetic field generates a high voltage in the secondary windings of the ignition coil. An HT lead transfers this voltage to the central electrode of the distributor cap and from there it passes through the spring and carbon brush to the rotor arm. The distributor is synchronized with the engine so that when the spark occurs the rotor arm is pointing to the electrode in the cap, which is connected to the sparking plug of the cylinder, which is at the point requiring ignition. The voltage passes through the side electrode along the HT lead to the sparking plug and ignition then takes place.

Combustion is not instantaneous and takes a finite, though extremely short, time to establish and reach optimum pressure. Allowance must therefore be made for the speed of the piston (proportional to engine speed over the short distance being considered) to ensure that maximum pressure always occurs at the correct piston position. Spring-loaded weights are fitted to the distributor shaft and as the engine speed increases these are moved outwards by centrifugal force. The weights are connected so that they turn the cam ahead of the distributor shaft to advance the ignition as the speed increases.

The combustion time will also depend on the quantity and quality of the mixture in the cylinder, which is a variable depending on engine load and throttle opening. The suction in the inlet manifold is dependent on the engine load and throttle opening and a vacuum unit on the distributor is connected to the manifold by a small-bore tube. The vacuum unit then rotates the baseplate of the distributor so that the ignition timing is altered.

3:2 Maintenance

The HT leads, distributor cap, and ignition coil top should be regularly wiped over with a soft clean cloth to remove any dirt or oil.

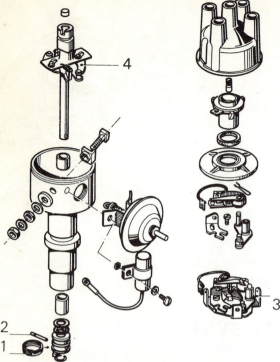

FIG 3:1 Typical distributor components

The sparking plugs should be cleaned at intervals of 10,000 kilometres (6000 miles) and renewed at intervals of 20,000 kilometres (see **Section 3:6**).

When renewing the sparking plugs the distributor should be lightly lubricated at the same time.

Distributor lubrication:

Excessive lubrication must be avoided otherwise the oil will spread onto the contact points and inside the distributor cap.

Free the clips and lift off the distributor cap. Firmly and squarely pull the rotor arm off the distributor shaft. Pour a few drops of oil onto the felt pad in the top of the distributor shaft. Lightly smear the lobes of the cam with a little grease so that the foot of the moving contact will be lubricated. If the moving contact is stiff the pivot post may be lubricated with a single drop of suitable oil, though it is more effective to remove the points and lightly polish the pivot post with fine-grade emerycloth.

Wipe away all surplus lubricant and use a separate clean cloth to wipe the rotor arm and inside of the distributor cap. Refit the rotor arm, making sure that it fits squarely into its slot and is pushed fully home. The distributor cap can then be clipped back into place.

Cleaning contact points:

The Ducellier distributor is fitted with self-cleaning points that wipe across each other. These points therefore do not require cleaning under normal conditions and should be renewed when excessively worn.

The SEV distributor is fitted with points that meet squarely, and with use there is a build up of metal on one contact and a matching pit formed in the other contact. This is perfectly normal and need not be cleaned off. When the build-up of metal reaches .3mm (.012 inch) the points should be removed, discarded and a new set fitted in their place.

If the contact are contaminated with oil or grease, shown by blackening and a smudgy black line on the baseplate under them, they should be removed and cleaned with a fine file, oilstone or ground down. **Do not use emerycloth as this leaves hard particles embedded in the points.**

The contact points must also be renewed as a set if the moving contact spring is weak or broken.

Adjusting Ducellier contact points:

The adjustment points are shown in **FIG 3:2**. The best and most effective method is to have the points set by an agent using a dwell meter. The meter measures the proportion of the circle during which the points are closed as the distributor turns through one revolution, while the engine is running.

If this method cannot be carried out then the points may be set using feeler gauges. The cam 1 is used for setting the vacuum advance and this should only be set using test equipment. Remove the distributor cap and rotor arm and then turn the engine until one of the lobes of the cam is directly under the foot of the moving contact and the points are at their widest gap. The correct gap between the points is .017 to .020 inch (.4 to .5 mm) and this clearance can be obtained by slackening the lockscrew 2 and moving the fixed contact mounting plate as necessary using the Ducellier tool or a screwdriver inserted in the notch 3. After adjusting, operate the vacuum advance mechanism by hand and check that the gap still lies within the specified limits.

Adjusting SEV contact points:

The adjustment points are shown in **FIG 3:3**. The best method of setting the points is to have them checked by an agent using a dwell meter, though feeler gauges can be used.

If feeler gauges are used remove the cap and rotor arm and turn the engine until the points are at their widest opening. Slacken the securing screw 2 and adjust the gap by turning the eccentric screw 1 with a screwdriver. **When inserting the feeler gauge between the points take care to keep it on the unworn portion otherwise it will bridge the pit and give a completely false reading.** Adjust to the correct gap of .4 to .5mm (.017 to .020 inch) and then tighten the securing screw 2.

Check that the gap has not altered while tightening the screw and that it is correct at the other three lobes of the cam.

3:3 Ignition faults

If the engine has a persistent misfire it can be caused by ignition faults.

Start the engine and run it until it has reached its normal operating temperature. Increase the idling speed to a fast-idle. On models fitted with emission control this can be done easily by disconnecting the grey lead from the solenoid flap valve. On other models either adjust at the throttle stop screw or prop the accelerator pedal down slightly. **Dry rags, thick gloves or special insulated tongs should now be used to prevent getting shocks from the leads.** Disconnect each lead from its sparking plug in turn, listening to the engine beat as the lead is disconnected. If the cylinder is firing correctly the misfire will become more pronounced with the lead disconnected, and the engine may even stop altogether. If the cylinder is not firing then there will be no difference in the engine running.

Having found the faulty cylinder, stop the engine and bare the end of the HT lead to that cylinder. Restart the engine and hold the lead approximately 5 mm ($\frac{3}{16}$ inch) from a convenient earth point on the engine (**but well away from the fuel system**).

If the sparks are regular with a healthy blue colour and they seem fat then the sparking plug is defective. Remove the sparking plug and either have it cleaned and tested or else fit a new one in its place. If this does not cure the misfiring then it is an engine fault such as a defective or incorrectly set valve that is the cause.

If the sparks are weak and irregular the fault lies in the ignition. Make sure that the HT lead is not perished, cracked or perishing and renew it if it appears defective. Remove the distributor cap and rotor arm for checking and cleaning. Use methylated spirits (denatured alchohol) to wash off dirt if required and wipe the parts clean with a soft cloth, paying particular attention to the crevices between the HT leads on the outside and those between the electrodes on the inside. Check the cap for cracks or 'tracking' and renew it if either defect is found. 'Tracking' shows up as thin black lines between electrodes or an electrode and the edge of the cap. Make sure that the carbon brush in the cap is not broken and that it moves freely against its spring pressure.

Weak sparks on all four cylinders can be caused by; defective ignition coil, defective HT lead between coil and cap, excessively worn and dirty contact points, or general deterioration of the insulation and dirt on the leads and parts.

Testing the low-tension circuit:

As a quick field test remove the distributor cap and turn the engine until the contact points are closed. Switch on the ignition and flick the points apart with a finger nail. If current is flowing a small low-voltage spark will be seen across the contacts.

As a more accurate test, disconnect the low-tension lead from between the ignition coil and distributor and reconnect it with a low-wattage test lamp in series. Switch on the ignition and slowly turn the engine over while watching the lamp. As the points open the lamp should go out and then come on again as the points close. If the lamp fails to light make sure that the contacts are clean and meeting and then use the test lamp to trace back through the wiring until the break is found.

If the lamp does not go out then there is a shortcircuit in the distributor. Check the internal wiring for frayed insulation or incorrect assembly. If no fault is found repeat the test with the capacitor disconnected and if the lamp now operates correctly the capacitor is shortcircuited and must be renewed.

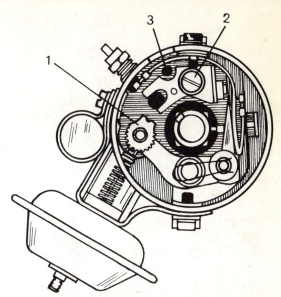

FIG 3:2   Adjusting points on a Ducellier distributor

Key to Fig 3:2   1 Vacuum advance cam   2 Locking screw   3 Notch for adjusting tool

Capacitor:

Capacitor failure is usually a fairly rare fault. The unit is made up of foil wrapped with paper as insulation and a break in the insulation allows the spark to erode away the foil in the area so that the capacitor is self-healing. A shortcircuited capacitor can be detected using the test lamp as instructed previously.

Open-circuit failure is more difficult to detect without special equipment though it may be suspected if starting is difficult and the points are excessively 'blued' or burnt. Substitution with a known satisfactory capacitor is the best test readily available.

3:4 Servicing the distributor

Removal:

Free the distributor cap and leave it hanging attached to the HT leads. When the distributor has been refitted the ignition timing should be reset, but this can be avoided if accurate aligning marks are made on the base of the distributor body and the crankcase. The engine can then be turned without losing the timing. Remove the clamp and screw, arrowed in **FIG 3:4**. Disconnect the low-tension lead from the distributor terminal and disconnect the small-bore tube from the vacuum unit. Withdraw the distributor from the engine with a sharp tug.

The distributor is refitted in the reverse order of removal. Make sure that the offset on the drive dog aligns with the offset in the drive gear. Turn the distributor body until the previously made marks are again in alignment and refit the clamp and its bolt. Refit the distributor cover, making sure that the rotor arm has not been omitted.

Dismantling:

A typical distributor is shown in **FIG 3:1**. Take out the screws that secure the vacuum unit and capacitor, disconnect the vacuum unit link, and remove the vacuum

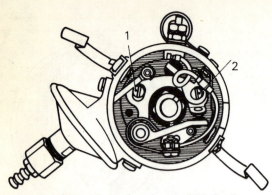

FIG 3:3   Adjusting the points on a SEV distributor

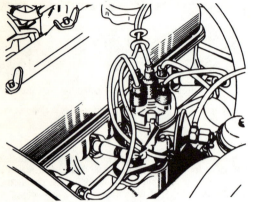

FIG 3:4   The distributor clamp bolt

unit. Free the wiring from the terminals and remove the contact breaker assembly. This is usually sufficient dismantling for all cleaning and servicing purposes.

If further dismantling is required, carefully note the relation of the slot for the rotor arm in the cam to the offset on the drive dog. Remove the retaining spring and drive out the pin. The drive dog and its thrust washers can now be slid off the shaft. Check that the shaft is free from burrs, polishing it with emerycloth if required, before sliding it out of the body.

If the cam is removed from the shaft take great care not to distort or bend the calibrated springs for the weights.

Reassembly:

The metal parts may all be washed in clean fuel, as should the felt pads. Lubricate all bearing surfaces lightly with oil and reassemble the unit in the reverse order of dismantling.

3:5 Setting the ignition timing

The ignition timing marks are shown by the pointer on the timing cover aligning with the notch in the crankshaft pulley. On all standard models the ignition is set to 0 deg. (TDC) on the firing stroke but models fitted with emission control are set **retarded**.

Turn the engine back until it is at TDC, indicated by the pointer on the timing cover with a hole in it aligning with the notch in the pulley. If the timing has been completely

lost turn the engine until it is at the TDC position with No. 1 (nearest clutch) cylinder firing. This position can be found by removing the rocker cover and setting the engine until the valves for No. 4 cylinder are at the point of balance. Another method is to remove the sparking plug and feel the rise in pressure with a thumb over the plug hole as the piston rises on its compression stroke. Slacken the distributor clamp bolt and turn the distributor body until the rotor arm is pointing at the electrode connected to No. 1 cylinder sparking plug. If the timing is reasonably accurate it will not matter about finding which cylinder is firing.

Disconnect the low-tension lead from between the distributor and ignition coil and then reconnect it with a low-wattage test lamp in series. Switch on the ignition and turn the distributor body until the point is found where the lamp has just gone out, indicating that the contact points have just opened. Tighten the distributor clamp in this position. Check by turning the engine a full revolution forwards and slow down the rate of turning near the end of the revolution while watching the light. The instant that the light goes out stop turning the engine and if the timing is correct then the marks will again be in alignment.

For emission-controlled models or for more accurate settings a stroboscopic lamp should be used with the engine running.

3:6 The sparking plugs

Removal:

Slacken each sparking plug using a well fitting box spanner and then blow away loose dust and dirt using an airline or tyre pump. Unscrew the sparking plug fully by hand.

Great care must be taken if the sparking plug is stiff otherwise the threads in the aluminium alloy cylinder head may be stripped. Lay a piece of rag around the base of the plug and soak it with paraffin or penetrating oil and leave at least overnight. Unscrew the plug to the point where it is very stiff and then run it in and out a few times to that point before trying to unscrew it a little further.

If the thread does strip then the cylinder head must be removed and special steel thread inserts fitted.

Store the plugs in the correct order for subsequent examination of the firing ends.

Examination:

The colour of the deposits on the firing ends will give a good guide to the conditions inside the combustion chambers.

If the deposits are light and powdery while ranging in colour from brown to greyish tan, coupled with light wear on the electrodes, then the conditions are normal. Much constant-speed or city driving will leave the deposits white or yellowish. Only cleaning and testing are then required.

If the deposits are wet and black looking, they are caused by oil entering the combustion chamber past worn parts. The only cure is an engine overhaul but fitting a hotter-running grade of sparking plug may help to alleviate the fault.

Dry black and fluffy deposits are caused by poor combustion. Excessive idling may be a cause but it may also be traced to defective ignition or running with too rich a mixture.

Overheated sparking plugs have a white blistered look about the central electrode and when lead-based fuels are used there may be glints of metal on the central insulator. The electrodes will also be excessively burnt away. Some of the possible causes are poor cooling, weak mixture, mistimed ignition, and running at high-speeds with the car overloaded.

When examining the sparking plugs reject out of hand any that have cracked insulators or excessively worn electrodes.

Cleaning:

Wash oily plugs in fuel to remove the oil. Clean the plugs on an abrasive blasting machine and then have them pressure tested after attention to the electrodes. Using a steel-wire brush will do it but it is not so effective.

Trim the electrodes square with a fine file and then adjust them to the correct gap of .6 mm (.025 inch). **Adjust by bending the side electrode only as bending the central electrode will crack the insulator.**

Clean the threaded portion with a wire brush. **If grease is used on the threads only graphite grease may be used as any other grease will bake hard and lock the plugs in place.** The external portion of the insulator can be cleaned with a piece of cloth dipped in methylated spirits.

Refitting:

If the plug is stiff to turn clean the threads in the cylinder head using a well-greased tap. Failing a tap use an old sparking plug with a cross-cut down the threads.

Check the sealing washers and renew them if they are compressed to less than half their original thickness.

Screw the sparking plugs fully back into place by hand. This ensures that any cross-threading or stiffness is immediately apparent. Tighten the plugs to a torque load of 3 to 3.5 kg m (22 to 28 lb ft). If a torque wrench is not available tighten them a further half turn from the hand-tight position. **Do not overtighten the sparking plugs.**

3:7 Fault diagnosis

(a) Engine will not fire

1 Battery discharged or terminals dirty
2 Distributor contact points dirty or out of adjustment
3 Distributor cap dirty, cracked or tracking
4 Carbon brush in cap defective
5 Faulty cable or loose connection in low-tension circuit
6 Rotor arm cracked or omitted on reassembly
7 Weak, broken contact spring or points stuck open
8 Water or dirt on the HT leads
9 Ignition coil defective
10 Defective HT lead between coil and distributor
11 Shortcircuit in distributor

(b) Engine misfires

1 Check 2, 3, 5 and 8 in (a)
2 Sparking plugs fouled, incorrectly set, loose or insulator cracked
3 Defective HT lead
4 Ignition too far advanced
5 Weak contact spring

CHAPTER 4

THE COOLING SYSTEM

4:1 Description

The engine is cooled by the passage of the coolant through its water passages and around the cylinder liners. Some heat is transferred from the bearings and parts by the oil circulation, heat being then lost from the sump. The coolant in the cooling system circulates through the engine picking up heat. It then passes out through the top radiator hose to the radiator, where it is cooled as it passes through the core by the passage of air over the radiator, before returning to the engine again. A natural thermo-syphon flow is set up but, as this is insufficient to ensure full cooling, a belt-driven centrifugal pump is used to circulate the coolant. The pump has fan blades mounted on its hub which ensure a positive passage of air through the radiator even when the car is stationary or travelling slowly. On the models with four-bladed cooling fans the blades are offset, and not at 90 degrees to each other, as this gives quieter operation.

A thermostat valve is fitted into the outlet pipe from the water pump. The valve stays closed when the coolant is cold and the coolant is prevented from passing to the radiator so it recirculates back to the engine through a bypass hose. This limits the quantity of coolant to be heated and the heat losses are minimized so the engine will warm up faster and reach its correct operating temperature sooner. As the coolant heats up the valve in the thermostat opens and allows the coolant to pass normally through the radiator.

The cooling system is sealed in use and should normally only require refilling at intervals of two years. An expansion chamber, with air valve, is fitted beside the radiator and as the coolant heats and expands the surplus passes through into the expansion chamber and it is then drawn back as the system cools.

Water alone is not used in the cooling system but a mixture of pure water and antifreeze, and this should be used in all climates. The antifreeze ensures protection against frost, as expected but it also contains inhibitors which prevent corrosion (essential with the light alloy used in the engine) and it raises the boiling point of the coolant.

4:2 Maintenance

The sealed cooling system should require no maintenance for two years and at the end of this time it should be drained, flushed and refilled with fresh coolant.

Topping-up should not be required unless there are leaks in the system. On models fitted with a clear expansion chamber the level is checked at the expansion chamber, which is marked with a cold maximum level.

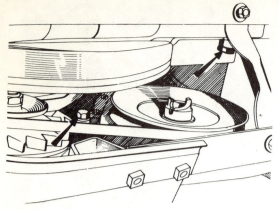

FIG 4:1 The cooling system drain plugs

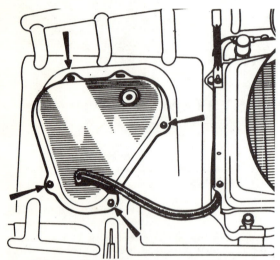

FIG 4:2 The R1130 type expansion chamber

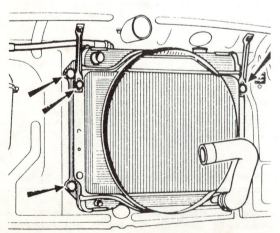

FIG 4:3 The R1190 type expansion chamber and radiator attachments

Never overfill the expansion chamber as coolant passing out through the vent valve will ruin the valve, requiring a new valve to be fitted.

At regular intervals check the fan belt tension (see next section).

Draining:

If the system is being drained so that work can be carried out on the engine, heater, or carburetter, the coolant should be drained into clean containers so that it can be used again. If the system is being drained for its two-yearly maintenance then the coolant should be discarded.

Remove or slacken the vent valve on the expansion chamber and then remove the radiator drain plug, shown in **FIG 4:1**. At first the coolant will flow slowly but when the rate speeds up, showing that the expansion chamber is empty, unseal and remove the radiator filler cap. Remove the engine drain plug (see **FIG 4:1**), make sure that the heater control is set to hot, and open the bleed screw on the heater as well as the bleed screw on the water pump if one is fitted. Note that if the bleed screws are removed new seals should be fitted on reassembly.

Flushing:

The system can be flushed through with clean water until it comes out clean from the drain plugs. If only water is to be used it will help to disconnect the hoses and flush through in a reverse direction. If need be remove the radiator, invert it, and flush through to clear any blockage from the water tubes.

The best method is to use a desludging agent, No. 806.542. Mix up the agent with slightly less water than the cooling system holds and then fill and bleed the system using this mixture, topping up as required with water. Mask off the bottom of the radiator and run the engine for 10 minutes at 2000 rev/min to warm it up rapidly. The engine should then be run for 2 hours with the car stationary or the car may be driven normally for a distance of 200 kilometre (120 miles). Leave the heater on hot so that this too is flushed and keep the coolant as hot as possible without actually overheating. Drain out the desludging agent when the system is hot, taking care not to get scalded, as a lot of the dirt will then still be in suspension. Flush the system with water and then fill and bleed it with water. Run the engine for 10 minutes at 2000 rev/min and drain out the water. Repeat the flushing, filling, running, and draining with water and if necessary do it again a third time. Finally carefully fill and bleed the system using coolant.

Filling:

A special funnel Mot.401 is made for filling the cooling system and this has a long hose so that by hanging the funnel under the bonnet a positive head of coolant is maintained. Whenever possible this funnel should be used.

Make sure that the radiator and engine drain plugs are fitted. With the valve out of the expansion bottle fill it to the maximum mark with coolant. On the R.1130 models with a triangular metal expansion chamber fill it with $1\frac{1}{2}$ litres (2.6 Imp pints, 3 US pints) of coolant and in all cases refit the valve.

Leave the bleed screws open and fill the system through the radiator. If difficulty is found in filling, then disconnect the top radiator hose from between the pump and radiator to allow air to escape, or take out the bleed screw on the pump (if one is fitted).

When the system is full start the engine. The water hose should be reconnected but the bleed screws left open. When coolant flows freely from the bleed screws they should be closed, keeping the coolant topped-up as its level drops. Wait until the thermostat opens, shown by turbulence in the filler neck and by the top radiator tank heating up. Top up the system fully and check that coolant comes out of the bleed screws immediately that they are opened. Refit the radiator filler cap.

Coolant:

This can be bought ready-mixed in drums. The advantage of buying it ready-mixed is that the water used is absolutely pure and soft. The ready-mixed coolant will protect the engine down to temperatures of —30°C.

If the coolant is to be mixed, use either Glaceol, Sexprot or Nyco antifreeze (or a suitable antifreeze recommended by an agent). Mix the antifreeze and water in equal amounts in a suitable container to make a 50 per cent mixture. Do not make up the mixture in the cooling system as inaccuracies are bound to occur and the components may not be well mixed. This coolant will protect the engine down to temperatures of —45°C, though in warmer climates the coolant may be made using 30 per cent anti-freeze which is of the same strength as the ready-mixed coolant.

4:3 The fan belt

The generator, or alternator, is pivoted at the bottom on its attachment bolt and the top end is attached to a slotted strut. By slackening the attachments the generator can be pulled away from the engine to tighten the fan belt, or pushed towards the engine to slacken the belt off.

The belt tension must be correct as if it is too slack the pump and generator will slip and if it is too tight the bearings will be damaged. The generator should be pulled out until the belt moves slightly at the centre of a run when moderate thumb pressure is applied and the generator cannot be turned with one finger in its cooling fan blades.

To remove the belt, slacken the generator right off and ease the belt off a pulley in the direction of rotation. If the belt sticks it can then be helped off by turning the engine with the starting handle. Once the belt is free from one pulley it can be lifted off the other two pulleys and over the cooling fan blades.

4:4 The radiator and cooling hoses

Cooling hoses:

At regular intervals check that the hoses are not perishing, cracking or the clips cutting into them. When flushing the system check the hoses with extra care and renew any that appear the slightest defective.

Special hose clips are fitted and they are tightened with the special tool No. Mot.336. Once the clips have been removed the owner may find great difficulty in tightening them satisfactorily and therefore before disconnecting hoses it is advisable to have a stock of new worm-driven hose clips.

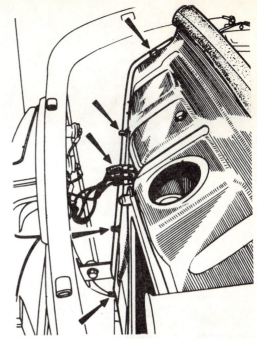

FIG 4:4   Removing the R1130 type radiator screen

Expansion chamber:

The expansion chamber for R.1130 models is shown in **FIG 4:2** and that for R.1190 models in **FIG 4:3**, also showing the radiator attachments after the screen has been removed. If the chamber needs to be removed, without draining the system, clamp the hose so that coolant cannot syphon out of the radiator and then take out the attachments that secure the chamber.

The vent valve will be damaged if coolant passes through it and it must then be renewed.

Refit the chamber in the reverse order of removal and fill it to the correct level with coolant.

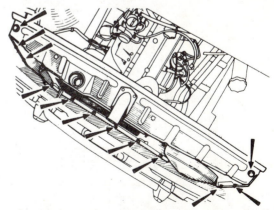

FIG 4:5   Removing the R1130 type radiator screen and panel assembly

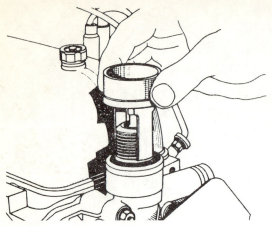

FIG 4:6 The thermostat

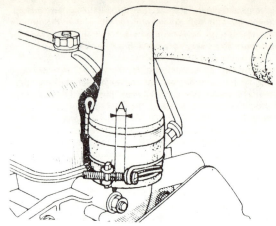

FIG 4:7 Refitting the thermostat

Radiator removal:

The radiator attachments on all models are very similar, and the actual attachments of the R.1130 models are shown in **FIG 4:3**. However, before the radiator attachments are accessible the radiator screen must be removed.

On all models drain the cooling system, disconnect the battery, and disconnect the air cleaner hose from the screen. Also disconnect the lower radiator hose from the pump and the upper radiator hose from the radiator. On the R.1190 models the screen can now be removed by taking off the four bolts that secure it to the radiator and the radiator can then be removed.

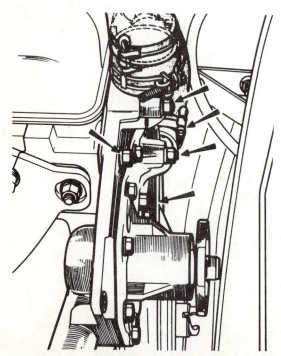

FIG 4:8 The water pump attachments

On the R.1130 models the screen attachments are arrowed in **FIG 4:4**. Once they have been disconnected the screen can be tilted rearwards and removed.

The radiator and screen is refitted in the reverse order of removal. Reconnect the hoses and then fill and bleed the cooling system.

When removing the engine take out the complete assembly after freeing the attachments shown in **FIG 4:5**.

Radiator maintenance:

This is not often required but if the car is driven in dusty conditions or in summer with a lot of insects, periodically blow through the fins, from the rear, with an airline or hosepipe to remove any accumulations of dirt. In extreme cases the radiator should be removed and soaked followed by scrubbing with hot weak detergent solution.

If the water passages are blocked with bits of scale after flushing then the radiator must be removed, inverted and flushed through in this position to blow out scale and dirt.

4:5 The water pump and thermostat

To remove either of these components the cooling system must be drained.

The thermostat, shown in **FIG 4:6**, is secured in the pump outlet by the top hose and clips. The thermostat can be checked by heating it in water and checking that the valve opens and closes correctly. If the thermostat is defective then it must be renewed as it cannot be repaired. When refitting the thermostat tighten the wire clip until the dimension **A**, shown in **FIG 4:7**, is correct at 7 mm ($\frac{9}{32}$ inch).

Water pump:

Disconnect all the hoses, except the top radiator hose, from the water pump. Disconnect the air cleaner from the screen and disconnect the top hose from the radiator. If the pump is to be dismantled then the top hose can be disconnected from the pump, but by disconnecting it from the radiator removal of the thermostat can be avoided. On the R.1130 models disconnect the screen and tilt it to the rear as far as it will go. Slacken off the fan belt and remove it. Take out the four bolts that secure the cooling fan and hub to the water pump. The water pump attachment nuts are shown in **FIG 4:8** and the pump can be drawn off its studs once these are removed.

The water pump components are shown in **FIG 4:9** and they can be separated after taking out the securing bolts. Sludge and dirt can be cleaned out and the pump should be reassembled with a new gasket 3. If the pump is defective or the castings damaged the pump cannot be repaired and a new unit must be fitted in its place.

4:6 The temperature switch

On some models a switch and warning light are fitted to indicate the dangerous limits of the cooling system. If the switch action is suspect, its operating end can be dipped into water and a lamp and battery connected in with the switch. Heat the water while stirring it with a thermometer and note the temperature at which the switch operates.

Before 1964 the switch had its own warning lamp. When the coolant is cold the light comes on and then goes out when the temperature reaches approximately 40°C (104°F). The light will then stay out in the normal operating range but it will come on again if the coolant overheats.

On later models the temperature switch operates the oil pressure warning lamp. The lamp will act as a warning of low oil pressure for the cold and normal operating temperatures of the cooling system. If the coolant overheats then the switch will operate the lamp. If the lamp comes on at speed leave the engine at idle and disconnect the lead from the temperature switch. If the light goes out then the coolant is overheating.

Check the oil pressure by increasing the engine speed slightly as with worn engines the light may sometimes be on at idling speed. **If the coolant is overheated or the oil pressure low stop the engine as soon as the check has been made and check for faults**

4:6 Fault diagnosis

(a) Internal water leakage

1 Loose cylinder head bolts
2 Defective cylinder head gasket
3 Cracked or distorted cylinder head
4 Defective liner seals

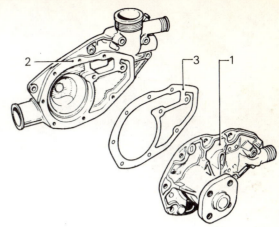

FIG 4:9   The water pump components

(b) Poor circulation

1 Perished or callapsed water hoses
2 Defective thermostat
3 Radiator or engine water passages blocked
4 Slipping fan belt

(c) Corrosion

1 Impurities in the water (preferably use distilled water only)
2 Infrequent draining and flushing
3 Using water only in the cooling system

(d) Overheating

1 Check (b)
2 Lack of coolant
3 Defective water pump
4 Radiator cooling fins blocked with dirt
5 Low oil level in engine
6 Sludge in crankcase and sump
7 Retarded ignition
8 Mixture too weak
9 Tight engine
10 Choked exhaust
11 Binding brakes
12 Slipping clutch

CHAPTER 5

THE CLUTCH

5:1 Description

All the models fitted with a manual gearbox are fitted with a mechanically operated clutch. There are slight differences between the various clutches but they will be dealt with in the text. On the earlier models the release bearing acts on a thrust plate held to the case by straps and the cover assembly is shown in **FIG 5:1**. On the later models the release bearing acts directly onto the fingers of the diaphragm spring and the clutch cover is shown in **FIG 5:2**. The parts as they are removed from the engine are shown in **FIG 5:3** and they cannot be dismantled further. The clutch cover assembly is bolted to the flywheel and revolves with the engine while the driven plate assembly is splined by its hub to the input shaft of the gearbox.

A sectioned view of the clutch assembly is shown in **FIG 5:4**. The diaphragm spring acts between the cover 9 and pressure plate 10 to force the pressure plate forwards. The driven plate 12 is then gripped, by its friction linings, between the face of the pressure plate 10 and that of the flywheel 13, so that it must rotate with the flywheel and transmit drive to the gearbox input shaft.

When the clutch pedal is pressed the cable 2 pulls the lever 1 so that its pivots about the point 3. Movement of the lever first brings the release bearings 4 into contact with the thrust plate 6 (directly with the fingers of the diaphragm spring on later models) and then moves the thrust plate so that the fingers move forwards. The diaphragm spring pivots about the points 7 and 8 on the cover and the outer end draws back the pressure plate 10 through the straps 11. The pressure on the driven plate is released and the driven plate and gearbox are free to rotate independently or even come to a stop together.

When the pedal is released normally the pressure on the driven plate builds up gradually, so that at first the linings slip between the pressure faces and drive is gradually taken up. Springs on the hub of the driven plate also damp the shock of take-up.

5:2 Maintenance

At regular intervals check the clutch adjustment. As the linings wear the clearance will alter, but there must be a clearance between the release bearing and fingers of the diaphragm spring when the clutch is released otherwise there will be excessive wear on the release bearings.

On all models the clearance is checked at the release lever (item 1 in **FIG 5:4**) and the end of the lever should

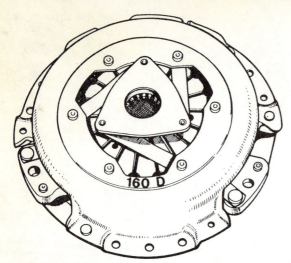

FIG 5:1 The earlier clutch cover assembly

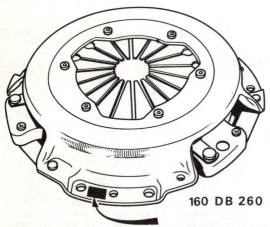

FIG 5:2 The later clutch cover assembly

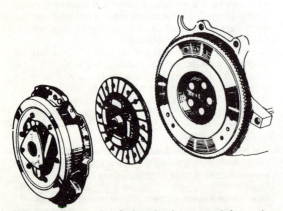

FIG 5:3 The parts of the clutch removed from the engine

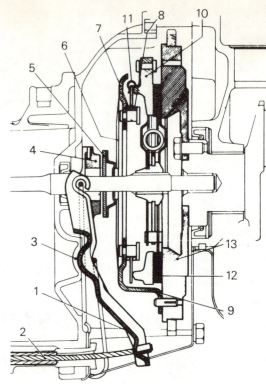

FIG 5:4 Sectioned view of the clutch

have a free movement of 2 to 3mm ($\frac{3}{32}$ inch). Remove the undertray to gain access.

On models fitted with 318 or 325 gearboxes the adjustment point is shown in **FIG 5:5**. Slacken the locknuts 1 and rotate the sleeve until the correct clearance is felt at the release lever. Tighten the locknuts and check that the adjustment has not altered.

On all other models the adjustment point is shown in **FIG 5:6** and the adjustment is set by turning the nut 2 after slackening the locknut 1.

If a grease nipple is fitted to the pedal pivot shaft this should be occasionally lubricated.

5:3 Clutch cable

318 and 325 gearbox types:

Remove the undertray and slacken off the locknuts 1 so that the sleeve 2 (shown in **FIG 5:5**) can be fully unscrewed. Disconnect the cable from the release lever, arrowed in **FIG 5:7**, and disconnect the cable from the hollow screw and clip. Push the cable cover end stop from its lug on the crossmember and remove the cable.

Refit the cable in the reverse order of removal and then set the correct clearance at the release lever.

All other models:

Remove the two undertrays. Disconnect the cable from the clutch pedal, by removing the clevis pin shown in **FIG 5:8**. Free the cable cover end stop from its lug on the crossmember, shown in **FIG 5:9**. Disconnect the cable from the release lever and free it from the hollow screw, rubber tube and clip to free it.

Refit the parts in the reverse order of removal and set the correct clearance at the release lever.

5:4 Pedal assembly

From inside the car remove the mat over the pedals and take off the coverplate. From underneath the car disconnect the cable from the pedal, by removing the clevis pin, unhook the return spring, shown in **FIG 5:10**, and then take out the bolt that secures the pedal shaft. Partially withdraw the pedal shaft and remove the pedal itself from inside the car.

Refit the pedal in the reverse order of removal and check that the clutch adjustment is correct.

5:5 Release bearing and lever:

To remove either of these parts the engine must be removed from the car. It is most advisable to check the bearing whenever the engine is taken out. To save taking the engine out again at a later date renew the bearing if it is at all suspect.

Release bearing:

The earlier type of attachment is shown in **FIG 5:11**. Later models do not have the tabs 1 as shown in the figure. To remove the bearing, withdraw the spring ends from the trunnions and lift the tabs, if fitted, so that the bearing can be slid off along the input shaft.

Before refitting the bearing, grease the trunnions with Molykote grease or graphite grease and on later models also lightly grease the contact areas on the diaphragm spring fingers. Refit the bearing in the reverse order of removal and if the tabs are fitted lightly knock them down, making sure that the bearing pivots freely.

Release lever:

The attachments on later models are shown in **FIG 5:12**. On earlier models a spring retaining lug is fitted. Remove the release bearing as described earlier and detach the cable from the lever. Unlock and remove the hollow bolt shown and remove the lever with its spring.

Lubricate the points, thrust pad guide, and pivot for the lever with Molykote or graphite grease.

On the earlier models the lever is automatically set and the bolt locked with a lockwasher. Refit the spring retaining lug after reassembly.

On later models use Locktite on the threads of the hollow bolt and make sure that the dimensions **C** are equal at 11 to 13 mm ($\frac{7}{16}$ to $\frac{1}{2}$ inch) before tightening the hollow bolt.

5:6 Servicing the clutch

The removal and refitting of the clutch has been dealt with in **Chapter 1**. Note that the bolts that secure the clutch must be tightened and slackened progressively and in a diagonal sequence, to avoid straining the cover, and that the driven plate must be centralized with a suitable mandrel when refitting the clutch.

The spigot bearing in the crankshaft should be checked every time that the clutch is removed and it should be renewed if it is worn or shows chatter marks.

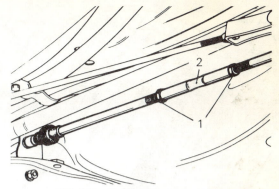

FIG 5:5   Clutch adjustment point

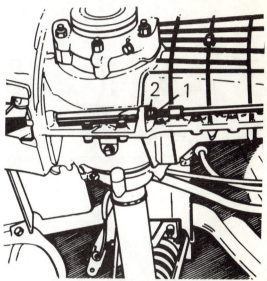

FIG 5:6   Clutch adjustment point

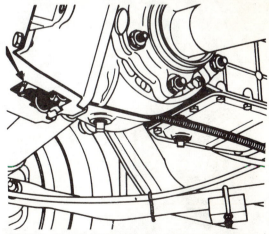

FIG 5:7   Attachment of the clutch cable to the release lever

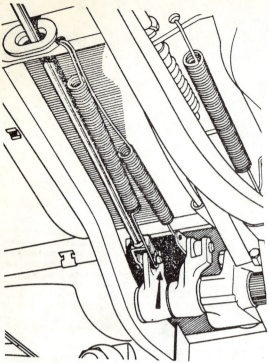

FIG 5:8 Attachment of the clutch cable to the clutch pedal

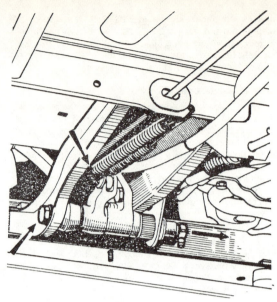

FIG 5:10 The attachments of the clutch pedal

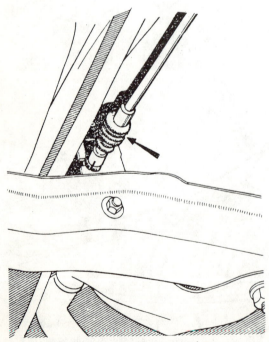

FIG 5:9 Outer cable cover end stop

Cover assembly:

This cannot be dismantled and it must be renewed if defective. **The unit must not be washed in solvent, as this will remove grease from the pivot points.** Loose dust and dirt should be removed with a brush and airline and if the assembly is excessively oily it should be wiped down with a cloth moistened in fuel.

Check the pressure plate face for scoring or burn marks. Check the cover and straps for cracking and distortion, paying particular attention to areas around rivets and attachment holes.

Driven plate:

The driven plate must be renewed if the linings are worn down nearly to the rivet heads, the linings are contaminated with oil, or the assembly is mechanically defective.

Do not attempt to rivet on new linings but always fit a factory-reconditioned or new unit.

Check the driven plate for loose rivets or damper springs. Slide it back onto the gearbox input shaft and check that it slides freely without excessive rotational play.

The linings are at their maximum efficiency when they have an evenly polished finish through which the grain of the material is clearly visible. Small amounts of oil will leave dark coloured smears while larger amounts will leave a dark glaze which hides the grain of the friction material. Large amounts of oil will be obvious from the oil-soaked appearance of the linings and the free oil in the housing. Provided that the grain of the material is still visible the driven plate may be used again, but if the grain is hidden then a new driven plate must be fitted. Do not forget to find and cure the source of the oil before reassembling the parts.

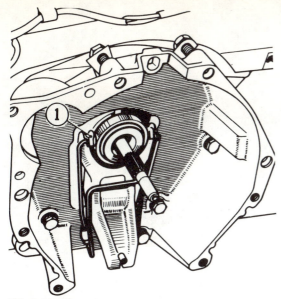

FIG 5:11 The release bearing attachments on earlier models

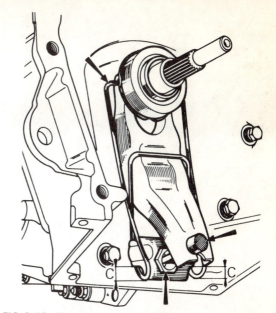

FIG 5:12 The release lever attachments on later models

5:7 Fault diagnosis

(a) Drag or spin

1 Oil or grease on the driven plate linings
2 Incorrectly adjusted cable
3 Binding spigot bearing in crankshaft
4 Distorted driven plate
5 Warped or damaged pressure plate

(b) Fierceness or snatch

1 Check (a)
2 Excessively worn clutch linings
3 Worn or loose driven plate hub

(c) Slip

1 Check 1 and 2 in (a) and 2 in (b)
2 Weak diaphragm spring
3 Sticking cable

(d) Judder

1 Check (a)
2 Pressure plate not parallel with flywheel face
3 Contact area of linings not evenly distributed
4 Buckled driven plate
5 Faulty or loose engine mountings
6 Defective rear suspension or drive shafts

(e) Rattles

1 Broken damper spring in driven plate
2 Worn release mechanism

(f) Tick or knock

1 Worn spigot bearing in crankshaft
2 Badly worn splines on input shaft or hub
3 Loose flywheel

CHAPTER 6

THE TRANSMISSION

6:1 Description

The transmission unit is mounted directly in front of the engine and contains the gearbox and final drive. The design varies slightly between different models but in all cases the basic principles are the same. All the parts are contained in four castings. The clutch cover is bolted to the rear of the unit and a front cover carries the mounting and selector input. All the main parts are contained in two castings bolted together along the longitudinal axis. A view of the 330 unit with one side casting removed is shown in **FIG 6:1**.

The average owner is advised to take the gearbox to an agent for repair work and adjustments, as dismantling will upset the adjustments of the crownwheel and pinion. Special tools and a press are required for dismantling and reassembling the transmission unit and all settings must be made with accuracy to ensure smooth and silent operation.

The drive to the transmission is taken in by an input shaft which is driven by the hub of the clutch driven plate. The primary shaft has the gears integral with it and is secured to the input shaft by a splined coupling. The gears are in constant mesh and those on the secondary shaft are free to rotate. A synchromesh unit connects the secondary shaft gear to the shaft itself when a gear is selected and drive then passes between the two shafts. The secondary shaft has the pinion for the final drive and this is in mesh with the crownwheel so that drive is transmitted to the differential and out through the drive shaft attachments. The various drives for the 330 unit in the selections are shown in **FIG 6:2**. Reverse speed is engaged by sliding an idler gear between the primary and secondary shafts.

The synchromesh outer sleeves are moved by selector forks attached to the selector rod. Each rod is held in its selected position by detent balls and springs and the disc 1, shown in **FIG 6:3**, prevents movement of the other two shafts when one shaft is moved into a select position.

6:2 Lubrication

The unit is partially filled with oil so that the gears dip into the oil. The parts above the oil bath are lubricated by splash thrown up by the gears as they revolve. The two types of gearbox filler and drain plugs are shown in **FIGS 6:4** and **6:5**. On all models the level is checked

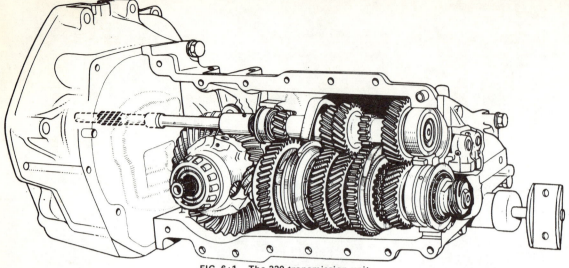

FIG 6:1   The 330 transmission unit

at the combined filler and level plug **A**. The unit is filled with EP.80 oil until the level is at the bottom of the hole for the filler plug. **Fill slowly to allow the oil to settle and fill all parts otherwise the oil may overflow from the filler plug before the unit is full.**

The drain plugs **B** and **C** are fitted for draining out the oil, noting that it is best to drain after a run when the oil is hot and will flow faster.

The oil capacity of the type of unit shown in **FIG 6:4** is 1.9 litre (3.5 Imp pint—4 US pint). The capacity of the type of unit shown in **FIG 6:5** is 1.6 litre (2¾ Imp pint—3½ US pint).

PART 1   325 and 318 TRANSMISSION

A sectioned view of this type of unit is shown in **FIG 6:6** and it can be identified by the sump fitted underneath. The actual one shown in the figure is type 318.

6:3 Removal

1 Disconnect the battery before carrying out any other work. Remove the air cleaner, disconnect the throttle cable from the bellcrank on the manifold and remove the silencer (muffler). Remove the engine floor compartment tray so that the starter motor can be disconnected and removed.

2 Slacken the rear wheel nuts and raise the car securely onto chassis stands and then remove the rear road wheels. Disconnect the handbrake cable from the caliper and then free the caliper from the suspension, without disconnecting the brake flexible hose (see **Chapter 11**). Drain the transmission.

3 Disconnect the tie bar at the wheel end and remove the damper and road spring, using a special tool to compress the spring and disconnecting one end of the rebound strap (see **Chapter 8**).

4 Free the starter electrical cable and throttle operating cable from their clips. Take out the side mounting pad securing nuts and bolts, shown in **FIG 6:7**, and remove the pads together with the accelerator cable support.

5 Mark the half shells, shown in **FIG 6:8**, relative to the differential carrier and housing so that the parts will be reassembled into their original position. Remove the remainder of the nuts that secure the half shells and pull off the half shells. Pull back the drive shaft tubes and secure the differential cover in place to the housing with two nuts on either side.

6 Remove the clutch protecting plate so that the cable can be disconnected from the release lever and housing. Disconnect the shift link and the speedometer drive cable, at the points shown in **FIG 6:9**.

7 Support the engine and gearbox with a jack and pad of wood placed under the engine sump. Remove the bolt, arrowed in **FIG 6:10**, which secures the transmission to the suspension sidemember. Lower the jack slightly so that the rubber pad can be removed. Support the transmission and take out the four bolts that secure the clutch housing to the engine. Still supporting the transmission, draw it forwards until the input shaft is clear of the clutch and then remove the unit. **Do not allow the weight of the transmission to hang on the input shaft or parts will be damaged.** Raise the engine back to its normal level after the transmission has been removed.

The transmission is refitted in the reverse order of removal. The end of the input shaft should be lightly greased and the thrust faces of the half-shells should be lightly smeared with jointing compound. Use the plain washers on the half-shell at the side mounting points. Do not forget to refit cable supports or refill the unit with fresh oil after it has been refitted.

6:4 Dismantling the 318 transmission

Only the general procedure will be given as special tools and a press are essential to ensure that the correct settings are made and that parts can be removed and refitted.

1 Remove the release bearing and lever (as instructed in **Chapter 5**). Take out the bolts that secure the clutch housing and remove it from the transmission.

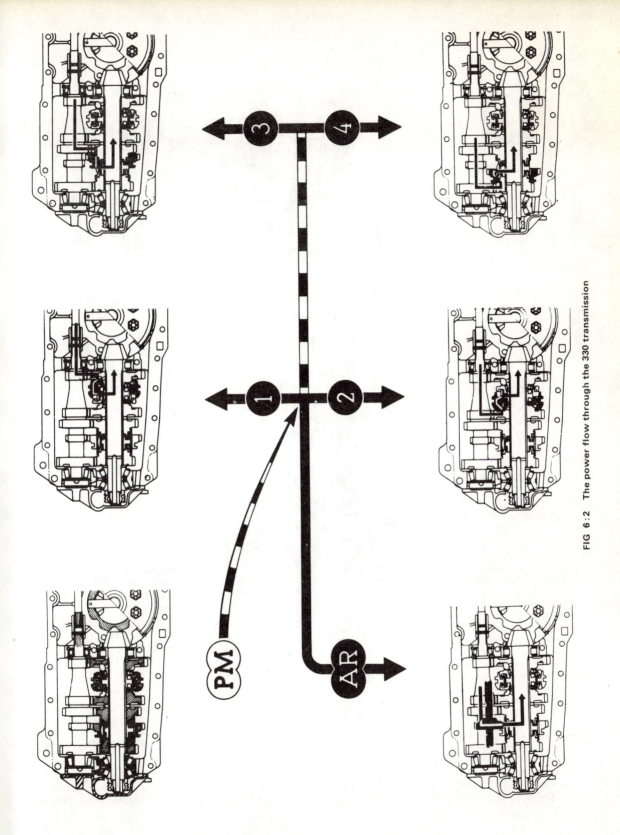

FIG 6:2   The power flow through the 330 transmission

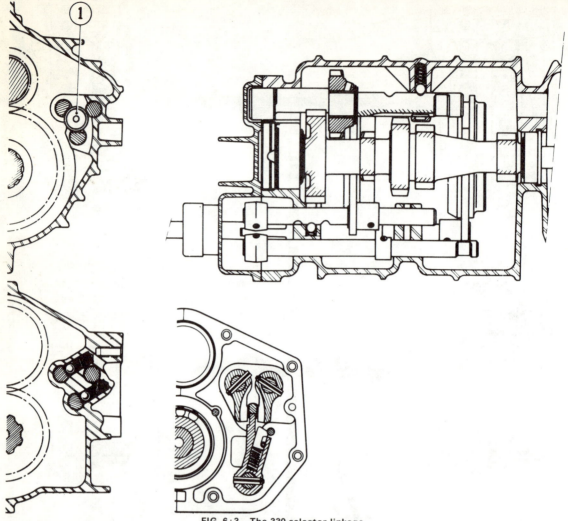

FIG 6:3 The 330 selector linkage

Remove the damping weights from the other end of the unit. Pull together the ends of the spring over the pin on the input shaft and slide the spring along the shaft to expose the pin. Drive out the pin and remove the input shaft from the primary shaft. Manoeuvre out the differential assembly through the aperture that was covered by the clutch housing.

2 Remove the bottom cover. Remove the nuts that secure the end cover. Take off the speedometer drive housing, engage second gear, and pull back the cover until it contacts the lug on the control rod, then drive out the pin, as shown in **FIG 6:11**. Remove the shaft and housing, then free the control lever. Return the gearbox to neutral and remove the spacer and primary shaft adjusting shims. Note that all shim sets should be tied together and labelled so that they can be refitted into their original positions.

3 Drive out the roll pins in the first/second and third/fourth shift forks. Unscrew the plug for the lock detent spring. Withdraw the first/second selector shaft and

carefully collect the lock plunger from between the shafts. Remove the third/fourth shaft and fork, leaving the fork for the first/second selector still fitted in the casing.

4 Move the selectors so that two gears are simultaneously engaged and the gearbox is locked. Unlock and unscrew the nut that forms the speedometer drive worm from the end of the secondary shaft. Return the gears to neutral to free the gearbox.

5 Remove the double-tapered bearing, adjusting washer and stop washer locking key. Gently tap the secondary shaft towards the differential end and pull the fourth speed gear to the case to expose the stop washer 22, shown in **FIG 6:12**. Turn the washer and then slide it off as shown.

6 Bring the fourth speed gearwheel against the synchromesh gearwheel to expose the stop washer 25 and then turn and slide the stop washer in a similar

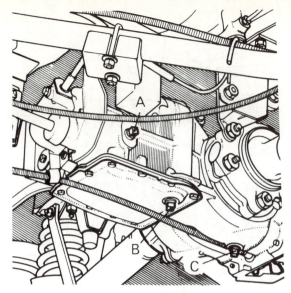

FIG 6:4 Filling and drain points on 318 and 325 transmissions

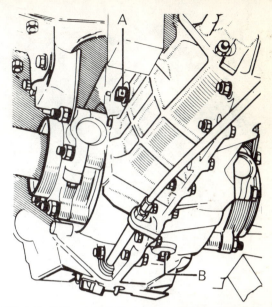

FIG 6:5 Filling and drain points on 330 transmissions

manner to the stop washer 22. Gradually pull the shaft out towards the differential end and remove the gears.

7 Remove the shaft bearing and reverse shaft stop plate. Take out the detent ball and spring after unscrewing the plug. Turn the shaft until the lever is free from the reverse sleeve and remove the sleeve, as shown in **FIG 6:13**. Drive out the roll pin that secures the fork to the shaft, as well as the circlip and washer that secure the reverse idler gear, and then remove the fork and gear. Remove the interlock plungers from the bores in the casting.

8 Push the primary shaft towards the differential end and lift out the outer track for the bearing. Remove the inner race of the bearing with a suitable extractor and the primary shaft can now be lifted out through the bottom aperture.

Reassembly:

The unit is reassembled in the reverse order of dismantling but before it is reassembled the pinion depth, crownwheel and pinion mesh and the differential bearing preload (no play if original bearings are used) must be checked and adjusted.

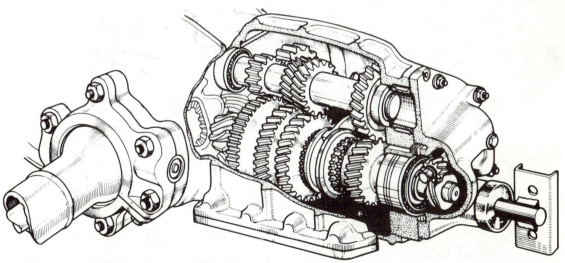

FIG 6:6 The 318 transmission unit

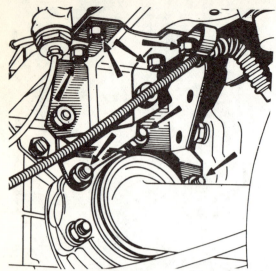

FIG 6:7   The side mounting pads

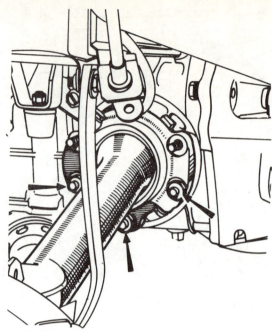

FIG 6:8   The half shell and axle tune attachments

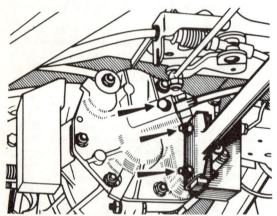

FIG 6:9   The speedometer drive cable and shift link

FIG 6:10   318 and 325 transmission attachment bolt

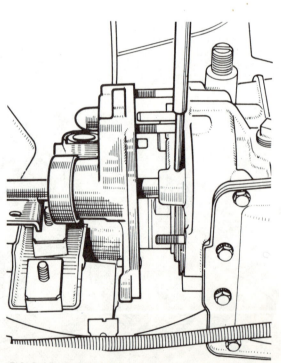

FIG 6:11   Freeing the speedometer housing, shown with the transmission still fitted

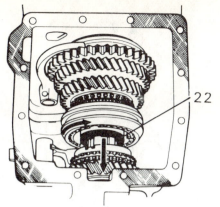

FIG 6:12 Removing stop washer

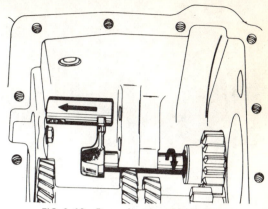

FIG 6:13 Removing the reverse sleeve

If the differential is dismantled note that new self-locking bolts must be fitted and that they must be further locked with a spot of electro-brazing or welding.

The components of the secondary shaft assembly are shown in **FIG 6:14**.

6:5 Dismantling the 325 transmission

This is very similar to the 318 transmission but it is only fitted with three forward speeds.

General dismantling is also very similar to the 318 transmission (see previous section).

The method of removing the selector mechanism is shown in **FIG 6:15**. Drive out the roll pins, unscrew the lock stop and then remove the spring and ball. Withdraw the first/reverse shaft and then remove the plunger 1 so that the second/third shaft can be removed, taking care not to lose the ball and spring.

The primary shaft bearing and the reverse shaft are secured by a plate, as shown in **FIG 6:16**. After the plate has been removed the reverse shaft can be withdrawn allowing the reverse gear to fall down into the casing.

6:6 Speedometer housing

On both types of transmission the speedometer housing can be removed, for curing oil leaks, without removing the transmission. Raise the car on stands and drain the transmission. Remove the damper weights and engage first gear. Disconnect the gearshift link and the speedometer drive cable and then remove the nuts that secure the speedometer housing. All the attachments are shown in **FIG 6:17**. Pull back the housing until it contacts the lug on the gear control shaft and then drive out the pin that secures the control shaft. Remove the shaft and housing and free the control lever.

The parts are refitted in the reverse order of removal, using a new paper gasket and roll pin.

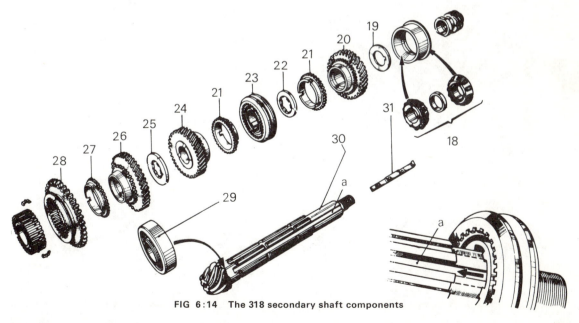

FIG 6:14 The 318 secondary shaft components

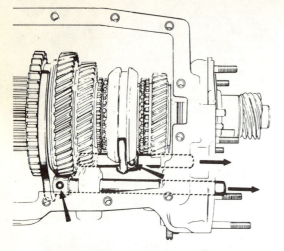

FIG 6:16 The primary shaft bearing and reverse shaft retainer on 325 transmissions

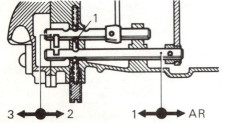

3 ◄—●—► 2   1 ●—► AR

FIG 6:15 The 325 transmission selector mechanism

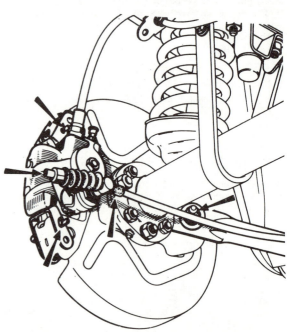

FIG 6:18 The brake and tie rod attachments

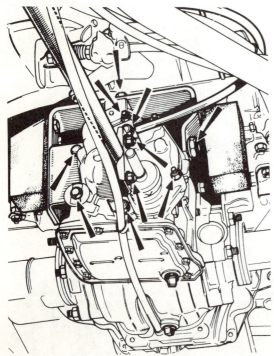

FIG 6:17 The speedometer housing attachments

FIG 6:19 330 transmission attachment bolt

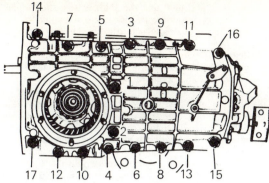

FIG 6:20 The sequence for tightening the nuts on 330 transmissions. Note that bolts 4, 10 and 12 are reversed

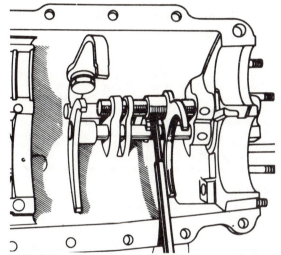

FIG 6:21 Driving out third/fourth selector roll pin

PART 2 THE 330 TRANSMISSION

6:7 Removal

1 Disconnect the battery. Remove the air cleaner and disconnect the throttle cable from the bellcrank on the manifolds. Remove the lefthand side engine compartment floor tray and then remove the silencer and starter motor.

2 Raise the rear of the car on stands, after slackening the road wheel nuts slightly, and once it is up remove the rear wheels as well as draining the transmission. Disconnect the axle tie bars, disconnect the handbrake cable and remove the brake caliper, by freeing the attachment points shown in **FIG 6:18**. The flexible brake hose does not need to be disconnected and further details of caliper removal are given in **Chapter 11**.

3 Remove the damper and road spring assembly (see **Chapter 8**). Free the starter electrical cable and throttle control cable from their clips. Mark the half-shells so that they will be refitted into their original positions and then remove the nuts that secure them to the differential casing as well as those that secure the side mounting pads. Remove the clutch cover and

disconnect the clutch cable from the release lever, then free the adjustable end fitting from the protective rubber. Disconnect the gearshift link and speedometer drive cable.

4 Support the unit with a jack and pad of wood under the engine sump and remove the bolt (arrowed in **FIG 6:17**) which secures the transmission to the suspension crossmember. Lower the jack and remove the rubber pad. Remove the four bolts which secure the transmission case to the engine and draw the transmission forward until the input shaft is clear of the clutch, **while supporting the weight of the transmission by hand.** Raise the jack to bring the engine back to its normal level so that its mountings are not strained.

The transmission is refitted in the reverse order of removal. The input shaft should be lightly lubricated on the splines and the half-shells lightly smeared with jointing compound.

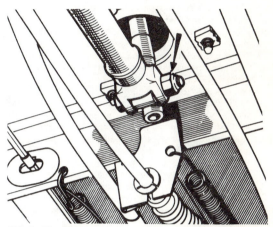

FIG 6:22 The attachment of the selector shaft to the gearlever

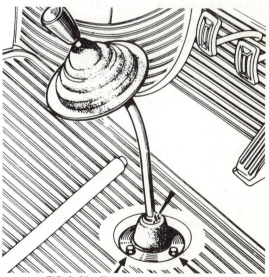

FIG 6:23 The gearlever attachments

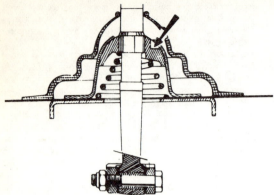

FIG 6:24 Sectioned view of gearlever ball joint

6:8 Dismantling

Special tools and a press are required to dismantle the unit completely and when the parts are being reassembled they must be set to the correct clearances and preloads to ensure that the unit operates smoothly and quietly.

1 Remove the clutch release bearing and lever. Remove the clutch housing by taking out the nuts and bolts that secure it.

2 Remove the nuts that secure the speedometer housing and pull it back until it contacts the lug on the control shaft. Drive out the roll-pin that secures the control shaft and remove the housing with the control shaft. Take out the primary shaft bearing shims and spacer, storing them safely for reassembly.

3 Slacken the bolts that secure the side casings in the same order as they are tightened (see **FIG 6:20**). Remove the bolts when they are slack and take off one of the side covers. It is advisable to remove the righthand side cover and leave the transmission lying on its lefthand side.

4 Lift out the secondary shaft assembly. **The synchromesh unit hubs are fitted hot to the shaft and for this reason the shaft assembly cannot be dismantled.** The bearings and fourth speed wheel can be renewed as these do not necessitate removing the synchromesh hubs, but no further work can be carried out on the remainder of the parts. Note that if a new assembly has to be fitted then the crownwheel must also be renewed as pinion and crownwheel are mated on manufacture.

5 Lift out the primary shaft assembly. The input shaft can be removed by drifting out the roll-pin. Lift out the differential and remove the differential carriers.

6 Drive out the roll-pin that secures the selector fork on the third/top selector shaft, as shown in **FIG 6:21**, and slide out the shaft with its end fitting, collecting the detent ball and spring. Remove the locking disc from between the shafts. Pull the reverse selector shaft out as far as it will go and then drive out the roll-pin that secures the first/second selector fork to its shaft. Remove the fork and then drive out the roll-pin that secures the end fitting to the reverse selector shaft. Remove the reverse shaft end fitting and slide out the first/second shaft, carefully collecting the detent ball and spring. Drive out the pin that secures the reverse fork to its shaft until it just touches the

housing, and then turn the shaft so that the pin can be fully pulled out with a pair of pliers, after the pin that secures the idle lever and lever have been removed. The reverse gear idler wheel can be removed after the retaining circlip has been taken out. Note that the idler gearshaft is fitted with a guide, friction washer and detent ball and spring as well.

The gearbox is reassembled in the reverse order of dismantling, after cleaning and checking the parts. If new parts are fitted then the pinion depth, crownwheel bearings, crownwheel and pinion backlash as well as the primary shaft end float must all be correctly adjusted. Do not forget to refill the unit with fresh oil after it has been refitted. Note that all the nuts are fitted on the righthand side except the nuts 4, 10 and 12 (see **FIG 6:20**) which are fitted on the left to clear the clutch control.

PART 3   THE SELECTOR MECHANISM

6:9 The selector mechanism

The linkage is similar on all the models covered by this manual. The selector shaft is attached by bolts between lugs at the transmission end and is disconnected as described in the sections dealing with removal of the transmission. The attachment to the gearlever is shown in **FIG 6:22**, though it will be necessary to remove the undertray to gain access. After the selector shaft has been disconnected the gearlever itself can be removed by lifting the floor covering and taking out the three bolts, arrowed in **FIG 6:23**, that secure it.

When refitting the parts always make sure that the identification mark, arrowed in **FIG 6:24**, faces the righthand side of the car as the lower part of the ball joint has an inclined plane which guides the lever to the first/second side.

6:10 Fault diagnosis

(a) Fault diagnosis

1 Broken or weak detent springs
2 Excessively worn detent groove in selector shaft
3 Worn synchromesh unit
4 Selector fork to selector rod pin loose

(b) Noisy transmission

1 Lack of lubricant or incorrect lubricant
2 Excessive end floats on shaft assemblies
3 Worn or damaged bearings
4 Worn or damaged gear teeth
5 Incorrectly adjusted crownwheel or pinion
6 Defective mountings

(c) Difficulty in engaging gear

1 Defective or incorrectly adjusted clutch
2 Stiff gearchange linkage
3 Worn synchromesh units
4 Bent or damaged selector shafts
5 Incorrect grade of lubricant

(d) Oil leaks

1 Defective gaskets and seals
2 Damaged joint faces on castings
3 Defective half-shells

CHAPTER 7

THE AUTOMATIC TRANSMISSION

7:1 Description

An automatic transmission can be fitted in place of the manually operated type.

The unit is basically a standard gearbox fitted with an electrically operated selector mechanism, controlled by push buttons and sensing units. An electro-magnetic clutch is also fitted so that the unit operates automatically once a selection has been made.

Driver-operated controls:

The driving range is selected by pressing the appropriate button out of the five buttons fitted on the dash.

On some models a Town/Country switch is also fitted, and usually this can be fitted as an optional extra using a kit supplied. By setting the switch to the town position the transmission is inhibited from changing down from second to first until the road speed has dropped below 11 km/hr (7 mile/hr). This reduces the number of downshifts into first-speed and therefore makes for more passenger comfort.

The use of the controls is explained more fully in the next section.

Decelerator:

The engine must be slowed temporarily while changing gear. This is done automatically by a solenoid-operated extra throttle valve. The parts are shown in **FIG 7:1**. When the solenoid is energized it pulls in the armature which is connected to the butterfly valve, and closes it so that the engine is decelerated irrespective of the position of the main throttle valve 7.

USA models are fitted with a special solenoid which cannot be fitted to other models.

Clutch and coupling:

A part-sectioned view of the unit is shown in **FIG 7:2**. Ferrous powder is used as the coupling medium. When current is fed through the field windings **P** a magnetic field is set up across the polepieces **N** and **R** which solidifies the ferrous powder to make the coupling rigid and transmit drive. When the current is cut off the powder loosens and drive is no longer transmitted.

By varying the current the strength of the magnetic field can be altered and therefore the clutch can be progressively engaged by progressively solidifying the ferrous powder. The relay unit increases the current over a period of 3 seconds to give this progressive increase and smooth engagement. When the clutch is released a light reverse current is fed through to overcome any residual magnetization in the ferrous powder and ensure full release.

The current to and from the windings is taken through slip rings **X** and brushes **Y**. **V** are the internal contacts and the input shaft of the gearbox **S**. A ballbearing **T** is fitted to reduce friction between the rotating parts.

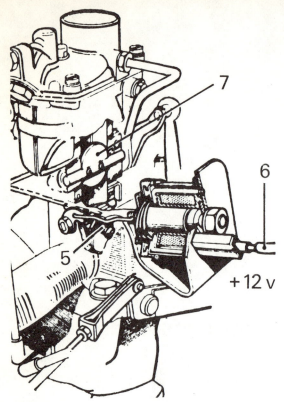

FIG 7:1 The decelerator mechanism. **5** is the adjusting screw

Gear selector mechanism:

The components are shown in **FIG 7:3**.

A solenoid **A** moves the plunger **P** when the contact **H** is operated by **G**. Interlock plungers **D**, **E** and **G** are fitted. The two levers **N** and **R** mounted on either side of the sliding gear **M** operate the fork shafts for the first/reverse and second/third gear shafts.

When the solenoid is energized the plunger **P** moves in the direction **X** thus freeing the plunger **D** which is pressed off the plunger **E** by the pressure of the spring **B**. The second/third gear shaft is locked in the neutral position by the plunger **E** and the reverse/first shaft is locked with the sliding gear **M** by the plunger **D**.

When the solenoid is not energized the plunger moves in the direction **Y** (spring **C** being stronger than spring **B**), and in this position the first/reverse shaft is locked in position while the second/third shaft is locked with the sliding gear **M**

As soon as a selection has been made the solenoid is again de-energized but the parts are held in position because the plunger **D** is no longer in line with the plungers **E** and **G**.

The actual movement of the selector mechanism is then carried out by a reversible motor driving through a gear assembly. The motor reverses when the direction of current is reversed and as soon as the current is cut a magnetic brake immediately locks the armature. A sectioned view of the motor is shown in **FIG 7:4**. When

the solenoid 7 is energized it draws the brake plate 3 in the direction **Y**, freeing the friction material 4 from the plate 5 attached to the armature so that the armature is free to rotate. As soon as the current through the motor is cut the solenoid releases the brake disc and the armature is prevented from rotating.

Control unit:

This is shown fitted in **FIG 7:5**. The unit integrates the input signals and produces the signals for the shifts and control of the solenoids. Car road speed is taken from the output shaft of the gearbox and throttle settings from the cam 12.

All the components of the system are set and adjusted at the factory and if a component is defective it must be removed and renewed as damaged parts cannot be repaired or adjusted without special equipment, held only by the fatory.

7:2 Operation

The function of the Town/Country switch (if fitted) has already been discussed in the previous section. The switch should always be set to the country position when out of towns, because the shift down to first will otherwise always occur at 11 km/hr, irrespective of the position of the throttle, and with heavy loads or on steep hills the downshift will be too late.

Starting:

The starter motor is isolated in all selections except when the **N** button is pressed. This is a safety precaution to prevent the car from moving off when the engine starts.

If the battery is flat the engine may still be started using the starting handle, but make sure that the **N** button is pressed with the Neuman anti-theft switch turned to its first position.

The car may also be started by pushing or running downhill. Leave **N** pressed until the road speed has reached 18 km/hr (12 mile/hr) and then press **A** while accelerating slightly.

Towing:

The car may be towed provided that the speed does not exceed 30 km/hr (19 mile/hr) and that **N** is selected. If the car has to be towed for long distances or at high-speed it is advisable to lock the front wheels in the straight-ahead position and tow with the rear wheels raised off the ground on a sling or dolly.

N button:

Pressing this button in puts the gearbox into neutral and there is no drive transmitted between the engine and rear wheels. This selection should always be made for starting the engine or when stationary with the engine running for long periods. **It must also be made when carrying out engine adjustments otherwise there is a danger of the car moving off when the throttle is opened.**

A button:

This button is pressed for all normal forwards driving. The car will automatically move off as the throttle is opened and then carry out the shifts at the appropriate speeds without any intervention from the driver. Applying

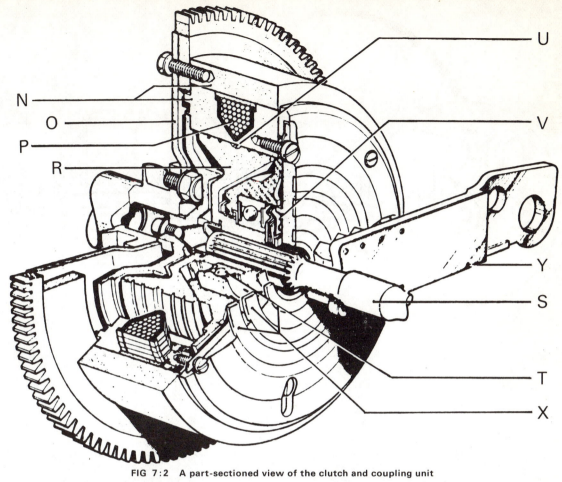

FIG 7:2 A part-sectioned view of the clutch and coupling unit

the brakes will slow the car, and downshifts will automatically take place until the car is stationary and ready to move off again when the throttle is opened again.

The shift points will depend on the throttle opening. If the throttle is fully open then the shift points will all take place at higher road speeds, ensuring that more torque is available and acceleration therefore faster. At small throttle openings the shift points will be at lower speeds with acceleration more gentle but increased economy. Use can be made of this when overtaking, as when the throttle pedal is fully depressed the shift point will be altered and the gearbox will then drop down a gear, if it is within limits, ensuring rapid acceleration and fast overtaking.

R button:

This is equivalent to reverse. The interlock mechanism prevents this button from being pressed when the car is in a forward gear. If reverse is to be used make sure that the car is stationary, press in **N** if a forward gear has been engaged, and then press in the **R** button. The car can then be driven backwards using the throttle and brake to control the speed.

Button 2:

Pressing in this button inhibits the upshift into third speed. The selection should only normally be used when descending steep hills when extra engine braking is required. The gearbox will change normally between first and second speeds but care must be taken not to overspeed the engine so **this selection should not be made at road speeds above 70 km/hr (45 mile/hr).**

This selection may also be used on winding roads, where the road speed does not exceed 70 km/hr, to prevent excessive changing up and down into third speed.

Button 1:

This button should rarely be used. When it is pressed the gearbox is locked into first gear only and will not upshift. **For this reason the selection must not be made at road speeds above 30 km/hr (20 mile/hr) or the car driven faster than this speed when the selection is made.** The selection can only be made after Button 2 has also been depressed so that both second and third speeds are inhibited.

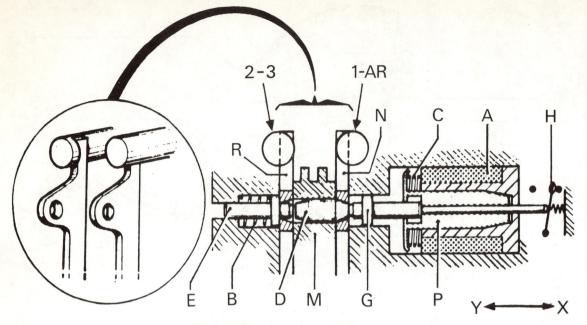

FIG 7:3   The selector solenoid mechanism

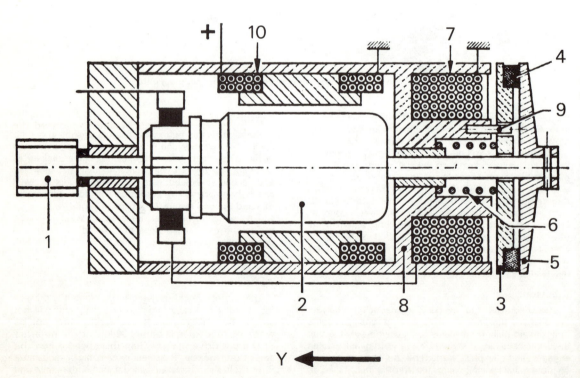

FIG 7:4   A sectioned view of the selector motor

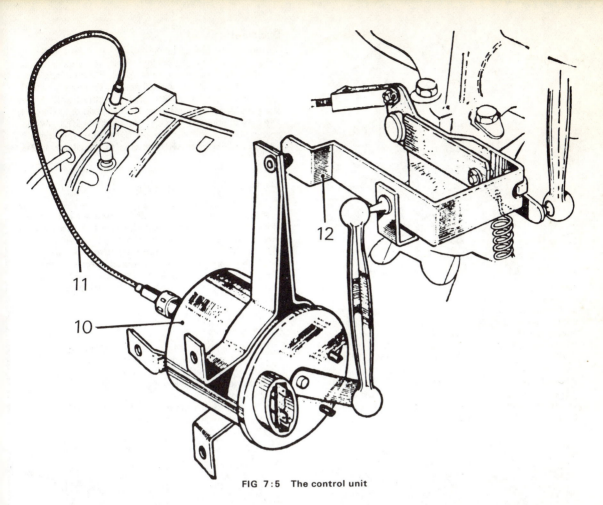

FIG 7:5 The control unit

The main use for this selection is when descending very steep and dangerous hills so as to give all possible engine braking but it can also be used when following slow-moving traffic up hills so as to cut out excessive hunting up and down through the speeds.

7:3 Maintenance

The lubricant in the gearbox should be checked as for a standard gearbox.

The brushes for the clutch should be checked at regular intervals. The brushes should be examined first at 30,000 kilometres (20,000 miles) and they should be examined regularly at intervals of 10,000 kilometres (6000 miles).

Remove the brush carrier assembly and check the lengths of the brushes. If the brushes have worn down to their minimum length of 8 mm ($\frac{5}{16}$ inch) then the complete brush carrier must be renewed.

If the brushes are not so worn as to require renewal but are still fairly short, the cover 7, shown in **FIG 7:6**, should be renewed. Remove the four clips 6 and take off the old cover. Fit the new cover back into place, making sure that the brushes are correctly positioned and once the cover is in place make sure that each brush slides perfectly freely in its holder.

When refitting the brush carrier make sure that the spacing washer between the gearbox and brush carrier is in position. **If this spacer washer is omitted the brush carrier will be rapidly damaged.**

In temperatures below 0°C the gearbox may not select down from second to first with the accelerator fully depressed. Provided that the gear does not grate and only refuses to engage then the gearbox is satisfactory. The cause is the drag of the lubricant and if the car is used regularly in climates below 0°C a mixture of SAE.75 oil and 30 per cent Rislone should be used. In all other cases use EP.80 oil.

7:4 Adjustments

Most of the adjustments require the use of a special test rig and therefore they should not be carried out by the owner.

Control unit linkage:

This must be adjusted every time the linkage between throttle and control unit (shown in **FIG 7:5**) is disturbed, such as when adjusting the slow-running or refitting the carburetter or control unit.

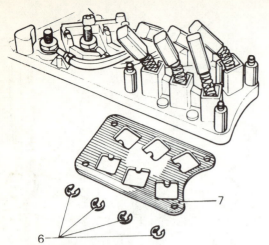

FIG 7:6 The clutch brush carrier assembly

Disconnect the plug from the control unit and connect a .2-amp 12-volt test lamp between the socket on the control unit and battery terminal on the control box, as shown in **FIG 7:7**. When the engine is at the idling position the test lamp should light. Adjust the position of the ball link support **A**, shown in **FIG 7:8**, by bending it slightly until the correct setting is obtained. The setting is correct when on depressing the accelerator pedal the test lamp just goes out when the dowel **B** is in the centre of its notch. Once the adjustment is correct remove the test lamp and reconnect the circuit correctly.

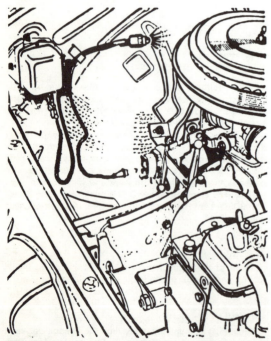

FIG 7:7 The test lamp connected for checking the control unit linkage setting. Do not use a bulb larger than .2 amp

Decelerator:

Run the engine until it is warm. Push the solenoid armature into the body so that the butterfly valve closes (see **FIG 7:1**) or energize the solenoid with a lead connected to the battery. Accelerate the engine and check that it does not stall. With the carburetter throttle open and the solenoid energized check the speed of the engine. The correct speed should be approximately 2000 rev/min and if necessary it can be set by altering the screw 5 which controls the closed position of the decelerator valve.

7:5 Renewing components

The positions of the components are shown in **FIG 7:9. Whenever leads are disconnected great care should be taken to prevent their ends from coming into contact with earthed metal parts, as a short-circuit will damage many of the components.** Whenever parts have been disturbed make sure that the wires and pipes run correctly as shown in **FIG 7:10** to avoid any danger of shortcircuits. Always disconnect the battery before removing components.

Brush support:

This has already been dealt with in **Section 7:3**. To remove the unit take out the attachment screw, spring washer and spacer, and then turn the engine until the brush carrier can be slid out over a smooth portion of the clutch, free from screws.

A special tool is made for refitting the brush support and this will make reassembly easier.

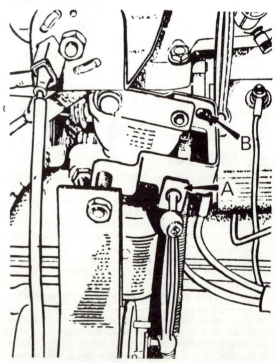

FIG 7:8 Adjusting the control unit linkage

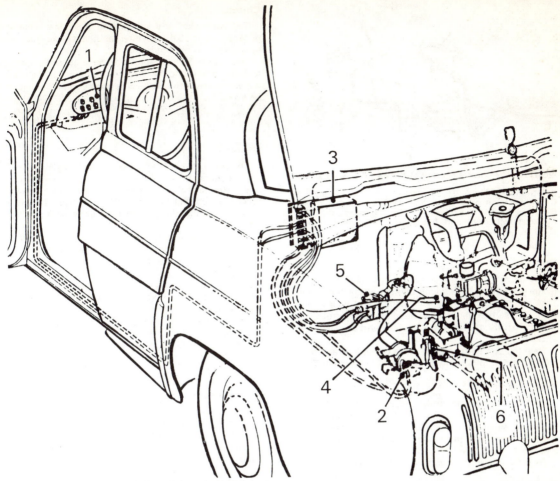

FIG 7:9 The components fitted to the car

Key to Fig 7:9   1 Push button control panel   2 Control unit   3 Relay box   4 Decelerator   5 Selector mechanism
6 Clutch coupling

Clutch:

**The clutch must always be kept upright and
never laid down.** In order to remove the clutch it is
necessary to take the engine out of the car. Engine
removal is described in **Chapter 1, Section 1:2**, but in
addition to these instructions disconnect and remove the
control unit and also remove the brush support unit as
well as disconnecting the decelerator cable. When lifting
the engine out take great care not to damage the clutch
slip rings or decelerator solenoid.

Once the engine is out, remove the sump and take out
the six bolts that secure the clutch to the driven plate,
noting that the bolts are at the back of the driven plate.

If necessary remove the driven plate by taking out the
five self-locking bolts that secure it·to the crankshaft. It
should be noted that if a spigot bearing is fitted to the
crankshaft then the bearing should be removed and
omitted on reassembly.

The parts are refitted in the reverse order of dismantling.
Red coloured marks should be present on both clutch and
driven plate and these should be aligned on reassembly
to preserve the balance. There is a white mark on the
clutch which is the reference point for refitting the brush
support.

The splines on the clutch should be lightly greased, but
take care not to put on too much grease as this may work
its way into the clutch. Wiping with an oily rag is usually
sufficient.

Push button selectors:

Disconnect the wiring harnesses, one to the relay box
and the other for the light, and then lift out the panel with
a blade. Remove the screws that secure the unit to the
support plate as well as the support plate and then draw
the assembly out to the rear and downwards to remove it.

The assembly is refitted in the reverse order of removal.

If the illuminating bulb has failed, lift the panel and pull
the old bulb straight out, without turning it. Press a new
bulb back into place and refit the panel.

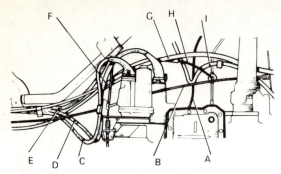

FIG 7:10   The correct routing of the harnesses and pipes

Key to Fig 7:10   **A** Governor cable   **B** Accelerator cable
C Selector motor feed   **D** Selector solenoid feed
E Control unit and clutch feeds   **F** Handbrake cable
G Starter motor cable   **H** Brake pipe   **I** Brush carrier feed

Control unit:

Disconnect the decelerator wire, operating rod, cable to the gearbox and the wiring harness at the connector. Take out the three attachment screws and remove the earth wire so that the unit can be lifted out. **Handle the unit carefully as it is very delicate and sensitive to shocks.**

Refit the unit in the reverse order of removal and then adjust the control linkage as described in **Section 7:4.**

Relay box:

Remove the housing on the lefthand side and disconnect all six wiring harnesses from the unit. Remove the clamp that secures the two selector wire harnesses to the cover and then take out the three attachment screws so that the unit can be removed.

Refit the unit in the reverse order of removal.

Decelerator:

Disconnect the feed wire and remove the air cleaner and carburetter. Take off the nut that secures the solenoid and withdraw the solenoid from its mounting. Disconnect the connecting rod from between the solenoid and valve.

Refit the parts in the reverse order of removal and then check the decelerator adjustment as well as the control unit linkage (see **Section 7:4**).

7:6 Road test

The owner is not the best person to carry out a road test unless he has had recent experience of a similar model fitted with an automatic transmission known to be in good working order.

Before carrying out a road test make sure that the ignition timing is correctly set and the carburetter adjusted. Check that the decelerator and control unit are correctly set and also make sure that all connections are properly in place.

If a new clutch has been fitted it must be allowed to run-in for a few hundred kilometres before fully smooth operation can be expected.

The road test should last a half-hour.

Clutch:

This is checked at the beginning of the test when the transmission is cold, then after the first quarter-hour, and finally again at the end of the test.

With the **N** button depressed accelerate the engine up to 2000 rev/min and then allow it to slow to 1500 rev/min. Select reverse. If the clutch is in good condition there will be no grating.

Gearbox:

The gearbox should be tested immediately after checking the clutch, provided that the clutch is satisfactory.

With the car stationary select **A** and press the accelerator fully down so that the car accelerates hard through the gears. Check that the gearbox upshifts without grating or noise.

Allow the car to slow down to 65 km/hr (40 mile/hr) and again floor the accelerator to make it downshift into second. Allow the car to slow down to 20 km/hr (12 mile/hr) and yet again floor the accelerator pedal to downshift from second to first. Provided that the changes all take place without grating then the synchronization of the gearbox is satisfactory.

Note that in cold climates, without special oil in the gearbox, the unit may refuse to downshift into first with full throttle but this does not signify a defect.

Shift speeds:

The shift speeds are given in the table that follows. The actual speeds given are the limits for the accelerator pedal fully released and fully pressed down. Shifts with intermediate throttle openings will take place between the limits given.

Accelerator position (engine torque)	Change-over speed in km/h			
	Change-up		Change-down	
	1st/2nd	2nd/3rd	3rd/4th	2nd/1st
Pedal fully released	$19{+3 \atop -3}$	$40{+0 \atop -3}$	$30{+0 \atop -3}$	$15{+0 \atop -3}$
Pedal depressed	$33{+1.5 \atop -1.5}$	$68{+1.5 \atop -1.5}$	$58{+1.5 \atop -1.5}$	$26{+1.5 \atop -1.5}$

7:7 Fault diagnosis

Before suspecting the transmission and its controls make sure that the fault does not lie with the engine, ignition or carburetter.

A special tester, Ele.16, is made for checking the operation of the controls and unit. In certain cases the tester can be plugged into the car, as it is a portable unit, and used to control the system so that the car can be driven to the garage for full checks and repairs.

Check the electrical system for a low battery or dirty battery terminals, the main fuse under the dash, and all electrical connections in the system.

(a) Engine stalls

1 Faulty or incorrectly adjusted decelerator

(b) Engine will not decelerate when changing gears

1 Check 1 in (a)

(c) No automatic change

1 Check control unit input leads
2 Defective motor or selectors

(d) Creeping with engine idling

1 Too high idling speed
2 Incorrectly adjusted control box linkage
3 Defective control unit auxiliary functions

(e) Poor acceleration, poor engine braking, impossible to tow-start

1 Check 3 in (d)

(f) Jerky engagement when changing down

1 Check synchronization contact

CHAPTER 8

REAR SUSPENSION, DRIVE SHAFTS AND HUBS

8:1 Description

The parts attached to the car are shown in **FIG 8:1** and the rear axle assembly complete with tie rods is shown in **FIG 8:2**. It should be noted that the complete assembly with the engine and transmission can be removed as a complete unit from the car (see **Chapter 1, Section 1:2**).

Drive shafts connect the transmission to the wheel hubs and a sectioned view of the rear hub assembly is shown in **FIG 8:3**. From this figure it can be seen that the drive shaft is splined to the hub and secured by a castellated nut and that the hub revolves about the tube using a ball-bearing. Also shown in this figure are the coil spring and concentric damper which support the weight of the car, take the road shocks, and control the oscillations of the suspension.

The axle tube is attached to the transmission at its inner end and is free to swivel in the half shells. A universal joint is fitted between the drive shaft and transmission to allow drive to be transmitted while the suspension moves. The tie rods locate the suspension in the fore and aft plane.

Disc brakes are fitted on all the models covered by this manual and full instructions on these are given in **Chapter 11. For most dismantling operations it will be necessary to remove the brake caliper and it should be noted that this can be carried out without disconnecting the flexible hose,** avoiding the necessity of bleeding the brakes on reassembly.

At intervals, grease the rear hub bearings through the grease nipple provided.

8:2 Damper and road spring

The damper is mounted concentrically inside the road spring and it is therefore necessary to remove them both if either requires checking or renewal. **A special spring compresser is essential.**

Removal:

1 Slacken the nuts for the road wheel slightly and then raise the car onto chassis stands. Remove the road wheel. Disconnect the handbrake cable and remove the brake caliper.

2 Refer to **FIG 8:4**. Unscrew the upper damper attachment nuts. Disconnect the rebound strap at one end only. Fit the special tool No. Sus.21 (Sus.364 can also be used on earlier models) and use the tool to compress the road spring.

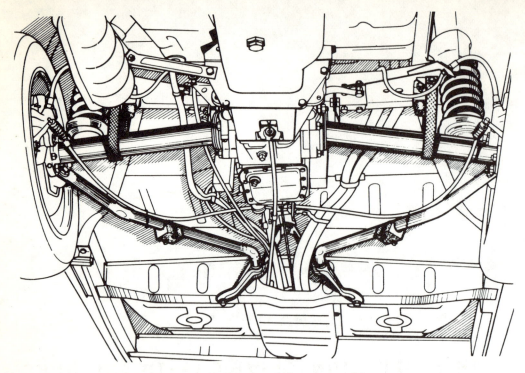

FIG 8:1   General view of the rear suspension

FIG 8:2   The rear suspension and drive shafts

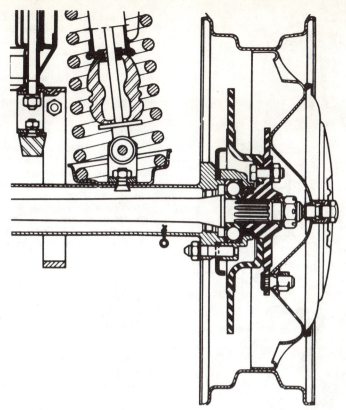

FIG 8:3   Sectioned view of the rear hub assembly

3 Free the spring and press it up as far as it will go so that it clears the lower damper attachment, shown in **FIG 8:5**. Disconnect the damper by removing the lower attachment bolt shown and then remove the parts from the car.

4 The components are shown in **FIG 8:6**. Do not slacken the pressure on the road spring until it has been fully removed from the car.

Checking road spring:

Data for the road spring is given in **Technical Data**. Measure the spring and check that it has not weakened with use. Check the spring carefully for hairline cracks or other damage and renew it if it is weak or defective.

Checking dampers:

Equipment is now coming into use which enables the agent to check the condition of the dampers without having to remove them from the car, but normally dampers have to be removed and checked on a special test rig. **The tests available to the owner will detect a faulty damper but will not ensure that the damper is operating at high efficiency.** Weak dampers should be suspected if the car continues pitching after it has passed over a bump in the road. As a rough check press down the corner of the car and release it suddenly. The oscillation should be rapidly damped out and if the car continues swinging up and down it is likely that the damper is defective.

As a rough check mount the damper vertically in the padded jaws of a vice, by the bottom eye, and pump it using short strokes about the midpoint. Gradually increase the length of the strokes until they are reaching the full travel of the damper. The resistance to motion should be constant and even in both directions. If there are pockets of no resistance, or if the damper is too stiff to move or it operates noisily, then it is defective. A damper will also be defective if it has physical damage, such as oil leaks, bent ram, or dented body. A defective damper cannot be repaired and must therefore be renewed.

It is most advisable to renew all four dampers (including two on the front suspension) at the same time as they will all have seen similar service and if not actually defective they will certainly have weakened. To preserve the suspension balance always renew the dampers in axle pairs.

Refitting:

The parts are refitted in the reverse order of removal. Make sure that all the rubber bushes and cupwashers are in good condition and renew any that are defective, worn or perished.

Note that on later models fitted with BOGE dampers the correct method of fitting the cupwashers is shown in **FIG 8:7**. If the cupwashers are fitted facing inwards then the suspension will rattle.

then take out the remainder of the nuts that secure them. Remove the drive shaft and hub assembly complete, taking care of the roller bearing track rings.

The assembly is refitted in the reverse order of removal. The faces of the half shells fitting against the differential carrier should be lightly smeared with jointing compound and the nuts tightened to a torque of 5 kg m (40 lb ft). Do not forget to refill the transmission with oil.

Universal joint:

A worn universal joint will make a 'clonk', particularly when the direction of drive is reversed. The joint is assembled in manufacture in such a way that if it is defective it cannot be repaired, and a new joint must then be fitted in its place.

To remove the universal joint first remove the drive shaft assembly as described previously, exposing the joint as shown in **FIG 8:10**. Withdraw the old joint and fit the new one, after lightly smearing it with grease, then refit the remainder of the drive shaft assembly.

Axle tube:

This can be removed without actually having to separate the drive shaft from the hub.

1 With the road wheel removed and the car on stands, take off the spring and damper assembly and also disconnect the tie rod from the wheel end. Note that the brake caliper must be removed. Drain the transmission.
2 Remove the nuts that secure the bearing track ring and steel brake deflector, shown in **FIG 8:11**. The complete brake disc and drive shaft assembly can then be drawn out from the tube. Carefully collect and store ready for reassembly any shims fitted between the axle tube and brake deflector.
3 Remove the appropriate side mounting pad and support, mark the half shells and remove them. The axle tube and bearing track rings can then be removed.

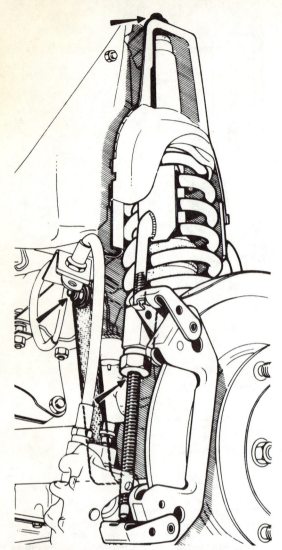

FIG 8:4 Removing the road spring and damper

8:3 Drive shaft assembly

1 Slacken the wheel nuts and raise the car onto suitable chassis stands. Remove the road wheel and then remove the brake caliper, without disconnecting the flexible hose. Remove the damper and spring assembly as instructed in the previous section. Drain the transmission.
2 Remove the side mounting pad and its support from the transmission. The lefthand side pad is shown in **FIG 8:8** and the attachment of the accelerator cable should be noted. The righthand side pad is shown in **FIG 8:9** and the attachment of the earth strap should be noted.
3 Disconnect the tie rod by taking out its attachment nut and bolt from the road wheel end. **Mark the half shells in relation to the differential carrier** and

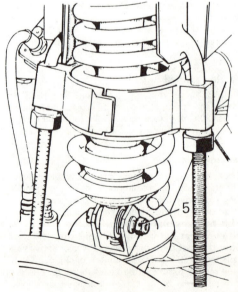

FIG 8:5 The damper lower attachment

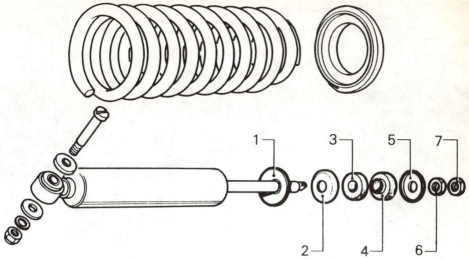

FIG 8:6   The damper and spring components

Check the tube visually for signs of deterioration or damage and if these are suspected the tube should be checked by an agent, using a special jig No. T.Ar.56A. Also make sure that the trunnions are not scored or damaged.

The parts are refitted in the reverse order of removal. If a new axle tube is fitted then the shims between it and the brake deflector must be selected so as to give the correct positioning of the brake caliper (see **Chapter 11**).

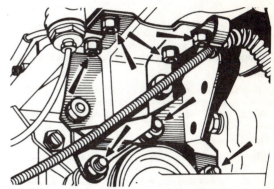

FIG 8:8   The lefthand side transmission mounting pad and support

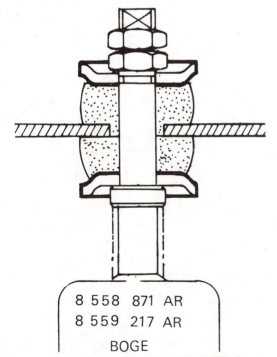

8 558 871 AR

8 559 217 AR

BOGE

FIG 8:7   The correct assembly of the BOGE damper

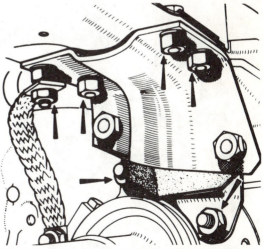

FIG 8:9   The righthand side transmission mounting pad and support

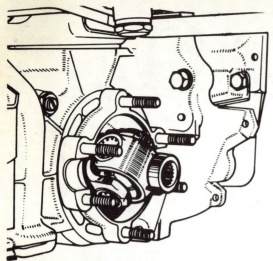

FIG 8:10 The drive shaft universal joint

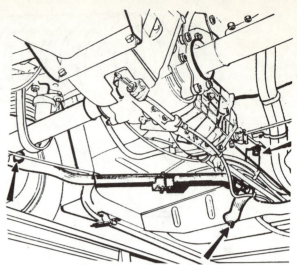

FIG 8:12 The tie rod attachments

8:4 Tie rod

The attachments of the tie rod are shown in **FIG 8:12**. To remove the righthand tie rod it is necessary to free the lefthand side one from its attachment to the floor.

Removal:

Remove the nut that secures the tie rod at the wheel end and then remove the two nuts securing it to the floor. Take out the tie rod and put the adjusting hexagon to one side.

Reassembly:

The parts are refitted in the reverse order of removal. The 'Belleville' washer is fitted with its concave side towards the nut and the nut is tightened to a torque of 9.5 kg m (70 lb ft).

8:5 Rear hub assembly

Removal:

1 Slacken the wheel nuts and raise the car onto chassis stands. Remove the road wheel and then free the brake caliper.

2 Disconnect the tie rod by taking off the nut that secures it at the wheel end. Remove the nuts shown in **FIG 8:11** (as for removing axle tube in **Section 8:3**). The drive shaft and hub assembly can now be withdrawn from the axle tube.

3 Support the assembly and unscrew the drive shaft securing nut so that the washer also can be removed. A sectioned view of the hub assembly is shown in **FIG 8:3**. Use the special tool No. T.Av.235 (Rou.09.A can be used on earlier models) to press the drive shaft

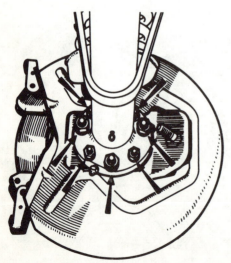

FIG 8:11 The axle tube attachments at the wheel end

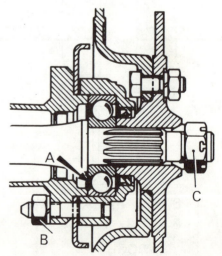

FIG 8:13 The correct fitting of the rear hub bearing

out of the hub. Mark the relative positions of the hub and disc and then separate them by removing the attachment nuts and gently tapping them apart with a copper or lead mallet.

Reassembly:

The parts are reassembled in the reverse order of dismantling. Make sure that the bearing is in good condition and pack it with grease. **When refitting the bearing make sure that the nylon seal A, shown in FIG 8:13, is on the side away from the castellated nut that secures the drive shaft.** The nuts **C** are tightened to a torque of $5 \pm .5$ kg m (35 to 40 lb ft), the hub nut **C** to 20 kg m (145 lb ft), the tie rod nut to 9.5 kg m (70 lb ft) and the caliper bracket attachment nuts to a torque load of 2 kg m (15 lb ft).

8:6 Suspension geometry

Damage to the bodywork or faulty parts can alter the rear suspension geometry. Incorrect geometry will cause poor handling characteristics as well as wearing out tyres at an excessive rate.

If incorrect geometry is suspected then the car should be taken to an agent for specialized checks using accurate gauges and test equipment. Without special equipment it is impossible to measure the settings accurately.

8:7 Fault diagnosis

(a) Noisy operation

1 Dry or worn rear hub bearings
2 Worn universal joints
3 Defective damper
4 Defective damper mounting bushes (rattles)
5 Loose attachments

(b) 'Bottoming' of suspension

1 Check 3 in (a)
2 Weak or broken road spring

(c) Excessive tyre wear

1 Incorrect suspension geometry
2 Damaged or defective tie rod

CHAPTER 9

FRONT SUSPENSION AND HUBS

9:1 Description

A sectioned view of the front suspension and hub assembly is shown in **FIG 9:1**. The figure actually shows the points that should be checked for wear throughout each unit but it also illustrates the parts. The front suspension fitted to the car is shown in **FIG 9:2**.

Each wheel is independently sprung using unequal length wishbones and coil springs. Sealed telescopic dampers are fitted concentric with each road spring to damp out the oscillations of the suspension. The inboard ends of the wishbones pivot about attachments on the crossmember and the stub axle pivots about the outer ends of the wishbones using ball joints. The inboard pivots ensure that the suspension can only move vertically while the outboard ball joints allow both the steering and suspension to move through their respective ranges. The road spring acts between the crossmember and the lower wishbone to take the weight of the car and the road shocks.

An anti-roll bar interconnects the lower two wishbones. When one suspension is at a different height from the other the anti-roll bar is twisted and exerts a restoring force between the two suspensions. This action reduces body-roll on corners and at the same time improves the road-holding.

The road wheel is attached to a hub that rotates about the stub axle on two tapered bearings.

There are adjustment points for altering the front suspension geometry but specialized equipment must be used for checking the accuracy of the settings.

9:2 Maintenance

On the early models, ball joints are fitted which have grease nipples. These models should have the ball joints regularly lubricated.

Later models have sealed-for-life ball joints that require no routine maintenance. However, on all models the dust covers over the ball joints should be examined at regular intervals. **If the covers are wearing or failing then they must be renewed before they actually split.** On the earlier models it may be possible to flush out any dirt that has entered by pumping grease through the grease nipple but on later models there is no method of removing any dirt and the ball joint must be renewed when dirt has entered it.

The wheel hub should be removed at regular intervals, cleaned, repacked with fresh grease and then refitted to the correct end float.

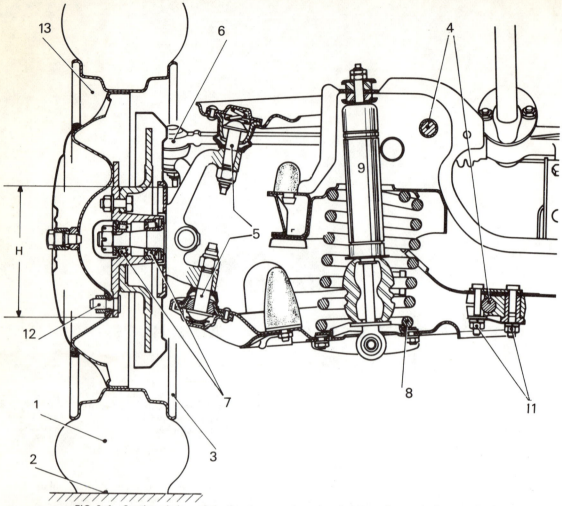

FIG 9:1 Sectioned view of the front suspension, showing the points to be inspected

Key to Fig 9:1   1 Tyre pressure   2 Even tread wear   3 Wheels for buckles   4 Play in pivots   5 Play in ball joints
6 Play in steering ball joints   7 Play in hub bearings   8 Spring condition   9 Damper efficiency   11 Security of pivots
12 Security of wheel studs and nuts   13 Wheel balance   **H** Height of steering ball joint

9:3 The wheel hubs

A sectioned view of the wheel hub assembly is shown in **FIG 9:1**.

The bearings and ball joints can be checked for wear after the front of the car has been jacked up, leaving the road wheels in place. Grip the tyre at the top and try to rock it in and out and then repeat the test gripping the tyre either at the front or rear, taking care not to confuse steering movement with play. Excessive play in the vertical direction will be caused by worn ball joints or bearings while play in the sideways direction will only be caused by worn bearings.

Spin the road wheel and check that it rotates smoothly and freely, taking care not to confuse noise from the disc brake with that from defective bearings. Jerky rotation, binding or grinding operation shows that the bearings are defective.

Removal:

The hub, brake disc, brake caliper and brake deflector shield must all be removed together because of the shape and design of the parts.

1 Jack up the car and support it on stands after slackening the road wheel nuts. Remove the road wheel. Carefully lever or pull off the grease cap so that the hub nut is exposed. Extract the splitpin and remove the hub nut with its thrust washer.

2 Remove the brake caliper, without disconnecting its flexible hose, and hang it safely out of the way so that the hose is not twisted or strained. Take off the four nuts shown in **FIG 9:3** and free the brake deflector and caliper bracket, carefully collecting any shims fitted between caliper bracket and suspension.

3 The hub and disc assembly can now be drawn off the stub axle, taking care to collect the inner race of the

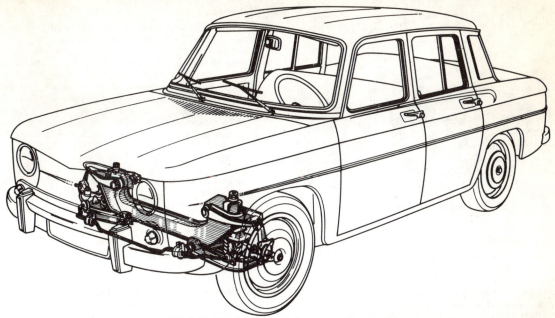

FIG 9:2   The location of the suspension parts

outer bearing as it comes free and not allowing it to fall into the dirt.

4 If necessary mark across the hub and disc and then take out the three nuts which secure the disc to the hub. Separate the disc from the hub using light blows of a copper or plastic mallet.

Cleaning and examination:

Use newspaper or rags to wipe out most of the old grease and then wash out the remainder using clean fuel. Wash the inner races of the bearings separately so that they do not pick up dirt. The inner race of the inner bearing should be removed using a suitable two-legged extractor though special tools are also made for the purpose.

Check the stub axle for wear or cracks, paying particular attention to the area on which the grease seal operates. Renew the grease seal if it is worn or defective.

Check the bearings for any sign of wear, chipping or pitting. Lubricate the bearings lightly with very thin oil and press them into their outer races. Apply firm pressure and oscillate the bearings backwards and forwards to check for any sign of roughness. If they feel rough, wash them again as dirt may be the cause but if cleaning does not make them rotate smoothly then they are defective. If the bearings are defective they must both be completely renewed. The outer races can be driven out and the new ones driven back using a suitable drift. Take care to drive the outer races evenly and squarely otherwise they will jam in position.

Reassembly and adjustment:

If the disc has been separated from the hub make sure that the mating faces are scrupulously clean. Refit the disc so that the previously made marks are again in alignment and tighten the attachment nuts to a torque of 4.5 ± 1 kg m (25 to 40 lb ft).

If the inner race of the inner bearing has been removed it should be pulled back into place using a suitable length of sleeve, a washer and the hub nut.

The parts are refitted in the reverse order of removal, making sure that the shims between caliper bracket and suspension are refitted into their original positions. Pack the inner races of the bearings liberally with grease before refitting them.

Use a moderate-length spanner and tighten the hub nut while spinning the hub. Tighten until slight drag is felt on the hub as it revolves and then slacken back the nut by $\frac{1}{6}$ turn and lock it with a new splitpin. Fill the grease cap $\frac{3}{4}$ full with grease and fit it back into position. Make sure that there is no grease on the brake disc and refit the brake caliper followed by the road wheel.

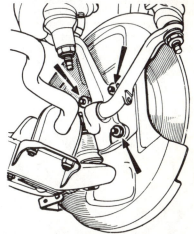

FIG 9:3   The brake deflector attachments

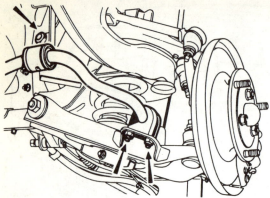

FIG 9:4   The anti-roll bar attachments

9:4 The anti-roll bar

The anti-roll bar attachments are shown in **FIG 9:4**. The car needs to be jacked up and the road wheels removed before the anti-roll bar can be removed or refitted and the suspensions should be at the same height so that there is no torsion in the bar.

Remove the anti-roll bar by disconnecting it from the lower wishbones first and then taking out the bolts that secure the bearings to the frame.

The anti-roll bar is refitted in the reverse order of removal. Make sure that the rubber bushes are all in good condition and renew them if they are worn, perished or cracked. Tighten the clamp nuts to a torque of .6 to .8 kg m (5 lb ft) and the bearing securing bolts to a torque of 2.5 $\pm$ .5 kg m (15 to 20 lb ft).

9:5 The dampers

Testing the damper is the same as for testing the rear dampers (see **Chapter 8, Section 8:2**).

The damper components are shown in **FIG 9:5**.

Removal:

Place the front of the car on stands and remove the road wheel. Slacken the locknut and remove the two nuts that secure the damper to the turret, shown in **FIG 9:6** and then remove the two nuts that secure the damper yoke to the lower wishbone. Withdraw the damper downwards, as shown in **FIG 9:7** and once it has been removed the yoke can be taken off.

Refitting:

The damper is refitted in the reverse order of removal. Note that the longer arm of the yoke faces outwards.

Before fitting the damper check to make sure that the eye bush and rubber bushes 2 and 3 are in good condition. On the Alliquant dampers the complete eye end is unscrewed from the damper shaft. Hold the damper shaft with the special tool No. Sus.22 to prevent it from becoming damaged. A new eye end can then be screwed back into place. On the other models the old eye-end bush can be prised out of the eye and a new bush pressed back in.

9:6 The road spring

With the car on stands and the road wheel removed, free the anti-roll bar from the lower wishbone. Remove the damper as instructed in the previous section.

Fit the spring compression tool Sus.20, as shown in **FIG 9:8** and use the tool to take the spring pressure. Remove the nut that secures the lower ball joint to the stub axle. Free the ball joint by pressing it out with the special tool T.Av.55.A as shown in **FIG 9:9**. Remove the nuts that secure the hinge pin bearings, arrowed in **FIG 9:8**, and slacken off the spring compressor so that the lower wishbone comes downwards and the spring pressure is relieved.

The spring is refitted in the reverse order of removal after checking it for damage, cracks or weakening. Once the parts have been refitted the suspension geometry should be checked.

9:7 The suspension ball joints

The original ball joints are riveted into place but when fitting new ball joints they are secured in place by nuts and bolts supplied with the new parts.

Check the ball joints for wear by rocking the top of the tyre in and out with the car raised off the ground. There should be very little movement indeed and if there is play make sure that it is not caused by loose wheel bearings. Worn ball joints cannot be repaired and they must be renewed.

In order to renew a ball joint it is best to remove the wishbone from the car and then work on the bench.

If care is taken the ball joints can be renewed with the wishbones fitted though it will be necessary to remove the stub axle assembly. When removing the stub axle take off the caliper and hang it safely out of the way on its hose and then also disconnect the steering ball joint from

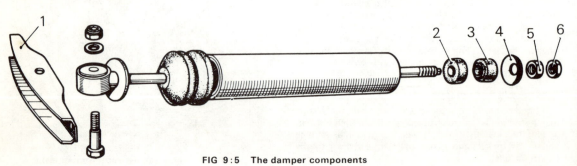

FIG 9:5   The damper components

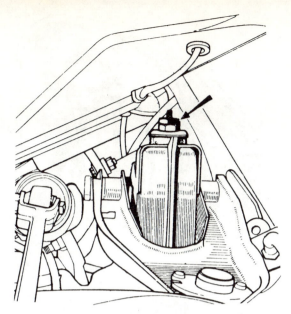

FIG 9:6 The damper upper attachment

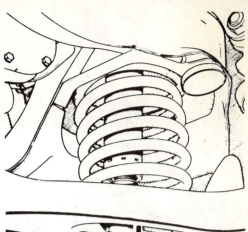

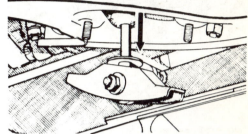

FIG 9:7 The damper lower attachment

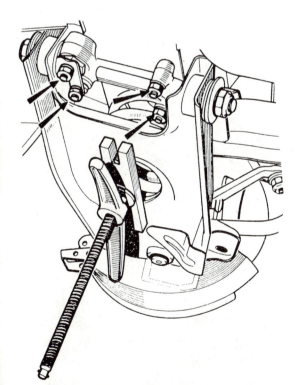

FIG 9:8 The road spring compression tool

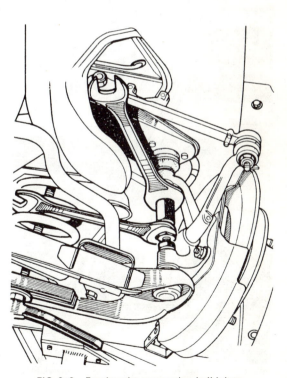

FIG 9:9 Freeing the suspension ball joints

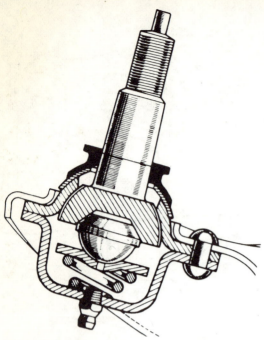

FIG 9:10 Sectioned view of a typical later ball joint

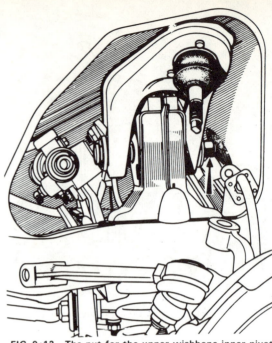

FIG 9:12 The nut for the upper wishbone inner pivot

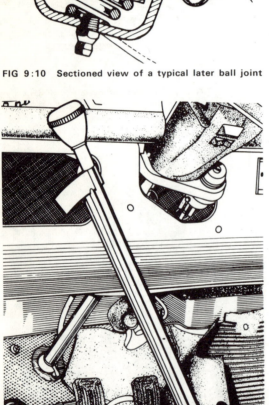

FIG 9:11 Access to the nut for the upper wishbone inner pivot

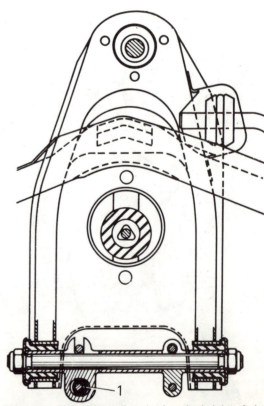

FIG 9:13 The adjuster for altering the height of the steering ball joint (castor)

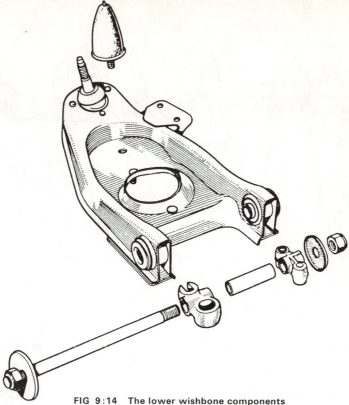

FIG 9:14　The lower wishbone components

the steering arm on the suspension. Again, when renewing ball joints, if care is taken then the caliper and steering ball joint can be left attached. The safest way of taking the spring pressure is to remove the damper and use the special tool Sus.20, as shown in **FIG 9:8**. Again if care is taken the suspension can be supported using a jack under the lower wishbone and the damper need not then be removed.

If the owner does not feel fully confident then he should remove the wishbones using the full correct procedure but if the special tool for compressing the springs is not available and he feels competent then short-cuts can be taken.

To remove the rivets that secure the ball joints carefully drill off the heads and then drive out the stems with a suitable punch. It is best to work from the ball joint side as then any mistakes will not damage the actual wishbone. File a flat on the rivet head and then make a starting mark with a centre punch. This will ensure that the drill can be started accurately without slipping off the head. Use a large drill which is just smaller than the head and stop immediately the head falls off or can be cleared off with a small cold chisel. The stem can then be driven out.

Refit the new ball joints using the bolts supplied tightened to a torque of .6 $\pm$ .1 kg m (4 to 5 lb ft).

When separating the ball joints from the stub axle, remove the securing nuts and use the special tool No. T.Av.55A pressing between the threaded studs of the ball joints to free them from the stub axle. Never hammer on

the end of the threaded portion as even with a slave nut fitted internal damage may be caused to the ball joint.

A sectioned view of a later typical ball joint is shown in **FIG 9:10**. Make sure that the rubber dust cover is securely in place. When renewing dust covers pack a little extra grease into the ball joint. Tighten the ball joint nuts to a torque of 9 $\pm$ 1 kg m (60 to 75 lb ft).

9:8 The upper wishbone assembly

Removal:

1 Slacken the road wheel nuts and raise the car onto stands. Remove the road wheel. As a safety precaution against straining the hose remove the brake caliper, leaving it hung safely out of the way still attached to its hose.

2 Remove the damper and use the special tool to take the weight of the suspension, or otherwise support it from under the lower wishbone using a small jack.

3 Remove the Nyloc nut from the upper ball joint and use the special tool T.Av.55A pressing between the threaded ends of the ball joints to free the upper ball joint from the stub axle.

4 From inside the car, as shown in **FIG 9:11**, use a socket spanner to remove the Nyloc nut from the pivot pin, arrowed in **FIG 9:12**. Turn the steering to its full lock in the opposite direction and push out the pivot pin so that the upper wishbone can be removed.

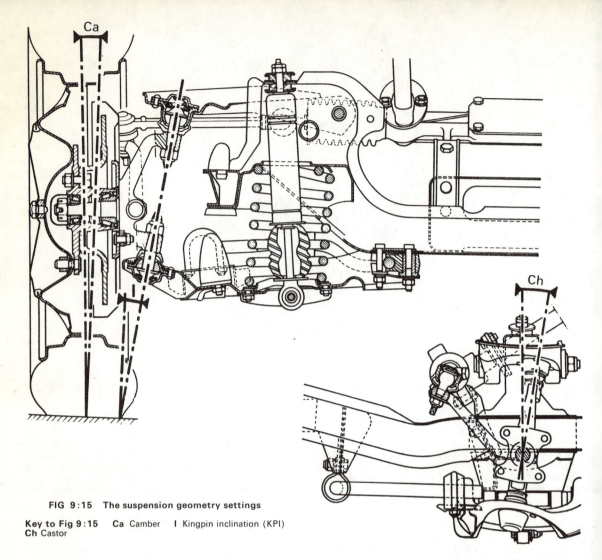

FIG 9:15   The suspension geometry settings

Key to Fig 9:15   Ca Camber   **I** Kingpin inclination (KPI)
Ch Castor

The upper wishbone is refitted in the reverse order of removal. Smear the pivot pin lightly with graphite grease before refitting it and run the nut fully down the threads without actually tightening it. The nut must only be fully tightened to a torque load of 6.5 $\pm$1 kg m (40 to 55 lb ft), as shown in **FIG 9:11**, when the suspension has been loaded to its normal working level.

Bushes:

Fluid-bloc bushes are fitted to the upper wishbone for it to pivot about. If the bushes are worn they should be pressed out, using a press, and new bushes pressed back into place. Special mandrels in a set No. T.Av.21 are made for this purpose.

Checking:

If it is suspected that the wishbone has become distorted or damaged then it should be taken to an agent for checking on a special jig.

9:9 The lower wishbone assembly

It should be noted that the rear bearing is fitted with an adjuster for varying the castor of the wheels. The adjuster 1 is shown in **FIG 9:13**, and it is altered by turning the thin hexagons on the rear bearing. The parts are shown in **FIG 9:14**.

Removal:

1 Jack up the front of the car and place it on stands, after slackening the wheel nuts. Remove the road wheel and damper. Compress the road spring, free the anti-roll bar and disconnect the lower ball joint, as instructed in **Section 9:6** for removing the road spring.
2 Take off the four nuts that secure the bearing assembly of the wishbone and release the pressure of the road spring. The wishbone assembly and road spring can then be removed.

3 If required the pivot pin can then be removed. Hold
one of the nuts in a vice and undo the other nut using
a spanner. Withdraw the pin and remove the bearings
and spacer. Mark the bearings and spacer so that they
will be refitted into their original positions.

Reassembly:

The parts are refitted in the reverse order of removal.
Smear the pivot pin lightly with grease before refitting it.
The Fluid-bloc bushes in the wishbone can be pressed out
and new ones pressed back into place, using a press and
the mandrel set T.Av.21. If it is suspected that the wishbone
itself is damaged or distorted then it should be taken to
an agent for checking on a special jig. When refitting the
parts do not fully tighten the pivot pin nuts until the suspension has been loaded to its normal working position.

Once the parts have been refitted the suspension
geometry should be checked and adjusted as required.

9:10 Suspension geometry

**Special gauges are essential for checking the
accuracy of the settings and for this reason the
owner should not attempt to set the geometry
himself but take the car to an agent.**

Incorrect suspension geometry will cause poor road-
holding, difficult handling characteristics and increase
the rate of tyre wear. The various settings that have to be
correct are shown in **FIG 9:15**. The height **H** of the
steering ball joint shank is a measure of the castor and
this is checked using the gauges T.Av.59 and T.Av.56A
(or T.Av.206 on later models) as shown in **FIG 9:16** and
is adjusted by the cam 1 shown in **FIG 9:13**.

Though the owner cannot check the actual settings he
can ensure that they are not altered by wear. The points
to check throughout the suspension are shown in **FIG
9:1**.

If full suspension checks are being carried out the
wheels should first be checked for buckles. The front and
rear axle parallelism is then checked followed by the
camber angle, castor and kingpin angles, and finally the
front wheel alignment and toe-in.

9:11 Fault diagnosis

(a) Wheel wobble

1 Worn hub bearings
2 Defective or worn suspension pivots
3 Unbalanced wheels and tyres
4 Slack or worn ball joints
5 Weak or broken front road springs
6 Loose wheel attachments

FIG 9:16 Checking the castor

(b) 'Bottoming' of suspension

1 Check 5 in (a)
2 Rebound rubbers worn or missing
3 Dampers defective

(c) Heavy steering

1 Neglected lubrication (earlier models only)
2 Defective suspension ball joints
3 Incorrect suspension geometry

(d) Excessive tyre wear

1 Check 2 in (a); 3 in (b) and 3 in (c)

(e) Rattles

1 Check 2 and 5 in (a)
2 Damper mountings loose or worn
3 BOGE damper attachments incorrectly assembled
4 Anti-roll bar broken or rubber bushes worn

(f) Excessive rolling on corners

1 Check 5 in (a); 3 in (b) and 4 in (e)

CHAPTER 10

THE STEERING GEAR

10:1 Description

The layout and positioning of the steering components are shown in **FIG 10:1**. All the models covered by this manual are fitted with a rack and pinion steering unit. A longitudinal sectioned view of the steering rack unit is shown in **FIG 10:2**. The steering wheel is splined to the column and the column is attached to the pinion shaft of the steering unit by a flexible coupling. As the pinion rotates it drives the rack of the unit from side to side. Steering links connect the end of the rack to the steering arms on the suspension units. The system has a minimum of moving parts and as all connections are as direct as possible there is the minimum of lost motion. The result is a precise steering.

10:2 Maintenance

On some of the earlier models grease nipples may be fitted to the steering ball joints and these should be greased at regular intervals.

At the same time as inspecting the suspension ball joints check the dust covers on the steering ball joints for damage or wear. The dust covers must be renewed before they split and allow dirt to enter the ball joint.

Play in the rack unit can be adjusted out but it is necessary to remove the unit from the car before adjusting it. On early models the steering unit is also fitted with a grease nipple.

10:3 Steering links and ball joints

The ball joints are integral with the links so if a ball joint is defective or worn a complete new link must be fitted. Note that the links are handed and cannot be interchanged between sides. The two different links are shown in **FIG 10:3**, **G** being the lefthand one and **D** the righthand one.

The attachment of the link to the end fitting on the rack is shown in **FIG 10:4**. The link can be freed from the end fitting 2 by taking out the pivot bolt 1.

Once the locknut 2 has been slackened and the link freed the end fitting 3 can be unscrewed from the rack. The toe-in of the front wheels is set by altering the position of the end fitting with reference to the rack. The bush in the end fittings 3 is renewable. A press and mandrel T.Av.28 are required to remove the old bush and the new bush should be fitted using a press and mandrels T.Av.21A and D.

The ball joint is separated from the steering arm on the suspension using the special tool T.Av.54, as shown in

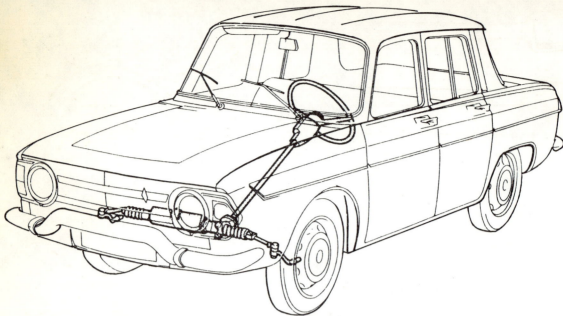

FIG 10:1   The steering components fitted to the car

FIG 10:5, after removing the securing nut. The tool fits between the arm and link while the bolt presses the tapers apart. **Under no circumstances hit on the end of the threaded portion, even with a slave nut fitted to protect the threads, as internal damage may be caused to the ball joint.** If the special extractor is not available, undo the securing nut to the last few threads and lever or firmly pull the link away from the steering arm. Lay a block of metal on one side of the tapered eye on the steering arm and hit on the other side with a copper mallet. The tapers will quickly free and the nut will prevent the link from flying off the arm.

10:4   Removing the steering rack unit

1 Jack up the front of the car and place it securely onto stands, after slackening the road wheel nuts. Remove the front road wheels making sure that the handbrake is applied and the rear wheels chocked. Remove the spare wheel from its stowage.

2 Disconnect the steering link ball joints from the steering arms on the suspension, as described in the previous section. Disconnect the steering column from the coupling on the pinion shaft by unscrewing the two nuts and withdrawing the two bolts, shown in **FIG 10:6**. Some models are fitted with castellated nuts that are locked with splitpins but other models use Nyloc self-locking nuts. The Nyloc nuts must be

renewed if they are worn so that they can be run up and down the threads using the fingers alone.

3 Remove the splitpins and take off the nuts 1 that secure the unit to the frame, arrowed in **FIG 10:7**, and remove the unit out through one side of the car as shown by the arrow.

Reassembly:

The unit is refitted in the reverse order of removal. **The bolts for the steering coupling must be fitted with the heads towards the steering unit and the washers fitted under the heads.** Tighten Nyloc nuts to a torque load of $.75 \pm .15$ kg m (5 lb ft) and castellated nuts to a torque of $.5 \pm .1$ kg m (4 lb ft).

Make sure that the pivot pins at the inboard ends of the steering links are parallel to the ground. The pivot pin nut is tightened to a torque of $2.5 \pm .5$ kg m (20 to 25 lb ft) and it is advisable to lightly lubricate the bore into which it fits.

The nut for the ball joint is tightened to a torque of $3.5 \pm .5$ kg m (25 to 30 lb ft). Discard all old splitpins and use new ones on reassembly.

If the flexible steering coupling is defective or damaged it should be renewed. Remove the coupling from the pinion shaft by taking out the two sets of nuts and bolts that secure it. Note that the heads of these bolts must face away from the steering unit.

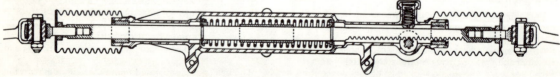

FIG 10:2   A sectioned view of the steering rack unit

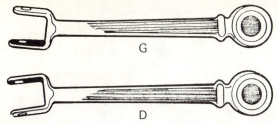

FIG 10:3 The steering links. **D** is the righthand link and **G** the left

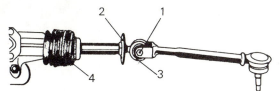

FIG 10:4 The attachments of the link to the steering rack

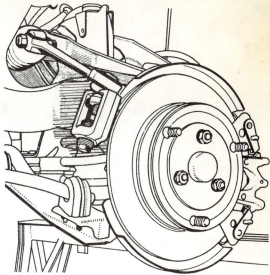

FIG 10:5 Freeing a steering ball joint

10:5 Servicing the steering unit

It should be noted that some special tools will be required, as well as a press for removing or refitting bearings.

Dismantling:

1 Remove the rack unit from the car. Remove the steering links by taking out the pins 1 shown in **FIG 10:4**, noting that the pins can be removed with the extractor T.Av.54 if they are stiff. Pull back the bellows 4, slacken the locknut 2 and unscrew the end fitting 3 from the rack.

2 Refer to **FIG 10:8**. Take out the two bolts that secure the coupling and its two end plates so that they can be removed. Remove the set bolt for the flange 10 and then withdraw the flange, after having marked its position in relation to the pinion shaft. Remove the circlip 11 and then take out the safety washer 12 and spacer 13. Remove the protective cap 5, extract the circlip 6 and withdraw the thrust washer 7, spring 8 and plunger 9. A sectioned view through the pinion shaft is given for guidance in **FIG 10:9**. Note that there are two different types fitted, some having a closed washer and the others a circlip.

3 Remove the seal washer 14, preferably using the extractor Dir.16 as shown in **FIG 10:10**. Remove the circlip 15, washer 19 and grease nipple 16 (if fitted). The pinion shaft can then be driven out of the housing using a suitable drift. The pinion shaft parts are shown in **FIG 10:11**, noting that a plain washer may be fitted in place of the circlip 21 Bis shown in the figure. Remove the circlip 21 Bis (if fitted) as well as the O-ring 20 after which the bearing 18 can be removed using a press.

4 Remove the circlips 22 and the cups 23, shown in **FIG 10:12**, from the ends of the rack after taking off the cover. Use a thin screwdriver resting against the

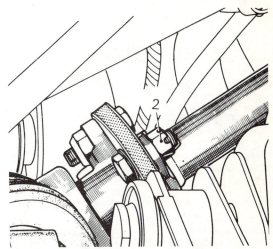

FIG 10:6 Disconnecting the steering column from the Staflex coupling

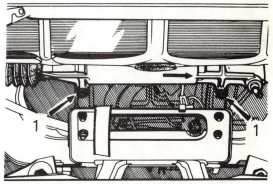

FIG 10:7 Removing the steering rack unit

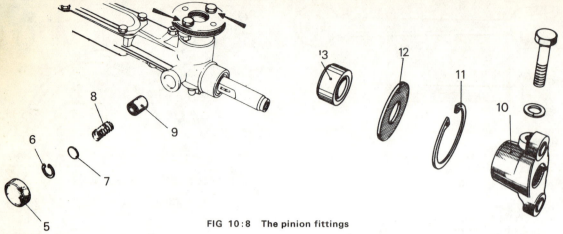

FIG 10:8   The pinion fittings

Key to Fig 10:8   5 Protective cap   6 Circlip   7 Thrust washer   8 Spring   9 Plunger   10 Flange   11 Circlip
12 Safety washer   13 Spacer

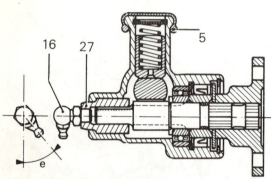

FIG 10:9   Sectioned view through the pinion shaft

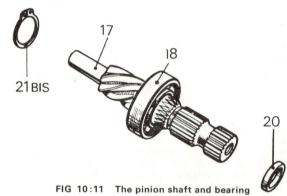

FIG 10:11   The pinion shaft and bearing

Key to Fig 10:11   17 Pinion shaft   18 Bearing
20 O-ring   21 Bis circlip (or plain washer on some models)

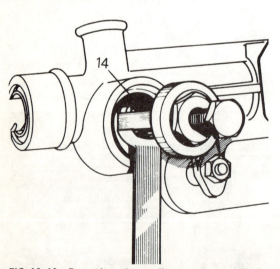

FIG 10:10   Removing the sealing washer with the special extractor

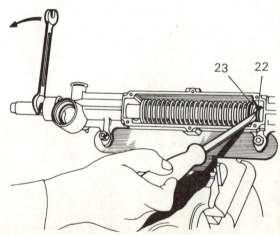

FIG 10:12   Removing the rack circlips

98

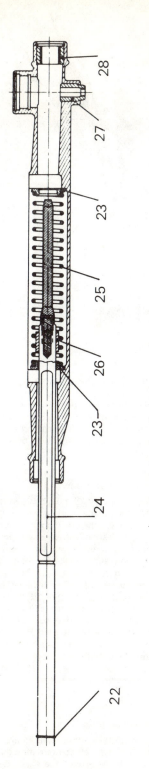

FIG 10:13   Reassembling the steering unit

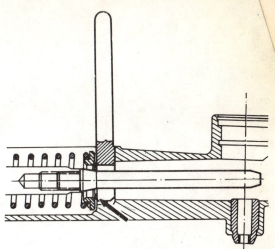

FIG 10:14   Using the special fork to hold the circlip in position while the rack is pressed through

side of the housing to lever out one end of the circlip on the end of the rack further from the teeth. Hold the screwdriver in place and rotate the rack with a 17mm spanner so that the circlip is freed from its groove. Pull the rack firmly out from the end nearest the teeth and the other circlip will then free from its groove. **All the circlips and seals must be discarded and new parts used on reassembly.** Free the spring from its seats and remove it together with the seat cups 23 and the rubber sleeve.

5 The lower bearing bush for the pinion shaft can be pushed out through the housing. If the bearing bushes for the rack are worn they should be pressed out using Mandrel Dir.17. Note that the bushes are identified by colour and the bronzed bush is fitted nearest the pinion end of the housing. Even if the bushes are not worn the bush furthest away from the pinion should be removed so as to make reassembly easier.

Reassembly:

All old seals, snap rings and circlips should be discarded and new parts fitted. Wash the parts in clean fuel and then check them for wear, paying particular attention to bushes and the teeth on the rack and pinion. Examine all circlip grooves to make sure that they are not worn, *paying particular attention to the groove for the circlip 6, shown in* **FIG 10:8**.

1 A sectioned view of the parts being reassembled is shown in **FIG 10:13**. Insert the rubber sleeve 26 back inside the spring 25 and then refit the spring into the housing so that its ends seat in the cups 23. Slide the bush 27 back into place. Grease the bush 28 and add some extra grease inside the housing behind the bush to act as a reservoir.

2 Fit a new snap ring 22 to the smooth end of the rack, making sure that it is fully seated in its groove. Slide in the special tool Dir.18C shown heavily shaded in the figure, followed by the rack 24, toothed end leading, and slide the parts far enough in to pass the rubber sleeve 26 over the rack end. Use the fork of the special tool Dir.18C to hold the other circlip 22 in place, as shown in **FIG 10:14** and then press the mandrel and

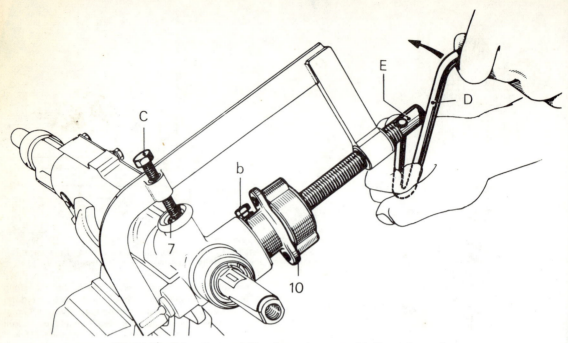

FIG 10:15   Using the special handpress to reassemble the pinion parts

rack through until the circlip slides along the mandrel and rack into its groove. Remove the locating fork and end-fitting mandrel.

3 Insert the remaining rack bush using a suitable tube. Pack the housing with grease (Carter F) and refit the cover using a new paper gasket.

4 Reassemble and refit the pinion shaft assembly in the reverse order of dismantling and removal. Make sure that the correct parts are obtained if new parts have to be fitted, as various slight modifications have been carried out. Use new seals and circlips and lightly oil the sealing washer 14.

5 Refit the parts shown in **FIG 10:8**. The hand press Dir.19 will be required, as shown in **FIG 10:15**. The pins on the end-fitting of the screw **E** align in the flange 10 and the pin on the leg aligns with the grease nipple hole. Do not yet tighten the bolt **b** which

secures the flange 10. The screw **C** is then used to press in the plunger 9, spring 8 and thrust washer 7 so that the circlip 6 can be fitted. On earlier models a plastic plunger 9 was fitted with a 25 kg (55 lb) spring. This earlier plunger should be discarded as well as its spring and the later steel plunger with 50 kg (110 lb) spring fitted instead.

Adjustment of pinion end play:

The special hand press Dir.19 must be used for this, as shown in **FIG 10:15**, for the models fitted with grease nipples. Fit the tool and use the bolt **C** so that it is tightened up against the thrust washer 7. Press down on the drive flange by tightening the screw **E** until the pressure on the special lever **D** is sufficient to make it contact the screw **E**. Tighten the bolt **b** to a torque of $2.25 \pm .25$ kg m (15 lb ft). On bolts marked with Y3 on the head the torque setting is increased to $2.75 \pm .25$ kg m (20 lb ft). Remove the tool and refit the protective cap and grease nipple.

On later models the adjustment is carried out with the flexible coupling fitted. Grease the bolts **P** and **S**, shown in **FIG 10:16** and tighten them to a torque of $1.6 \pm .1$ kg m (10 lb ft), and on these models the tool Dir.325 can be used instead of the hand press to refit the plunger assembly when reassembling the parts.

10:6 The steering column

The components of the steering column are shown in **FIG 10:17**, and the typical column attachments are shown in **FIG 10:18**. Note that the exact design will vary slightly between models.

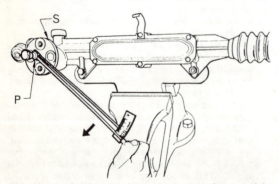

FIG 10:16   Setting the pinion clearance on later models

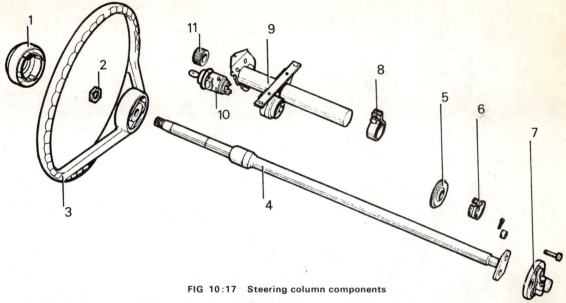

FIG 10:17   Steering column components

Key to Fig 10:17   1 Embellisher   2 Nut   3 Steering wheel   4 Steering column   5 Grommet   6 Split bearing
7 Staflex coupling   8 Lower clamp   9 Upper clamp   10 Anti-theft switch   11 Upper bush

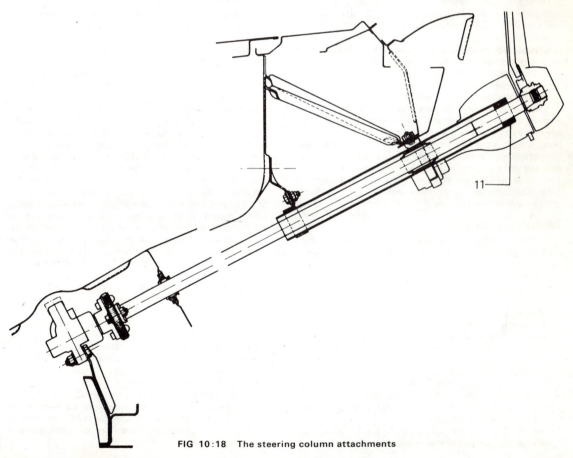

FIG 10:18   The steering column attachments

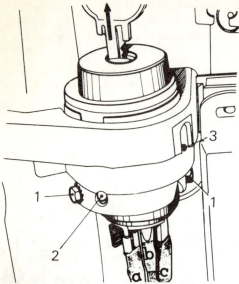

FIG 10:19 The anti-theft switch

Steering wheel:

To remove the steering wheel, first prise out the embellisher 1 and then unscrew the nut 2. Mark across the hub of the steering wheel 3 and splines of the shaft 4 so that the steering wheel will be refitted into its original position. It may be possible to remove the steering wheel by giving even blows with the palm of the hand on the base of the spokes but if this does not free the splines then the special extractor Dir.21A must be used to draw the steering wheel off the shaft.

Refit the steering wheel in the reverse order of removal, aligning the previously made marks. If a new steering wheel is being fitted or the alignment marks lost, then the front wheels must be turned into exactly the straight-ahead position and the steering wheel refitted so that both spokes make the same angle to the horizontal. The centre position of the rack can be found by turning the steering column until the rack stops make contact with the return spring.

Removing steering column:

On the R.1190 models this will be slightly easier if the steering rack unit has already been removed, as less panels need to be removed. On all models it will be necessary to remove instrument panels and glove box, as required, in order to gain access to the column mounting brackets.

1 Disconnect the battery and remove the spare wheel. Remove the steering wheel and disconnect all the electrical leads from the horn, lighting switch and anti-theft switch. It is advisable to label each lead as it is disconnected to save confusion when the time comes to reconnect them.

2 Disconnect the steering column from the Staflex coupling by taking out the two sets of nuts and bolts, noting that on some models Nyloc nuts are fitted while others have castellated nuts.

3 Remove the nuts and bolts from the upper clamp 9 as well as the nut and bolt from the lower clamp 8.

4 Pull back the carpets and floor covering. Free the grommet 5 and remove the half-bushes 6 (if fitted). The steering column can then be removed from inside the car.

The parts are refitted in the reverse order of removal. The upper bush 11 can be removed and renewed after the column has been removed or it can be extracted with the column in place. The upper bush should only be lubricated with Spargraph grease. **When refitting the column do not tighten the clamp nuts and bolts fully until the assembly is completely in place and correctly aligned.**

Anti-theft lock:

Disconnect the battery and remove sufficient panels to gain access to the switch attachments. Disconnect the three leads shown in **FIG 10:19** and take out the two attachment bolts 1. Turn the lock to the 'Garage' position and remove the key. Press the locking ball 2 and pull the lock out as far as it will go while keeping the ball depressed with a piece of rod. On some models the lock will come free but on other models an additional lock tab 3 is fitted. Press on this tab using a scriber and fully withdraw the lock assembly.

The unit is refitted in the reverse order of removal.

10:7 Steering geometry

On all models the front wheel alignment should be set between the limits of 1 mm ($\frac{1}{32}$ inch) toe-out to 2 mm ($\frac{5}{64}$ inch) toe-in with the car laden to the half-laden position. To ensure that the suspensions are at the correct height gauges T.Av.56A are fitted between the frames and upper wishbone and the car is laden until the gauges are held in position. The adjustment point is at the inboard ends of the steering links, shown in **FIG 10:4**. A complete turn of the end fitting on the rack will alter the setting of that wheel by 3 mm ($\frac{1}{8}$ inch). **The alignment must be half the correct value at each wheel so that the total is correct between the wheels.**

If the tyres wear with a characteristic feathered edge to the tread pattern then the front wheel alignment is incorrect. It is just possible for the owner to adjust the tracking himself but some form of trammel will be required, to measure the distance between the wheel rims at wheel centre height. If the adjustment is to be checked roll the car forwards on level ground with the front wheels in the straight-ahead position. Measure, as accurately as possible, the distance between the two wheel rims at wheel centre height and at the front of the wheels. Mark the positions from which the measurements were taken and roll the car forwards so that the wheels turn exactly half-a-revolution and the marks are again at wheel centre height but at the rear of the wheels. Measure the distance apart again and the difference between the two dimensions represents the wheel toe-in or toe-out. **The car must always be rolled forwards when taking measurements and if a mark is overshot the car should be rolled forwards until the mark is again in the correct position.**

Because of the setting of the suspension height using special gauges it is advisable to take the car to an agent, who will also have accurate equipment for checking the track and the remainder of the steering and suspension geometry.

10:8 Fault diagnosis

(a) Wheel wobble

1 Unbalanced wheels and tyres
2 Slack steering ball joint
3 Worn hub bearings
4 Excess play in steering unit pinion
5 Incorrect suspension or steering geometry
6 Defective suspension

(b) Wander

1 Check 2, 4, 5 and 6 in (a)
2 Uneven tyre pressures or tyre wear
3 Weak dampers or springs
4 Front axle assembly out of line from rear axle assembly

(c) Heavy steering

1 Check 5 in (a) and 2 in (b)
2 Extremely low tyre pressures
3 Neglected lubrication
4 Steering rack incorrectly adjusted
5 Steering column bent or out of alignment
6 Defective bearings in steering column

(d) Lost motion

1 Check 2, 4 and 6 in (a)
2 Defective Staflex coupling
3 Loose steering wheel or badly worn attachment splines
4 Worn bush for steering link attachment

CHAPTER 11

THE BRAKING SYSTEM

11 : 1   Description

All the models covered by this manual are fitted with swinging-caliper disc brakes on all four wheels. All four brakes are hydraulically operated when the brake pedal is pressed. The brake pedal is connected to the master cylinder by a pushrod which presses the piston down the bore of the unit to generate hydraulic pressure. This hydraulic pressure is pressed through a system of metal and flexible pipes to each brake caliper, as shown in **FIG 11 : 1**. The hydraulic pressure then moves the piston in the caliper to clamp the rotating brake disc between the friction pads and thus exert a retarding force.

A brake limiting valve is fitted into the hydraulic circuit to the rear brakes. Up to a certain pressure the pressure in the rear brakes increases at the same rate as that for the front brakes but above this setting the rear brake pressure increases at half the rate of the front brakes. This ensures that under heavy braking, with the weight of the car transferred forwards, the rear wheels do not lock.

The rear brakes only are operated from the handbrake, using levers on the rear calipers, and a system of cables to clamp the disc between the friction linings. The same friction pads are used for the handbrake as for the main brakes.

A sectioned view of a brake caliper is shown in **FIG 11 : 2**. The caliper 1 is a light alloy casting mounted in swinging links on the brake caliper bracket. When hydraulic pressure is applied into the bore of the caliper, the piston 2 is forced outwards into contact with the brake disc. The reaction and the pressure of the hydraulic fluid acting on the base of the cylinder forces the caliper in the opposite direction so that an equal force is applied to each of the brake pads 4 with their friction linings 5, and they clamp the disc between them. The seal 3 performs the dual function of sealing around the piston and also ensuring that it returns when the pressure is released. When pressure is applied the seal distorts slightly and with pressure released this distortion disappears and draws the piston back slightly from contact with the brake disc. The disc rotating then ensures that both the caliper and piston are pushed back to an adequate clearance. The automatic wear system 6 is fitted to ensure that the clearance between disc and pads stays constant and does not increase as the pads wear. The assembly is bolted to the caliper and has a snap ring which is a tight fit inside the piston. The snap ring fits loosely into the groove formed between two plates on the adjuster and on normal operation the snap ring moves backwards and

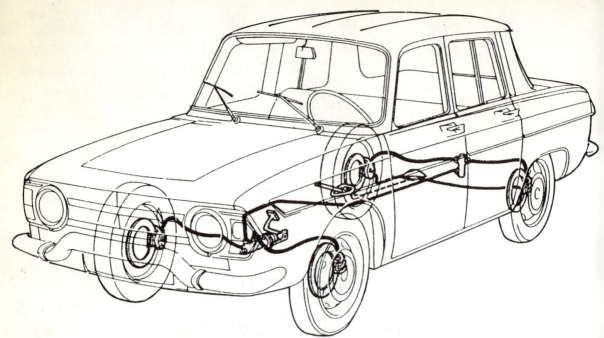

FIG 11:1   The layout of the pipe runs for the braking system

forwards in this groove. When the pad wears the snap ring is pressed firmly against the outer plate, the hydraulic pressure overcomes the resistance, and the snap ring slides inside the piston to allow the piston to move further out. The maximum return movement is controlled by the snap ring abutting against the inner plate.

A sectioned view of the handbrake operating mechanism is shown in **FIG 11:3**. When the cable is pulled, by applying the handbrake lever in the car, the lever moves the cam 3 so that it applies pressure to the friction pad and the reaction then draws the caliper so that the disc is clamped between the friction pads.

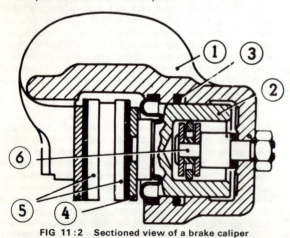

FIG 11:2   Sectioned view of a brake caliper

Key to Fig 11:2   1 Caliper   2 Piston   3 O-ring seal
4 Brake pads   5 Friction linings   6 Automatic adjuster
assembly

11:2 Maintenance

Adjustments:

The disc brakes are self-adjusting and therefore no routine adjustments need to be made. **After renewing pads or refitting brake calipers, the brakes should be pumped hard several times to set the correct clearances before the car is driven.** If this precaution is not observed there may be so much clearance that the brakes will not apply on the first few applications when driving.

Handbrake:

When correctly adjusted the handbrake lever travel should be 5 to 6 notches to the fully on position. If the travel becomes excessive the handbrake should be adjusted at the point shown **FIG 11:3**. Lubricate the adjusting screw and cable end lightly with Spargraph grease. Slacken the locknut 1 and turn the adjusting screw 2 until the cam 3 is in light contact with the brake pad. Slacken off by turning the adjusting screw back by a $\frac{1}{2}$ turn. Check that the road wheel rotates freely with it jacked up off the ground. As little as a $\frac{1}{4}$ turn may be sufficient on some models but never exceed more than $\frac{3}{4}$ turn. Operate the handbrake several times to make sure that it releases correctly. **The handbrake should not be adjusted at any other point and both wheels should be equally adjusted.**

Fluid level:

At regular intervals check the fluid level in the master cylinder reservoir. The level will slowly drop as the friction pads wear but an increase in the rate of dropping must be investigated immediately as it can be caused by a leak

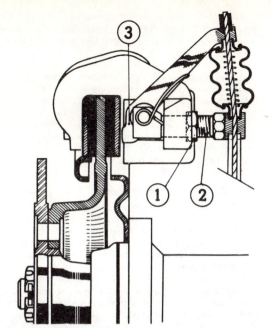

FIG 11 : 3 Sectioned view of the handbrake operating mechanism on rear brakes

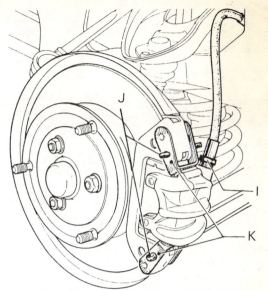

FIG 11 : 5 Attachments of a typical caliper

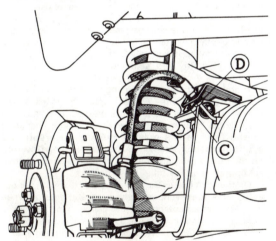

FIG 11 : 4 Attachments of a typical brake hose

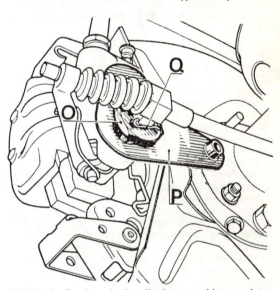

FIG 11 : 6 Freeing the handbrake assembly on a later caliper

in the system. Wipe the cap and top of the reservoir clean before removing the filler cap to prevent any dirt from falling into the reservoir. On earlier models fluid to specification SAE.70.R1 is used but on later models the specification was changed to SAE.70.R3. **The correct specification for use is marked on the filler cap. Do not mix fluids.**

Preventive maintenance:

At regular intervals check the thickness of the friction linings on the pads and renew the complete pads if their total thickness is less than 5.5mm (.217 inch) at any point, or if they are contaminated with oil or grease.

The brake fluid used is hygroscopic and over a period of time absorbs moisture from the air, even through the small vent fitted to the filler cap of the reservoir. The water content will reduce the boiling point of the fluid so that it may boil under heavy brake application. For this reason the fluid should be drained out through the bleed nipples in the system at intervals of 18 months and the system filled and bled using fresh hydraulic fluid.

At intervals of three years the system should be drained, flushed through with methylated spirits and all components removed and dismantled. Discard all the old seals, examine the parts and renew any components that are defective. The parts should then be reassembled using all

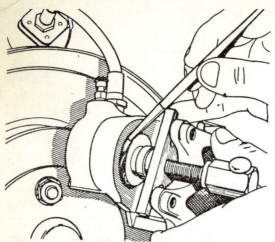

FIG 11 : 7 Cleaning and lubricating the piston. Note the special tool preventing excessive movement of the piston

new seals and the system filled with fresh fluid. While the system is dismantled examine all the metal pipelines carefully and renew any that show signs of corrosion or have been dented by stones.

11 : 3 Flexible hoses

These are fitted between the suspension and frame to allow the pressure to be transmitted while the suspension moves. When removing or refitting flexible hoses great care must be taken not to twist or strain the flexible portion otherwise the hose will be damaged. The hoses must also be refitted without twisting them otherwise they will move the brake caliper, causing the friction pads to rub against the disc.

A typical hose-to-frame attachment is shown in **FIG 11 : 4**. Before removing or disconnecting a hose either drain the hydraulic system or seal off the reservoir so that fluid does not flow out. Hold the hexagons of the hose with a spanner and then undo the union nut **D** with another spanner, making sure that the metal pipe does not twist with the union nut. Once the union is disconnected remove the clip **C** and free the hose from the bracket. The other end of the hose can then be unscrewed from the brake caliper, allowing the flexible portion to rotate freely.

Refit the hose in the reverse order of removal. Special tools are made for checking the angle of the bracket to ensure that the hose will clear the road wheel under all positions of the suspension and steering.

The flexible hoses should be renewed after a life of five years, even if they still appear sound.

11 : 4 Removing brake calipers

Only if the caliper requires dismantling or complete removal from the car does the flexible brake hose have to be disconnected. If the caliper is being removed for attention to the suspension then the hose should be left connected, as this will save having to bleed the brake system after the parts have been reassembled. If the hose is disconnected then the brake system must be bled after reassembly.

The attachments of a front caliper are shown in **FIG** in **FIG 11 : 5**. To remove the caliper, extract the pins **J** and swing back the clamps **K** so that the caliper can be removed.

The removal of the rear calipers is similar but it is necessary to disconnect the handbrake cable. On later models it will be necessary to unscrew the nut **O** and free the guide plate **P**, shown in **FIG 11 : 6**, before the cable can be disconnected by removing the pin **Q**.

When refitting the caliper use new pins and anti-rattle rubber tubes. Refit the caliper in the reverse order of removal, making sure that it is correctly positioned and that all the parts are clean and free from oil or grease.

11 : 5 Renewing friction pads

The pads should be renewed when their total thickness is less than 5.5 mm (.217 inch) and they must be renewed before the lining is so worn that there is metal to metal contact. **Pads must not be renewed individually, but always in axle sets. Do not intermix brands or different grades of lining material.**

Remove the caliper as described in the previous section, without disconnecting the flexible hose. **Remove only one caliper at a time and make sure that the brake pedal is not pressed with the caliper free.** Remove the old brake pads.

Use a blunt-nosed tool to carefully prise out and remove the dust seal from around the piston. Pour a little methylated spirits over the end of the piston to wash away dirt and allow it to air dry. Fit the tool Fre.12A, as shown in **FIG 11 : 7**, to prevent the piston from coming out too far and gently press on the brake pedal so that the piston comes out by approximately 3 mm ($\frac{1}{8}$ inch). Use a paint brush and methylated spirits to wash away any dirt remaining and when the parts are dry grease the piston all round the circumference, using the brush to apply the grease as shown in the figure. Tighten the screw on the special tool so that the piston is pressed fully back into the cylinder. **During this operation check the level of the fluid in the master cylinder reservoir and syphon out any excess to prevent it overflowing.** Fit the new brake pads and refit the brake caliper before starting work on the other brake calipers.

On the front brakes the pads may be fitted with flanges at the ends, to prevent excessive wear and bruising when the pads make contact with the caliper. On the earliest models no flanges may be fitted while on the latest models there may be flanges at either end. On the intermediate stages flanges were fitted to one end only and in such cases the flanges should be fitted to make contact with the top of the caliper, as shown in **FIG 11 : 8**.

On the rear brakes lubricate the threads and eye of the adjuster as well as the pivot point of the lever and contact point of the spring.

11 : 6 Servicing a caliper

A sectioned view of the caliper is shown in **FIG 11 : 9**. **The parts of the automatic adjuster must not be dismantled, or removed from the piston.**

1 Remove the caliper from the car and disconnect the flexible hose. Take out the brake pads and brush away all loose dust and dirt. If need be wash with methylated spirits.

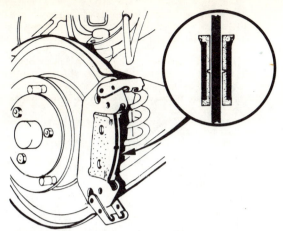

FIG 11:8 The correct method of fitting brake pads with only one flange

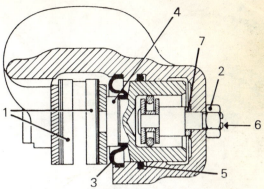

FIG 11:9 Sectioned view of a brake caliper

Key to Fig 11:9 1 Friction pads   2 Nut   3 Dust seal
4 Piston   5 Seal   6 Adjuster screw   7 Copper seal

2 Carefully prise out the dust cover 3 using a thin flexible tool that has no sharp edges. Hold the screw 6 with a screwdriver and unscrew the nut 2 using a 14 mm ring spanner. Gently push out the piston and adjuster assembly from the bore of the caliper, using a drift made of soft-metal such as bronze and not larger than 7mm ($\frac{9}{32}$ inch) in diameter. If necessary tap lightly on the end of the drift, using a plastic mallet so that the drift acts on the end of the screw 6.

3 Use a thin, flexible tool to remove the O-ring 5 from its groove in the cylinder bore, **taking extreme care not to score or scratch the surface of the bore.** Unscrew and remove the bleed screw.

4 Wash all the parts in methylated spirits. The only other solvent that may be used for cleaning is hydraulic fluid but this will take longer than methylated spirits to remove dirt. **The use of any solvent is dangerous as some may remain to contaminate and rot the new seals.**

5 Examine the bore of the cylinder for wear, scoring or any other damage. If the bore is not perfectly smooth and polished then a complete new caliper must be fitted. The piston and adjuster assembly must be renewed if the piston surface shows any signs of scoring or damage. Discard all the old seals, including the copper seal 7, and fit new ones on reassembly.

6 Wet the O-ring 5 with a little clean hydraulic fluid and fit it back into its groove. Use only the fingers and make sure that the O-ring is fully and squarely seated. Fit a new copper seal 7 onto the shoulder of the adjuster. Lubricate around the piston with a little hydraulic fluid and carefully enter it back into the bore. **Take great care not to cock the piston so that it jams and damages the bore.** Carefully press the piston down the bore **using only thumb pressure, as shown in FIG 11:10. The piston must not be tapped or forced to insert it.** Use a thin screwdriver through the hole in the caliper to guide the screw 6 of the adjuster through. The caliper and piston should be held vertical during this operation.

7 **The gap in the snap ring of the adjuster must be in line with the bleed screw otherwise air inside the piston cannot escape and bleeding**

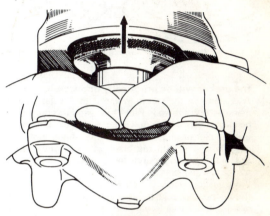

FIG 11:10 Pressing the piston back into the cylinder

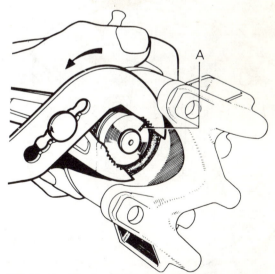

FIG 11:11 Aligning the mark on the piston (indicating the gap in the snap ring of the adjuster) with the bleed screw

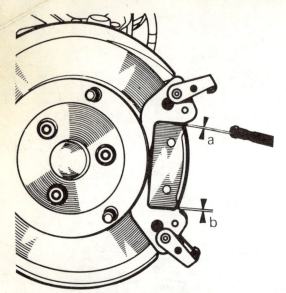

FIG 11:12 Checking the end clearance of the friction pads

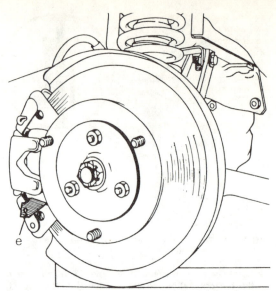

FIG 11:13 Shims fitted to reduce excessive pad end clearance

the brakes will be practically impossible. A mark **A** is made on the piston in line with the gap during manufacture, shown in **FIG 11:11**, and this mark may be electro-etched or a drill point mark. Turn the piston using a pair of grips as shown in the figure until the mark is in line with the bleed screw. Lightly brush Spargraph grease around the outer circumference of the piston and press it fully back into position. Hold the adjusting screw 6 with a screwdriver, to prevent the piston and adjuster assembly from rotating, and refit the nut 2 to a torque load of 1.5 kg m (10 lb ft).

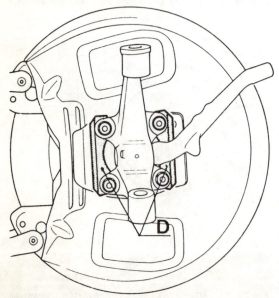

FIG 11:14 Shims for adjusting the caliper bracket on front wheels

8 The caliper should be tested using air pressure while immersed in a bath of methylated spirits. Any air leaks indicate a defect. Prevent the piston from moving out by using the special tool Fre.12A or a suitable bar of metal. The test pressure should be progressively raised and leaks checked for at each test pressure. Start at .7 kg/sq in (10 lb/sq in) and increase the pressure by 5 lb/sq in at each test until the maximum pressure of 1.5 kg/sq cm (20 lb/sq in) is reached. Because of the equipment required it is best to leave the testing to an agent but, provided that the parts have been carefully checked and reassembled, a calculated risk can be taken and the pressure test dispensed with. If the test is carried out the lubrication with Spargraph grease should be left until after the test.

9 Refit the dust cover 3. **Before refitting the caliper refill it with fresh hydraulic fluid, as this will make subsequent bleeding easier.** Leave the bleed screw out when filling and tilt the caliper around to remove as much air as possible. Refit the caliper in the reverse order of removal, remembering to use a new copper seal for the union of the flexible hose.

11:7 The brake discs

Because of the design of the hubs and discs it is impossible to remove the brake discs without removing the hubs. The removal of the front brake discs is dealt with in **Chapter 9, Section 9:3**, while the removal of the rear brake discs is dealt with in **Chapter 8, Section 8:5**. Before freeing the disc from the hub make alignment marks so that the parts will be reassembled in their original positions.

Slight concentric scoring will occur with normal use and wear but deep scores or radial scores will adversely affect the braking efficiency. **The discs must not be machined** and if they are so scored or distorted as to affect braking then new discs must be fitted.

If the discs and pads are dirty or lightly contaminated with oil or grease they should be cleaned with triclorethylene and deposits removed by gentle rubbing with emerycloth.

When the brake discs have been refitted they should be checked for runout. Mount a DTI (Dial Test Indicator) on the suspension so that the stylus rests vertically on the outer operating face of the disc. Rotate the hub and disc through one complete turn and check the runout on the disc. The runout should not exceed .3 mm (.012 inch) at a diameter of 250 mm ($9\frac{7}{8}$ inch). If the runout is excessive try rotating the disc in relation to the hub and if this fails to cure excessive runout then a new disc must be fitted.

11 : 8 The caliper bracket

For effective and quiet brake operation it is essential that the brake pads and caliper are accurately positioned in relation to the rotating brake disc.

Use feeler gauges to measure the clearance **a** between brake pad and caliper bracket, as shown in **FIG 11 :12**. The clearance should lie between .15 and .30 mm (.006 to .012 inch). If the clearance is excessive then shims can be fitted as shown at **e** in **FIG 11 :13** to reduce the clearance.

Shims can be fitted between the suspension and brake to ensure that the disc runs centrally between the caliper. The shims fitted for the front brakes are shown in **FIG 11 :14**. Only one shim may be fitted at each position on the front brakes but it is permissible to use only one shim per brake so as to correct any tilt and the shims are only available in .05 mm (.020 inch) thickness. The rear brakes must be shimmed parallel using one shim at each position, shown in **FIG 11 :15**. Shims for the rear brakes are available in three different thicknesses, .05 (.020, 1 (.040), and 1.5 (.059). To check on the shim thicknesses required, measure with feeler gauges between the disc and caliper at the points **a** and **b** shown in **FIG 11 :16**. The shims must be adjusted so that the gaps are both within the correct tolerances of 2.5 ± .5 mm (.079 to .118 inch).

It should be noted that if the caliper brackets require removal then the complete hub assemblies must also be removed, as for removing brake disc (see **Chapters 8 and 9**).

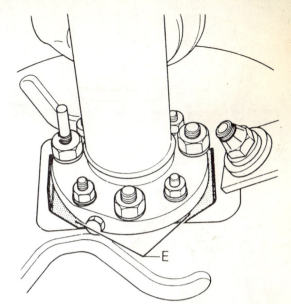

FIG 11 :15   Shims for adjusting the caliper bracket on rear wheels

Swinging links :

These can be checked for position but special gauges are required so the work should be left to an agent. If the links are worn or damaged they can be removed by carefully drilling out the rivet that secures them. The inner side of the caliper bracket should then be drilled out to 8 + .1 + .2 mm (.319 to .323 inch) as shown at **A** and the other side slightly chamfered as shown at **B** in **FIG 11 :17**. The swing link is then secured using a new pin and the pin peened using the special tool No. Fre.17

11 : 9 The brake pressure distributor

On the earlier models the valve limits the maximum pressure reached in the rear brake circuit. If the valve is fitted with a white plug then the pressure is limited to 50 + 8 — 0 kg/sq cm (710 to 820 lb/sq in) but if the valve

FIG 11 :16   Checking the shimming for the caliper bracket

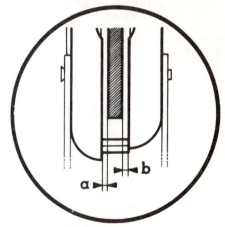

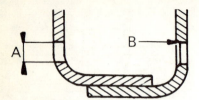

FIG 11:17 Drilling the bracket for fitting new swinging links

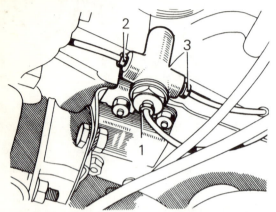

FIG 11:18 The brake pressure distributor valve

has a yellow plug then the pressure is limited to $56 + 0 - 6$ kg/sq cm (710 to 800 lb/sq in). The pressure limit is also stamped on one of the flats of the inlet union.

On later models a slightly different valve is fitted. Up to a pressure of $25 + 5 - 0$ kg/sq cm (355 to 425 lb/sq in) the pressure in both front and rear brakes remains identical but above this pressure the rear brakes only increase at half the rate of the front brakes.

Testing:

Special pressure gauges Fre.244 or Fre.214 are made for checking the operation of the valve. These gauges have an adaptor which screws into place off the bleed screw on a rear brake, and they are fitted with a pipe and bleed screw so that the gauge and system can be bled after the gauge has been fitted. While one operator watches the gauge the other operator applies gradually increasing pressure to the brake pedal.

If the valve does not operate correctly at the pressures given, or it leaks, then it must be renewed as no repairs can be carried out. The attachments of the valve are shown in **FIG 11:18**.

Disconnect the pipes 1, 2 and 3 and then remove the two nuts that secure the valve. The valve is refitted in the reverse order of removal but it is essential to bleed the brake system.

11:10 The master cylinder

The tandem master cylinders fitted to later USA models will be dealt with separately in **Section 11:13**, though it should be noted that many points of servicing are similar on both the types of master cylinder.

The components of the standard master cylinder are shown in **FIG 11:19**, and the method of operation in **FIG 11:20**. When the master cylinder is in the released position fluid can enter the bore through the port from the reservoir. As soon as the piston moves initially, under the action of the pushrod, the port is blocked off by the seal and pressure builds up in front of the piston. The fluid passes through the valve 7 to the brake calipers and operates the brakes. When the pedal is released the fluid returns through the four holes in the valve and finally the interconnecting port is again uncovered so that there is no residual pressure in the system. **If a new valve is fitted, make sure that the four return holes are present otherwise the brakes will lock after application.** A pressure-operated switch is mounted on the end of the master cylinder so that when there is hydraulic pressure in the system the contacts close and operate the brake lights.

Adjustment:

To ensure that the interconnecting port is always open when the brakes are released it is essential to have a small clearance **K** between the pushrod and master cylinder piston, with the brakes off. The adjustment is set at the pushrod so that there is a free movement of the brake pedal of approximately 5 mm ($\frac{3}{16}$ inch). Slacken the lock-nut on the pushrod with a thin spanner and then set the correct adjustment by turning the pushrod with a special spanner Fre.07, as shown in **FIG 11:21**. The special spanner is required because of the limited access room to the pushrod itself.

The adjustment should be checked occasionally but normally it does not require setting other than when the master cylinder or brake pedal assembly has been worked on.

Removal:

1 Disconnect the battery. Remove the spare wheel and undertray. Disconnect the leads to the stoplight switch after labelling them.
2 Drain the hydraulic reservoir, or fit a sealed filler cap or fit a clean plug into the outlet. Unscrew the stop light switch from the end of the master cylinder and disconnect the feed pipe 1 shown in **FIG 11:22**. Disconnect the pipes to the brakes by undoing the union nuts.
3 Remove the attachment bolts, shown in **FIG 11:23**, and slide the unit off the pushrod so that it can be removed from the car.

Servicing:

1 Lightly press the piston assembly down the bore using a suitable tool such as a pencil. Slide back the bellows and remove the snap ring 1 and stopwasher 2. The internal parts can then be removed by tapping the end of the cylinder onto the palm of the hand and once exposed can be gripped with the fingers and fully withdrawn.
2 Remove the seals from the piston, using only the fingers. Wash the parts in methylated spirits. **If any other solvent is used on the metal parts then they must be given a final swill in methylated**

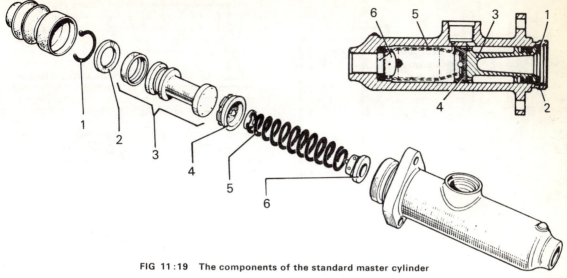

FIG 11:19 The components of the standard master cylinder

Key to Fig 11:19   1 Snap ring   2 Stop washer   3 Piston assembly   4 Cup seal   5 Return spring   6 Valve

spirits to remove all traces of other solvent. Examine the bore of the cylinder and if it is not perfectly smooth, polished and free from scores, wear or defects then the complete assembly should be renewed. Discard all old seals and fit new ones supplied in a service kit. Fit a new piston if the old one is worn or damaged.

3 Dip the seals into hydraulic fluid and refit them wet, using only the fingers and making sure that they are fully and squarely seated. Once assembled dip the internal parts into hydraulic fluid and slide them back into place while wet. Secure them in place with the stopwasher and snap ring. Check that the piston assembly returns freely under the action of the spring.

Refitting:

The master cylinder is refitted in the reverse order of removal. Once it is in place the pedal free movement must be correctly set and the brakes then filled and bled. Apply the brakes several times and check that all four wheels rotate freely once the pedal is released.

11:11 Bleeding the brakes

This is not routine maintenance but it must be carried out whenever air has entered the system, either through allowing the level in the reservoir to fall too low, because of leaks, or after dismantling and reassembling the system.

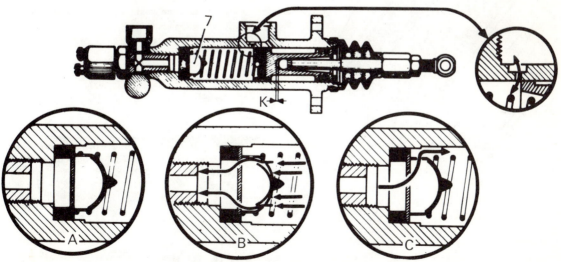

FIG 11:20 Operation of the master cylinder

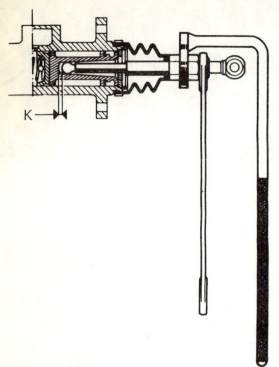

FIG 11:21 Adjusting the pushrod clearance on the master cylinder

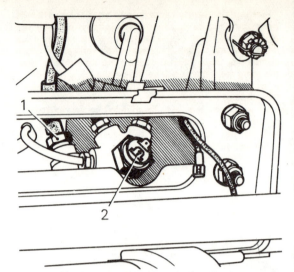

FIG 11:22 The hydraulic inlet tube **1** and brake pressure switch **2**

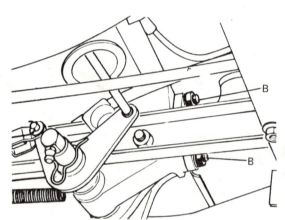

FIG 11:23 The master cylinder attachments

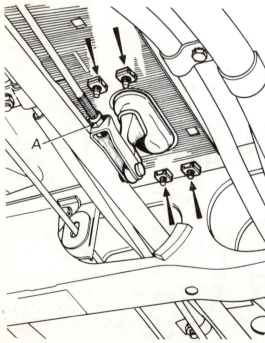

FIG 11:24 The handbrake lever attachments

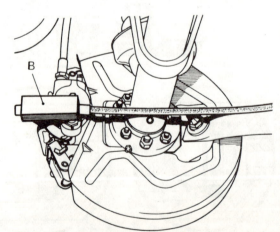

FIG 11:25 The special tool fitted to the rear brakes when setting the handbrake rod adjuster

Renault strongly recommend that the system is pressure bled using special equipment held by the agent. The system can be bled using the brake pedal but it will be a long task and may not be fully satisfactory when completed, though the more care and time that is taken the more satisfactory will be the result.

Before starting bleeding fill the reservoir right up using the grade of fluid specified on the filler cap. Keep a constant watch on the level as bleeding progresses and top up before the level falls too low.

Fluid that has been bled through the system is best discarded, unless it comes out perfectly clean. If the fluid is clean store it in a sealed container for at least 24 hours to allow all air bubbles to rise and disperse. **Fluid from bleeding must never be returned directly to the reservoir.**

Attach a length of small-bore tube to the bleed screw and dip the other end of the tube into a little clean fluid in a clean glass container. Note that the brakes are best bled in the order of decreasing pipe runs, starting with the brake that has the longest run to it.

Open the bleed screw and have an assistant slowly press down the brake pedal. Close the bleed screw when the pedal reaches the end of its travel and then have the assistant allow the pedal to return slowly. Carry on this sequence until only fluid, free from any air bubbles, comes out of the bleed tube. It may be necessary to press the brake pedal down fairly fast but in all cases it should be allowed to return slowly. When the brake has been bled make sure that the bleed screw is closed and then remove the bleed tube.

Bleed the remainder of the brakes by the same method. Provided that the car is safe to use it may help, after bleeding, to use the car for a few days and then bleed the system again when all the tiny bubbles have had a chance to coalesce into larger ones that are easier to bleed out. After bleeding make sure that the reservoir is topped up to its correct level.

11:12 The handbrake

Adjustment of the handbrake is covered in **Section 11:2**.

Handbrake lever:

The attachments are shown in **FIG 11:24**. Extract the splitpin and remove the clevis pin that secures the fork to the lever. The lever assembly can then be removed by undoing the four bolts that secure it to the floor.

Refit the lever assembly in the reverse order of removal.

Note that the adjuster A, is only used for setting the cables and must not be used for adjusting the handbrake. It is advisable not to alter the adjuster unnecessarily.

If the adjuster is slackened or altered it must be set using made-up sheet metal gauges Fre.15 fitted over the springs on the cables, as shown at **B** in **FIG 11:25**. Disconnect the handbrake rod from between the handbrake lever assembly and equalizer by removing the nut 5 shown in **FIG 11:26**. Fit the special gauges so that the cable lengths are set and then alter the adjuster **A** on the rod (shown in **FIG 11:24**) until the eye end of the rod fits easily back onto the equalizer without having to apply any pressure. Tighten the nuts on the adjuster **A** in this position and remove the gauges from the cables.

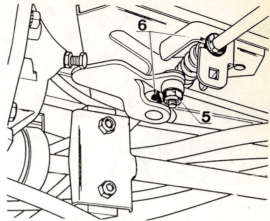

FIG 11:26   The handbrake equalizer attachments

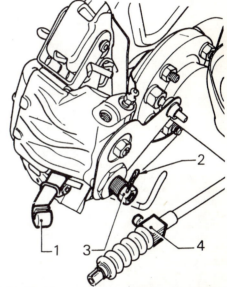

FIG 11:27   The attachment of the handbrake cable to earlier calipers

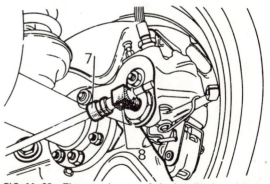

FIG 11:28   The attachment of the handbrake cable to later calipers

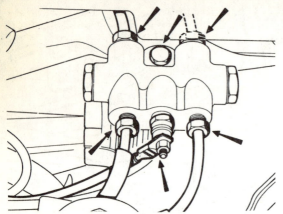

FIG 11:29   The pressure drop indicator

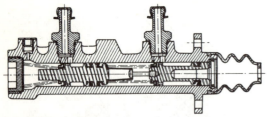

FIG 11:30   Sectioned view of the tandem master cylinder

Cables:

The attachment to the brake on earlier models is shown in **FIG 11:27** while that on later models is shown in **FIG 11:28**. In both cases free the clips that secure the cable to the tie rod and disconnect the cable from the operating lever on the brake. On the earlier models remove the pin 2 so that the guide stop 4 can be removed from its location 3. On the later models remove the cable cover end stop 7 from its location 8. In both cases remove the nut 5 from the equalizer and then push out the stops 6 to completely free the cable.

Refit the cables in the reverse order of removal and adjust the handbrake at both rear wheels.

Care must be taken in obtaining new parts as they have been modified slightly from time to time.

11:13 USA models

Later models destined for the North American market are fitted with a tandem master cylinder and dual-circuit brakes. A pressure drop indicator is fitted and this valve operates the warning light if there is an excessive pressure differential between the two systems, such as will occur if there is a hydraulic leak.

Pressure drop indicator:

The attachments of the unit are shown in **FIG 11:29**. Before removing the unit disconnect the battery and drain out the fluid from the reservoir or fit a sealed filler cap. Disconnect the electrical lead to the switch and then the four hydraulic pipes. The unit can then be removed by taking out its attachment bolt.

Refit the unit in the reverse order of removal and bleed both braking systems. If the unit is defective or leaks it cannot be repaired and a new one must be fitted in its place.

Master cylinder:

A sectioned view of the master cylinder is shown in **FIG 11:30**. The primary piston operates normally from the pushrod while the secondary piston is operated by the build-up of hydraulic pressure between the two pistons. If there is a failure in the circuit served by the secondary piston then the secondary piston will move fully forward until it mechanically contacts the cylinder end and pressure can then build up normally between the two pistons to operate the other circuit. If the circuit served by the primary piston fails then the primary piston will move forward until it mechanically contacts the secondary piston and pressure can then build up normally in front of the secondary piston. The pressure differential will operate the pressure warning switch to light the lamp and warn the driver, though the fault should be obvious by the further movement required from the brake pedal.

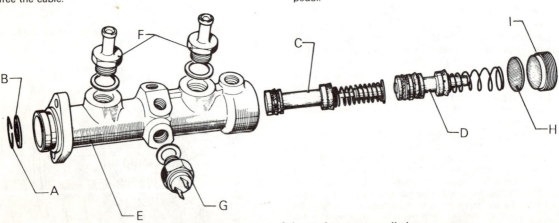

FIG 11:31   The components of the tandem master cylinder

Key to Fig 11:31   A Snap ring   B Stop washer   C Primary piston   D Secondary piston   E Body   F Inlet adaptors
G Stoplight switch   H Copper seal   I Plug

The removal and adjustment of the tandem master cylinder is very similar to the method used on the standard master cylinder (see **Section 11:10**).

The components of the master cylinder are shown in **FIG 11:31**. Remove the master cylinder and mount it in the padded jaws of a vice. Unscrew the two inlet unions **F** and stoplight switch **G**. Unscrew the stop plug **I**, using a steel blade. Remove the copper seal **H** and withdraw the secondary piston assembly **D**. Lightly press the primary piston assembly **C** down the bore and remove the snap ring **A** and stopwasher **B**. The primary piston assembly can then be withdrawn. Remove the old seals using the fingers.

Clean the parts in methylated spirit and check them for wear, paying particular attention to the bore of the cylinder. Renew the complete assembly if the bore is scratched or damaged.

Discard all the rubber and copper seals and fit all new ones on reassembly. Dip the rubber seals into hydraulic fluid and refit them to the pistons, using only the fingers and making sure that the lips face in the correct directions.

Refit the stopwasher **B** and snap ring **A**. Lubricate the primary piston assembly **C** with hydraulic fluid and press it back into the bore from the plug end. Follow it by the secondary piston assembly, **taking great care not to damage or bend back the lips of the seals that face into the bore.** Fit a new copper seal **H** and screw in the closure plug **I** to a torque of 10 kgm (75 lb ft). Lightly press the pistons down the bore from the snap ring end and fit the stoplight switch **G**, using a new copper seal. Refit the inlet unions **F** using new seals. Check that the pistons return freely under the action of the return springs.

11:14 Fault diagnosis

(a) Spongy pedal

1 Air in the system
2 Hydraulic leak
3 Excessively low fluid level in reservoir
4 Worn master cylinder

(b) Excessive pedal movement

1 Check (a)
2 Excessive pad wear
3 Incorrectly adjusted front hub bearings
4 Excessive clearance on master cylinder pushrod

(c) Brakes grab or pull to one side

1 Wet or oily pads
2 Cracked or distorted brake disc
3 Worn out friction pads
4 Faulty or seized caliper
5 Seized handbrake cable or brake lever assembly
6 Mixed pads of different grades
7 Defective suspension or steering
8 Unevenly worn tyres

CHAPTER 12

THE ELECTRICAL SYSTEM

12:1 Description

It should be noted that the models destined for the North American and Scandinavian markets are fitted with a generator and control unit made by Bosch.

All models are fitted with a 12-volt electrical system in which the negative (—ve) terminal of the battery is earthed.

A generator driven by a belt from the crankshaft pulley supplies the needs of the system and the charging current for the battery when the engine is running. The battery, which is of the lead/acid type, supplies the extremely heavy current required by the starter motor for starting the engine as well as supplying the ancilliaries when the engine is stopped. The output of the generator is regulated to the demands of the system by a control box but the battery also serves a vital part in stabilizing the voltage.

A 12-volt test lamp and leads, or any voltmeter that reads above 12-volts, may be used for checking the continuity of circuits and tracing wiring faults. **Cheap and unreliable instruments must not be used when checking performance, or adjusting components, as they are incapable of reading to the accuracy required.** For accurate checks high-grade (and preferably moving-coil) instruments must be used.

Wiring diagrams are shown in the **Appendix** to this manual to enable those with electrical experience to trace and rectify wiring faults.

Instructions for servicing components are given in this chapter but it must be realized that it is a waste of both time and money to attempt to repair items that are seriously defective, either electrically or mechanically. A patched-up unit will always be liable to trouble and failure, so in the long run it will be found better to fit a new or reconditioned unit in its place.

12:2 The battery

The battery is the heart of the electrical system and if the battery is poor or defective then the operation of the whole electrical system will also suffer. The battery is also the first component of the electrical system to suffer from neglected maintenance.

Maintenance:

1 Always keep the top of the battery clean and dry. Wipe away any spillage or dampness with a clean cloth and then discard the cloth as it will have acid on it. If dirt or moisture are allowed to accumulate they will form a leakage path for the charge to drain away and this current drain will also cause galvanic

corrosion to the battery metal surrounds. If corrosion is present then remove the battery and wash the area with dilute ammonia or baking powder dissolved in warm water. Flush with plenty of clean water and when the parts are dry paint them with anti-sulphuric paint.

2 Keep the battery terminals clean and tight. Poor contact here is one of the commonest causes of poor starter motor operation. Wash away any corrosion using dilute ammonia, followed by flushing with clean water. Oxides can be cleaned off with a wire brush or by careful scraping with a sharp knife. Smear the posts and connectors with petroleum jelly as a preventive against further corrosion.

3 At regular intervals check the electrolyte level in the individual cells. The water will evaporate more rapidly in hot weather, therefore the checks should be more frequent. Excessive requirements of distilled water indicate overcharging or a cracked case. If the level is low top-up to just above the separators, using distilled water only. **Additives that are said to improve battery life or recharge batteries should not be used and acid must never be added directly to the battery.** Electrolyte of the correct specific gravity should only be added to replace spillage or leakage.

Charging:

The best rate of charging is a current that is equal to 10 per cent of the battery capacity, though a trickle charger giving 1 to 2 amps will be quite sufficient for boosting the battery or even recharging it. Garage boost chargers should be avoided if possible, as they charge at a rate of up to 100 amps and a poor battery will be completely ruined by this type of treatment.

The battery charge can be checked with a hydrometer but it is fully charged when it gasses freely on the charging current. **Never examine the battery with a naked flame as the gases given off are explosive. When refitting a newly charged battery avoid sparks as these can set off the gas mixture.**

A poor battery can quite often be reclaimed by giving it a series of discharges and charges. Connect the battery across a lamp bank which takes approximately 5 to 6 amps and discharge it until the lamps dim perceptibly and then recharge it fully. Carry out this sequence for two or three cycles and then charge it ready for use.

Electrolyte:

If electrolyte is spilled or leaks out it is best to buy ready-mixed electrolyte to top-up with. If electrolyte has to be mixed then use distilled water and pure sulphuric acid, mixing them in an earthenware or heatproof glass container. Heat is given off so allow the mixture to cool before checking the specific gravity. For the same reason **always add the acid to the water, as drops of water falling into the acid will instantly turn into steam and spatter out the acid.** Acid or electrolyte on the skin or clothing should be immediately neutralized with baking powder followed by flushing copiously with water. If acid or electrolyte splashes into the eye, hold the eye open under a running tap and **obtain medical assistance immediately.**

Testing:

Provided that the battery has not just been topped-up with distilled water the state of charge of the battery can be checked using a hydrometer. If the battery has just been topped-up, the car should be used for at least half-an-hour to ensure full mixing of the distilled water and electrolyte. Draw up sufficient electrolyte into the instrument to ensure that the float is clear of the bottom and sides, and then take the reading at eye level. At the same time check the appearance of the electrolyte as dirt, specks or cloudiness are indications of a defective cell. This will be confirmed by the specific gravity reading differing radically from the five other cells. The readings give the following indications:

For climates below 32°C (90°F):

1.270 to 1.290	..	..	Cell fully charged
1.190 to 1.210	..	..	Cell half-charged
1.110 to 1.130	..	..	Cell discharged

Replace spillage with electrolyte of 1.270 specific gravity.

For climates above 32°C (90°F):

1.120 to 1.230	..	..	Cell fully charged
1.130 to 1.150	..	..	Cell half-charged
1.050 to 1.070	..	..	Cell discharged

Replace spillage with electrolyte of 1.120 specific gravity.

The figures are given assuming a standard electrolyte temperature of 16°C (60°F). If the actual temperature is different from standard then convert the reading to the standard temperature equivalent by adding .002 for every 3°C (5°F) rise in temperature and subtract for every increment drop in temperature.

If the intercell connectors are accessible the battery can also be tested using a heavy duty discharge tester. Do not use this type of tester on a battery known to be low in charge or in poor condition.

Storage:

Short-term storage presents no problems provided that the battery has been well-maintained. If the battery is to be stored for long periods make sure that it is fully charged, the top dry and any exposed metal portions well covered with petroleum jelly. Keep the battery stored in a cool dry place well away from extremes of temperature.

At monthly intervals give the battery a freshening-up charge and at three-month intervals discharge it using a lamp bank and fully recharge it. If this is not done the battery will slowly self-discharge and the plates sulphate up, to the ruination of the battery.

12:3 Servicing electric motors

All the motors fitted to the car operate on the same principles and are basically very similar in constructional detail. It should be noted that the generator can be considered as a specialized form of motor in which the inputs and outputs are reversed, in that mechanical power is fed in and electrical power drawn out.

The removal and dismantling of the various motors will be dealt with in the relevant sections but to save constant repetition general instructions for servicing all motors are collected into this section.

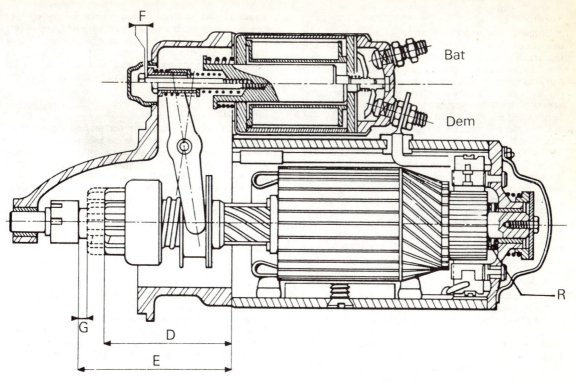

FIG 12:1   A sectioned view of the Ducellier starter motor

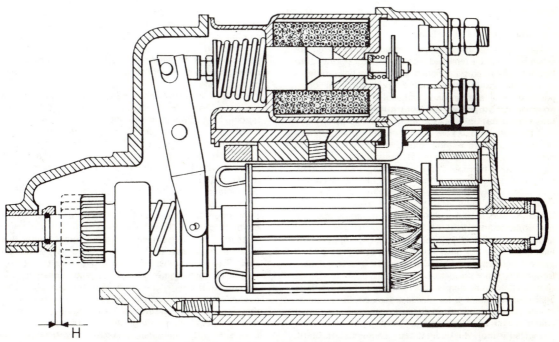

FIG 12:2   A sectioned view of the Paris-Rhone starter motor

Brushgear:

Dismantle the motor sufficiently for the brushgear to be exposed. **Great care must be taken not to damage the brushes on the commutator** and on some motors it will be necessary to lift the brushes up in their holders and hold them up with the brush springs resting against the sides of the brushes, instead of on top. On some generators it will be necessary to slide shims between the brushes and commutator so that as the brushes are slid out they do not become chipped on the edge of the commutator.

Renew the brushes if they are excessively worn. On motors where the connector is soldered into place, grip the connector with a pair of pliers to prevent the solder from creeping up it and making it stiff.

Check that the brushes slide freely in their holders. If the brushes stick then remove them and polish their sides lightly on a fine file. Clean the brush holder with a piece of cloth moistened in fuel before refitting the brush. To preserve the bedding-in the brushes should be refitted into their original positions and facing in the original directions.

Check the brush springs and renew them if they are weak or distorted.

Not all brushes are supplied ground to shape on the end and they should therefore be bedded-in. Make up a wooden rod of the same diameter as the commutator and wrap this with fine-grade glasspaper. Alternatively the actual commutator itself can be used, wrapped with glasspaper. Fit the brushes around the glasspaper in their holders and rotate the commutator or mandrel in the opposite direction to normal rotation for a few turns to grind the brushes to shape.

Before reassembly blow out and brush away all loose dirt and dust. Wipe the commutator over with a piece of cloth moistened with fuel.

Commutator and armature:

If the commutator is worn or scored then the armature assembly must be removed from the motor. Light score or burn marks can be polished off using a fine-grade of glasspaper, though note that a commutator in good condition will appear dark and polished. **Never use emerycloth to polish the commutator as this will leave hard particles embedded in the copper.**

If the wear or marks are deep then the damage should be skimmed off in a lathe, provided that the minimum diameter of the commutator is not reached. Use the highest speed possible and a very sharp tool. On some generators and starter motors the insulation between the commutator segments is undercut. Grind the sides of a hacksaw blade until it is the exact thickness of the insulation and then use the blade to squarely undercut the insulation to a depth of .8 mm ($\frac{1}{32}$ inch). Take a light final skim cut using a diamond, or carbide-tipped tool. Failing such a tool, polish the commutator with a very fine grade of glasspaper. Remove all swarf and metal dust from the commutator before reassembly.

Very little can be done to the remainder of the armature apart from checking it for physical damage. Shortcircuits in the coils can be tested for but a special instrument called a 'growler' is required, though they can be suspected if individual commutator segments are burnt. Check that there are no loose laminations, segments or wiring as well as checking the laminations for scoring. Scoring all round the laminations indicates excessively worn bearings or loose polepieces while scoring on one side only indicates a bent armature shaft. **A defective armature cannot be repaired and it must not be machined or straightened,** so fit a new armature and discard the old one.

Field coils:

On some smaller motors permanent magnets are fitted in place of the field coils. Care must be taken when dismantling this type of motor as the magnet is attached inside the cover and tends to draw the armature out with it, to the possible damage of the brushes.

The field coils can be tested using a 12-volt test lamp and battery across the terminals. By connecting the lamp between a terminal and the motor body the insulation can also be checked. A better method is to use an ohmeter and measure the actual resistance. An ammeter can be used instead of an ohmeter. Connect the ammeter in series with a 12-volt battery and note the current that flows. The resistance can then be calculated using Ohm's law (Voltage/current=Resistance).

The field coils on starter motors and generators are held in place by the polepieces which are in turn secured by large screws. The screws must be tightened to a high torque on a special wheel screwdriver and then staked to prevent them from slackening. As an ordinary screwdriver cannot tighten the screws sufficiently, renewal of the field coils should be left to a service station.

Bearings:

Either ballbearings or bushes may be used. The ballbearings are usually held in place by a riveted retainer plate. To remove rivets use a drill larger in diameter than the stem but smaller than the head. File a flat on the head and then centrepunch it in the centre as a guide. Drill carefully until the head is so weakened that it can be knocked off using a small cold chisel and then use a suitable punch to drive out the stem. Before fitting ballbearings make sure that they are packed with grease of the correct grade.

On larger motors bushes made of porous bronze alloy are used. Sometimes these can be extracted by gently tapping them out with a drift but if they are in blind holes then screw a tap into them and withdraw them on the tap. In extreme cases a thread will have to be cut in them with the tap and then an extractor made out of a suitable piece of tube, large washer and correct sized bolt.

Before fitting new bushes they should be soaked for 24 hours in engine oil. The period can be reduced if the oil is heated over a bath of boiling water but even then they should be allowed to soak for 2 hours and not taken out of the oil until it has cooled. Refit the new bushes using a stepped mandrel whose spigot is slightly longer than the bush and of exactly the same diameter as the armature shaft. The spigot must also have a high finish on it.

Smaller motors are often fitted with spherical self-aligning bearings. These are held in the end plate by a riveted retainer, and usually spares cannot be obtained if they are worn. Check that such bearings move freely in their retainers (otherwise the shaft will bind) and that the bore is not worn. Lubricate the bearings with a few drops of oil before refitting them.

Insulation:

Clean away all metal and carbon dust from the parts as this type of dust can form a leakage path for the electricity. Use a brush and airline, or tyre pump, and wipe away excess grease with a piece of cloth moistened with fuel. **Under no circumstances dip the armature, brushes or field coils into solvent.** Methylated spirits can also be used as a cleaning solvent but fuel is more readily available.

The best way of testing insulation is to use some form of resistance meter through a 12-volt test lamp and battery can be used. A 110-volt AC supply with Neon test lamp will be more effective than the lower voltage test but the owner is warned against using the full 240 mains voltage used in many countries. In all cases the lamp should not light when connected across the insulation.

12:4 The starter motor

Two main types of starter motor are fitted as standard to the models covered by this manual. The two types are Paris-Rhone D.8.E41 or D.8.E60 and Ducellier 6128A or 6172. A sectioned view of a Ducellier starter motor is shown in **FIG 12:1** and that of a Paris-Rhone starter motor in **FIG 12:2**. The method of operation is the same in both cases.

When the starter switch is energized current flows through the starter solenoid coil and the solenoid draws in the plunger. The lever then moves the pinion assembly along the spiral path on the armature shaft so that it is rotated and pressed into mesh with the teeth on the fly-wheel. If the teeth abut edge to edge then the spings compress and the teeth mesh on initial rotation of the starter motor. At the same time the solenoid plunger closes the heavy duty contacts in the solenoid allowing current to flow to the starter motor. Lost motion springs are fitted which ensure that the contacts open fractionally before the drive is disengaged. An overrun clutch is fitted into the drive and this ensures that when the engine starts the starter motor is not driven at high speed by the engine. If loose wiring, segments or laminations are found on the armature then the overrun clutch should be checked as it is possible that it is defective and the starter motor has been over-speeded.

On some models brake washers are fitted to the armature. These are weak enough not to slow the armature under power but as soon as the current is cut they bring the armature to a rapid halt to ensure that it is not rotating if the engine stalls and has to be restarted rapidly.

Starter fails to operate:

1 Check the state of charge of the battery and make sure that the battery connections are clean and tight. At the same time it is advisable to check the connection of the heavy duty cable to the starter solenoid and the earth strap to the frame.
2 Switch on some lights that can be seen from the driving seat and again operate the starter switch. If the lights go dim then the starter motor is taking current. No rotation of the motor can be caused by an internal fault or by the pinion jamming in mesh. Select a gear and rock the car backwards and forwards to free a jammed pinion. If this fails then the starter motor must

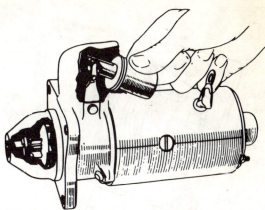

FIG 12:3 Removing or refitting the solenoid plunger on a Paris-Rhone starter motor

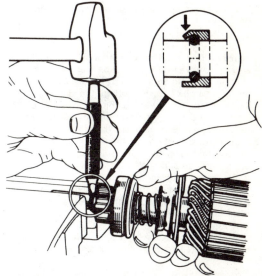

FIG 12:4 Peening the stop ring on a Paris-Rhone starter motor

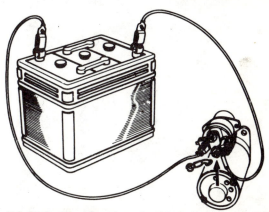

FIG 12:5 Checking the solenoid setting on a Paris-Rhone starter motor

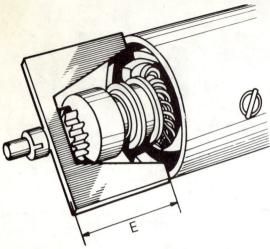

FIG 12:6 Checking the pinion setting on a Ducellier starter motor

be removed for further examination. The motor should also be removed for examination if it jams regularly, checking the pinion and teeth on the flywheel. The flywheel can be checked through the aperture for the starter motor while turning the engine over on the starting handle, but if the teeth are damaged then the transmission must be removed in order to gain access.

3 If the lights do not go dim then listen for the click as the solenoid operates. If the solenoid does not click use a test lamp or voltmeter to check the supply to the solenoid, tracing back until the fault is found if no current is reaching the solenoid terminal. If current is reaching the solenoid terminal, use a thick piece of metal to short across the heavy-duty solenoid terminals and if the solenoid is at fault the motor will spin freely and at high speed. A defective solenoid must be renewed as repairs cannot be carried out to it.

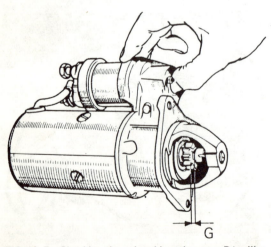

FIG 12:7 Checking the solenoid setting on a Ducellier starter motor

Removal:

Disconnect the battery first and then disconnect the leads and cables from the starter solenoid. It may be necessary to remove both the silencer assembly and engine floor panel in order to gain access to the parts. Remove the nuts and bolts that secure the starter motor to the engine and withdraw the starter motor.

Refit the starter motor in the reverse order of removal, reconnecting the battery only after all other connections have been made.

On later models the starter motor is located by hollow dowels through which the attachment bolts pass. This point must be remembered when removing the starter motor as the motor will have to be partially pulled straight out to free the dowels. A new starter motor can be fitted to an old type clutch housing by means of the special spacer bushes No. 6.084.203. If an old starter motor has to be fitted to a new type of clutch housing then the end plate of the starter motor must be changed, using a new plate No. 8.705.241 which has provisions for dowels in it.

Servicing:

The brushgear is accessible after removing the cover-band (if fitted) and can be serviced after the through-bolts have been released and the end cover taken off. The solenoid can be removed after taking out the nuts or bolts that secure it to the drive end bracket. On the Paris-Rhone models the solenoid plunger will separate from the solenoid body and it is refitted, or removed, as shown in **FIG 12:3**.

On both models the pinion drive is removable, as a complete unit, from the armature shaft. Check the teeth on the pinion and renew the assembly complete if they are badly worn or scored, at the same time checking the teeth on the flywheel. Similarly renew the assembly if the overrun clutch does not rotate freely in one direction and still takes up drive immediately in the other direction. On the Paris-Rhone models the pinion assembly is held in place by a snap ring covered with the stopwasher. Use a suitable piece of tube to drive the stopwasher down the shaft towards the armature and then remove the snap ring so that the parts can be slid off. When refitting the parts use a new stopwasher and peen it down at four or five places to trap the snap ring, as shown in **FIG 12:4**.

Adjustments:

The dimensions shown in **FIGS 12:1** and **12:2** must set in order to ensure that the motor operates correctly and quietly.

On the Paris-Rhone starter the gap **H** is set with the solenoid energized using a 6-volt battery as shown in **FIG 12:5**. **Do not use a 12-volt battery, and note that the lead to the motor from the solenoid has been disconnected.** Energize the solenoid and measure the gap with feeler gauges. If the gap is incorrect then remove the solenoid and screw the clevis fork in or out of the plunger to adjust the gap to the correct limits. The gap **H** is correct between .5 and 2.5mm (.020 to .099 inch).

On the Ducellier starter motor the pinion must be checked for position at both the energized and at rest positions. The dimension **D** should be $59 \pm .6$mm ($2\frac{5}{16}$ to $2\frac{11}{32}$ inch) when at rest. The dimension **E** is set to 70.5 ± 1 mm ($2\frac{3}{4}$ to $2\frac{13}{16}$ inch) by screwing down the front stop and the best method of checking this setting is using the gauge Ele.05, as shown in **FIG 12:6**. The gap **G** should be adjusted to .05 to 1.5 mm (.002 to .060 inch) by turning the control bolt on the solenoid while keeping the solenoid in the energized position as shown in **FIG 12:7**. The gap **F** should be .1 to .5 mm (.004 to .020 inch) but this will be partially controlled by the setting **G** and the main aim is to keep **F** as small as possible while setting **G**.

Testing:

For full and accurate checks a torque rig and accurate meters are required. The performance of the various motors is given in **Technical Data**.

The solenoid windings can be roughly checked by connecting them across a battery, as shown in **FIG 12:5**, with the lead to the motor disconnected. The solenoid should pull in firmly and rapidly and it should be noted that a fairly high current will be taken so if the contact is not good the solenoid will chatter in and out.

The motor can be tested by clamping it in a vice and connecting it to a 12-volt battery using heavy duty leads. The motor should spin freely and rapidly while taking a large current.

Reconnect the lead between motor and solenoid and then the complete unit can be tested, using heavy-duty leads between motor body and battery positive terminal and between solenoid terminal and battery negative terminal. A third lead, of fairly thick construction, is then connected between the battery negative terminal and solenoid control terminal. The solenoid should then operate and the motor spin. If the motor is not firmly held it will kick heavily as it starts.

12:5 The generator

As for the starter motor two makes of generator can be fitted as standard; Paris-Rhone or Ducellier. It should be noted that on later models the brushes are not radial but held at a slight angle to the commutator, as shown in **FIG 12:8**. This ensures better commutation at high speed.

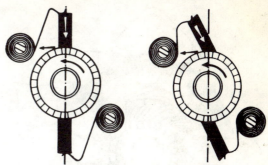

FIG 12:8 The earlier and later brush angles on the generator

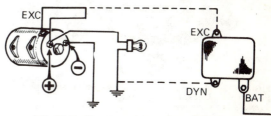

FIG 12:9 Testing the generator for output

Generator fails to charge or battery low:

1 Check the tension of the drive belt, as described in **Chapter 4, Section 4:3**. If the belt is defective or slipping then the generator output will be reduced.
2 Make sure that the low charge of the battery is not just due to heavy demands being made on the electrical system, such as in winter conditions, and the car only being used for short-mileage journeys where the generator has not got the time to recharge the battery. If these conditions apply then a boost charge on a trickle charger at about monthly intervals will prevent the battery from going flat.

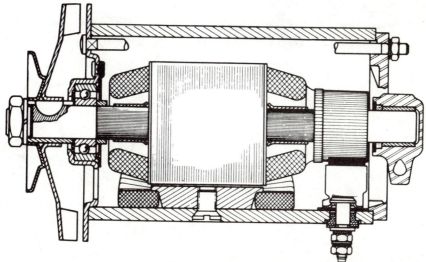

FIG 12:10   A sectioned view of a Ducellier generator

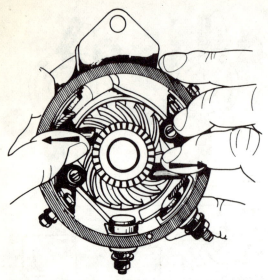

FIG 12:11 Holding out the brushes while removing the body from a Ducellier generator

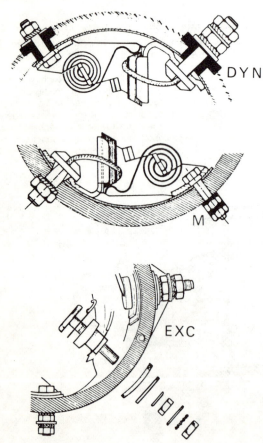

FIG 12:12 The terminals on a Ducellier generator

3 Check all the connections and wiring in the charging circuit. Pay particular attention to the battery connections and the earth points in the system. Lightly tug on wires to check for loose connections and shake them to check for frayed or defective insulation.

4 If the actual output of the generator is suspected to be low then Renaults recommend that both the generator and control box are removed and tested on a test bench. As a brief test of the generator disconnect the two leads at the generator and connect a jumper lead between the terminal **D** and **EXC** terminal on the generator. Make sure that the —ve terminal is earthed and then connect a voltmeter or test lamp between the **D** (+ve) terminal on the generator and a good earth on the car. The circuit is shown connected in **FIG 12:9**. Start the engine and gradually increase its speed. **If a test lamp is used do not exceed 1000 rev/min of engine speed, otherwise the lamp will burn out.** If a voltmeter is being used then the voltage should rise steadily and without fluctuation as the engine speed rises. **Do not race the engine in an attempt to get a reading and do not increase the engine speed beyond the point where the voltmeter reads 20 volts.**

5 If a new generator has been fitted or the old one dismantled and reassembled it is possible that the residual magnetism in the coils has been lost. The same circuit as shown in **FIG 12:9** can be used to re-energize the generator. Instead of connecting the lamp to earth as shown, brush a lead connected to the positive terminal of the battery across the positive terminal on the generator. If the fan belt is off then the generator will operate as a motor, if the lead is held in place, and this will be a further check that the generator is operating satisfactorily.

Dismantling Ducellier generator:

A sectioned view of the unit is shown in **FIG 12:10**. Loosen the pulley and cooling fan without actually removing the assembly. While slackening the nut hold the pulley with the special spanner Ele.04. Unscrew the two

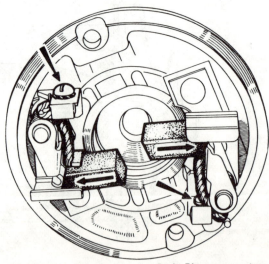

FIG 12:13 The brushes on a Paris-Rhone generator

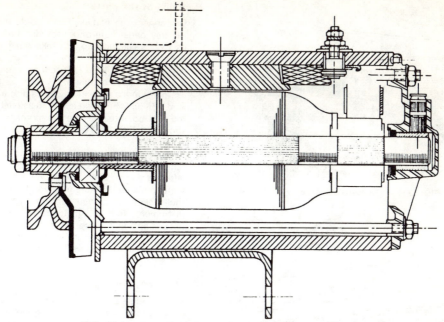

FIG 12:14   A sectioned view of a Paris-Rhone generator

tie rods and remove the rear end plate. Hold the brushes away from the commutator, as shown in **FIG 12:11** and remove the body from around the armature.

Normally this is sufficient dismantling for servicing purposes but if further dismantling is required remove the pulley and its key so that the front end plate can be removed. The attachments of the various terminals are shown in **FIG 12:12**.

The generator is reassembled in the reverse order of removal but note that if new brushes are fitted they must be bedded-in as described in **Section 12:3**.

Dismantling Paris-Rhone generator:

The general method is the same as for the Ducellier generator. The difference is that the brushes are secured in their holders to the rear end plate, as shown in **FIG 12:13**. A sectioned view is shown in **FIG 12:14**. After the pulley has been slackened and the two tie rod nuts removed, insert strips of metal to hold the brushes away from the commutator, as shown in **FIG 12:15**, to prevent the brushes being damaged as the end cover is being removed. These strips should also be used when refitting the end cover.

12:6 The windscreen wipers

The attachment of the wiper arms to the wheelbox spindles is shown in **FIG 12:16**. To remove the arm lift it off the glass so that the hook end 1 frees the spring plate 2 and the arm can be drawn off the splines. Refit the arm making sure that the blades park 6 cm ($2\frac{3}{8}$ inch) away from the windscreen frame. If the park position is not satisfactory then the arms should be removed and then refitted correctly.

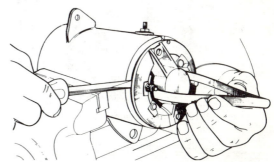

FIG 12:15   Removing the end plate from a Paris-Rhone generator

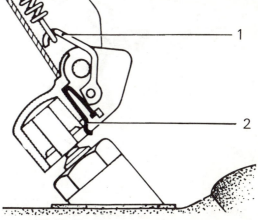

FIG 12:16   The wiper arm attachments

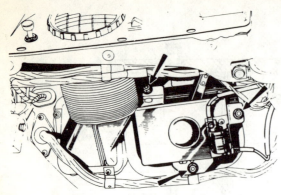

FIG 12:17   The wiper protector

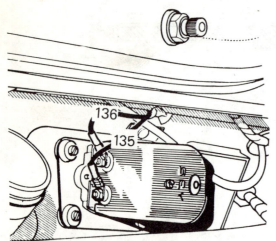

FIG 12:18   The wiper motor attachments

FIG 12:19   The tank unit

Removal of the parts:

1 Disconnect the battery. From inside the car remove the tray panel from under the dashboard, by freeing its twelve securing points. Take out the windscreen wiper protector by removing the three securing nuts arrowed in **FIG 12:17**. Disconnect the wiper motor from the linkage coupling.

2 From inside the ventilation casing disconnect the grey lead 135 and the green lead 136 as well as taking out the four bolts that secure the motor to its backplate, shown in **FIG 12:18**. The motor itself can now be removed.

3 If the backplate requires removal it is necessary to remove the heater (see next chapter) as well as the lefthand side cool air ventilation nozzle. Remove both wiper arms and spindle nuts and bushes. Disconnect the speedometer drive cable from the back of the instrument. Pull the plate downwards to free the bushes and motor support and then swing the plate through 180 degrees and remove it towards the left. The parts are refitted in the reverse order of removal.

12:7 The fuel gauge

If the gauge gives inaccurate or varying readings, check carefully through the wiring looking for loose or defective connections and defective insulation or broken wiring.

If the wiring is not at fault, and current is reaching the system, then either the gauge or tank unit are defective. Without specialist equipment for testing the best method is to renew one item and then see if the system operates correctly.

The gauge must be removed with the instrument panel (see next chapter) and the attachments of the tank unit are shown in **FIG 12:19**. Before carrying out work on the system disconnect the battery. Remove the parcel shelf bottom lining and then take out the access panel to expose the tank unit. Disconnect the lead and then take out the three securing screws so that the tank unit and its leather seal can be removed from the tank. **When withdrawing the tank unit take care not to bend or damage the float arm.**

Refit the tank unit in the reverse order of removal, making sure that the gasket is in good condition.

12:8 The direction indicators

A flasher unit is fitted to operate the lights and its connections are shown in **FIG 12:20**. The flasher unit is a delicate piece of equipment that will be damaged by careless handling, dropping or incorrect connection. Once damaged the unit cannot be repaired and a new one must be fitted in its place.

Flashers fail to operate satisfactorily:

Check all the bulbs as if one bulb has blown the flash rate will be completely altered on that side.

If the lights fail to operate at all then check the supply to the flasher unit, using a voltmeter or test lamp. If the input is live, disconnect all three leads from the flasher unit and connect them together. Operate the direction indicator switch in both directions and check the lamps.

The lamps should operate correctly but without flashing. If the lamps do operate correctly then the flasher unit is at fault and must be renewed. If a lamp (or lamps) does not light then check through the wiring that leads to that lamp, as well as the earth points. Use the test lamp or voltmeter connected between suitable terminals and a good earth on the car to determine which parts of the circuit have current reaching them. When a terminal is found to be dead trace the wiring between this and the previous terminal and find the fault or break. Test on both sides of the switch to ensure that the fault does not lie with the switch.

12:9 Fuses

Two fuses are fitted into a fuse box to protect the circuits from overloads or shortcircuits.

If a fuse blows briefly check the circuits protected by that fuse and then fit a new fuse. Operate each circuit in turn and if the new fuse blows then carefully check through the circuit that was live at the time. If the fuse does not blow then it is likely that the old one had weakened with age. Before renewing the second blown fuse make sure that the fault has been found and rectified. Intermittent but persistent blowing of fuses is likely to be caused by chafed insulation which earths under vibration. If this is the complaint, check each circuit in turn and at the same time move the wiring about so that the fault has a chance to re-occur.

Under no circumstances fit a fuse of a higher rating than called for. If there is an overload there will be a danger that the fuse does not blow and wiring will be damaged instead.

12:10 The headlamps

Sealed-beam units are fitted as standard. In these the headlamp is a bulb where the filaments are sealed through the reflector. The lens and reflector are integral and the interior of the unit is filled with inert gas. This type of lamp has a longer life than a bulb and is also far less prone to darkening. If a filament does burn out or the lens is cracked then the complete unit must be renewed.

The adjustment points, accessible after the embellisher has been removed, are shown in **FIG 12:21**. The screw **A** alters the horizontal adjustment the screw **B** the vertical. The two screws are so arranged that they do not interact. When removing or refitting the headlamp take care not to alter the adjustment screws.

Beam setting:

This can be carried out with the car standing squarely to and a few metres away from a plain wall. This method should only be used in emergency and to ensure that the lights meet all legal requirements the car should be taken to an agent for the lamps to be correctly set using beam-setter equipment.

12:11 Lighting circuit faults
Lamps give insufficient light:

Check, or have checked, the settings of the lamps. If the lamps or reflectors have darkened with age then they should be removed and new units fitted.

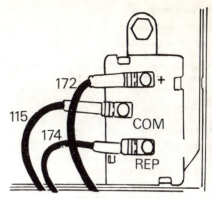

FIG 12:20   The flasher unit

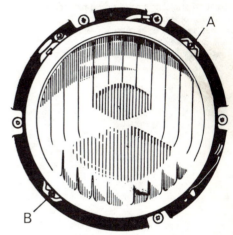

FIG 12:21   Headlamp beam adjustment screws

On long journeys mud and dirt thrown up from the road will slowly spread over the lenses to cut down the light. At stops give the headlamps a wipe over with a piece of cloth. Do not forget to clean the rear lights as well.

Bulbs burn out frequently:

If there is also a frequent need for topping-up the battery then it is most likely that the charging current is too high. Have the generator and control box checked.

Lamps light when switched on but gradually fade:

Check the battery as it is incapable of supplying current for any length of time. With this fault the car will also be difficult to start.

Lamp brilliance varies with speed of car:

Check the condition of the battery. Check all the connections in the charging circuit, paying special attention to the battery connectors.

12:12 Fault diagnosis

(a) Battery discharged

1 Terminals loose or dirty
2 Insufficient charging current
3 Shortcircuit in part of circuit not protected by fuse
4 Accessories left on
5 Insufficient mileage to allow generator to charge battery

(b) Battery will not hold charge

1 Low electrolyte level
2 Battery plates sulphated or ineffective
3 Electrolyte leakage from case

(c) Generator output low or nil

1 Drive belt broken or slipping
2 Control box defective
3 Insulation standing proud on commutator
4 Commutator worn, dirty or burnt
5 Brushes sticking or excessively worn
6 Weak or broken springs
7 Armature or field coils defective

(d) Starter motor lacks power or will not operate

1 Battery discharged, terminals loose or dirty
2 Starter pinion jammed in mesh
3 Defective starter switch
4 Defective starter solenoid
5 Brushes excessively worn or sticking
6 Connectors to brushes broken or shorting
7 Weak or broken brush springs
8 Commutator worn or dirty
9 Defective armature or field coils
10 Starter motor mechanically defective
11 Engine abnormally stiff

(e) Starter runs but does not turn engine

1 Defective overrun clutch
2 Incorrect adjustments
3 Broken teeth on pinion or flywheel

(f) Starter motor rough or noisy

1 Check 2 and 3 in (e)
2 Loose polepieces
3 Loose mountings
4 Excessively worn bearings

CHAPTER 13

THE BODYWORK

13:1 The bodywork

Large scale repairs to the bodywork are best left to experts. Even small dents can be tricky as too much or injudicious hammering will stretch the metal and make things worse instead of better.

The body itself is of monocoque construction and any distortion of this must have specialist attention. If a wing or door is damaged consideration should be given to fitting a new panel rather than trying to repair the old one, taking into account the extent of the damage and cost of repairs. The attachments of the wings on R.1130 models are shown in **FIGS 13:1** and **13:2** while those on R.1190 models are shown in **FIGS 13:3** and **13:4**.

The best method of repairing dents and damage available to the owner, other than fitting new panels, is to fill the dents and then spray. Deep dents can be lightly tapped out to reduce their depth without trying to make them flush. Fillers are readily available and paint can be bought in self-spraying cans of matching colour. It should be remembered that paint fades with age and therefore fresh paint will stand out on an old finish. This problem can be partially overcome if a complete panel is sprayed, rather than a patch in the middle, as any mismatch will then not be so obvious. The original lustre and colour on the remainder of the car can be partially restored by using a mild cutting compound to remove the top layer of faded paint, but it must be remembered that paint is removed by this treatment and therefore it must not be carried out too often.

Wash the area to be sprayed with white spirits to remove any wax polish, noting that even more drastic treatment will be required to remove silicone-based polishes. Lightly scuff the area to give a good key for the new finish and rub off any corrosion down to bare bright metal. Apply a coat of primer and then build up flush to the original surface, using filler or paste-stopper as required. When the surface is dry rub it down using 400 grade 'Wet and Dry' paper and clean water. If required use further coats of filler or stopper to achieve a perfect result. Spend plenty of time and patience at this stage as the finish at this point controls the final gloss finish. When the surface is smooth wash it down with plenty of clean water and leave it to dry. Check the surface for blemishes, correcting them as required, and wash off any slurry that may have been missed in the first wash.

Mask off surrounding areas using newspaper and masking tape. A better finish will be obtained if handles and trim are removed rather than masked over when they are in the spray area.

Spray a complete panel evenly all over, but if only a patch is being sprayed then the paint should be 'feathered' at the edges. Apply two or more thin coats, rubbing down

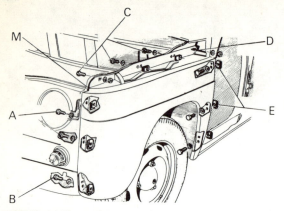

FIG 13:1   The attachments of a front wing on a R1130 model

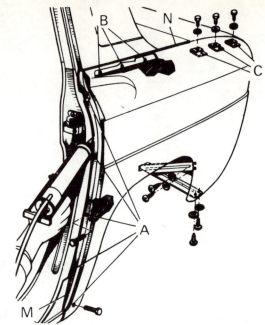

FIG 13:2   The attachments of a rear wing on a R1130 model

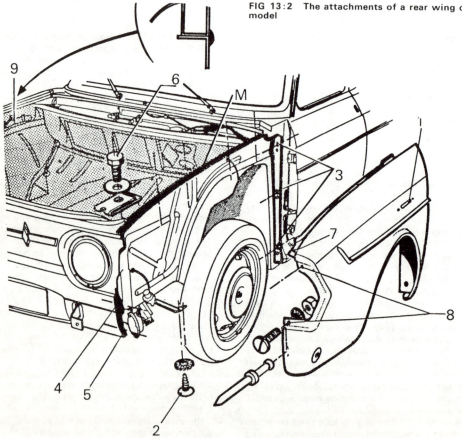

FIG 13:3   The attachments of a front wing on a R1190 model

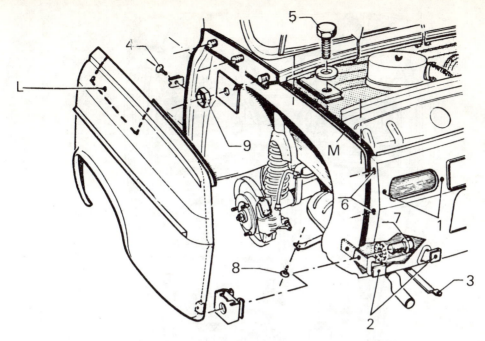

FIG 13:4   The attachments of a rear wing on a R1190 model

lightly between each, rather than one thick coat which may run.

Remove the masking and leave the paint to dry for as long as possible and then use a mild cutting-compound to lightly polish the surface and remove any spray dust. Leave the paint to harden completely for a period of weeks before applying wax polish.

13:2 Seat belts

Strong points for attaching the seat belts are built into the frame, as shown in **FIGS 13:5** and **13:6**. Full instructions for fitting the seat belts are supplied with all Renault approved seat belt kits.

If non-standard seat belts are to be fitted or the owner does not feel absolutely competent to carry out a first-class and safe installation then the car should be taken to an agent for the seat belts to be fitted.

13:3 Fasteners

TACL or Pozidrive screws may be found on the later models covered by this manual. Pozidrive screws are very similar to Phillips-head screws though they differ from the Phillips screws in that they have additional recesses **C**, shown in **FIG 13:7**. A Phillips screwdriver will work Pozidrive screws but it is far better to use the correct Pozidrive screwdriver which is designed for the task.

A TACL screw is shown in **FIG 13:8**. This type of screw has the advantage of forming a waterproof seal, using its Nylon washer **N**, without causing damage to paintwork. A special TACL screwdriver should be used

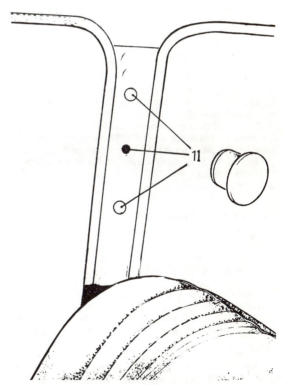

FIG 13:5   The door pillar strong points for seat belts

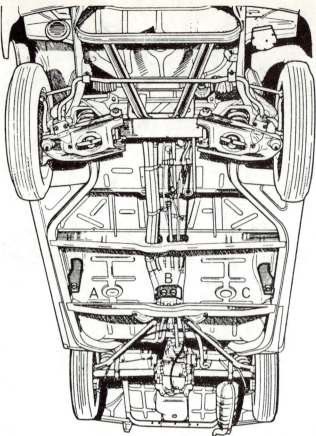

FIG 13:6   The under body strong points for seat belt attachment

and the drive is then so positive that enough force can be applied so as to shear the shank, though this much torque should obviously not be applied.

Plasti-rivet clips are also used to secure trim in place. The rivet is fitted as shown in **FIG 13:9** and the trim then pressed into place on the rivet, as shown in **FIG 13:10**. To secure the rivet, push it through the 5 mm hole and then lock it by pushing in the pin. The rivet can be removed after the pin has been pushed out.

13:4 Doors and door fastenings

Door removal:

The correct method of removing a door is shown in **FIG 13:11**. Compress the spring on the door restraint with the special tool Car.40 and use the short end of the special tool Car.07A to push out the hinge pins as shown.

Refit the door in the reverse order of removal. Check that the drain holes in the bottom of the door are clear and if a new door is being fitted make sure that the inside of the outer panel is covered with soundproofing compound.

Door trim panel:

The attachments of the later window regular handle are shown in **FIG 13:12**. On early models a clip is used instead of the Pal nut otherwise the design is the same.

Carefully prise off the cover 24, taking great care not to scratch or distort it. The nut or clip will then be exposed and can be removed to free the handle.

With the handle removed, use a broad-bladed screwdriver or steel rule to carefully lever out the clips that secure the trim panel to the door frame. Get the tool as near to the clip as possible before levering, otherwise there is a danger of pulling out the clips from the panel instead of from the door. When all the clips are free lift off the panel. Unstick and remove the plastic sealing panel from behind the trim panel.

The parts are refitted in the reverse order of removal. The plastic panel must be glued back into position otherwise there is a danger of water leaking in.

Front door window:

The parts are shown in **FIG 13:13**. Remove the trim panel and plastic panel in order to gain access to the parts. Lower the glass and remove the outer weatherstrip 1, which is crimped to the door. Remove the two rollers 2 from the window bottom channel, tilt the glass and remove it through the window aperture.

The regulator mechanism is secured to the inner door panel by the three nuts 3, and it can be removed through the aperture in the inner door panel after the nuts have been taken off.

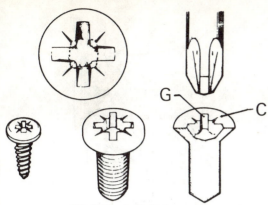

FIG 13:7 A Pozidrive screw

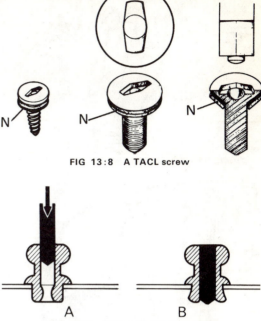

FIG 13:8 A TACL screw

If necessary remove the inner weatherseal 4, which is retained by four clips. The glass run channel is secured by four staples inside the door and four tags on the window aperture frame.

The parts are refitted in the reverse order of removal. If the glass bottom channel has been removed it should be smeared with soap (as a lubricant), and then pressed back onto the glass so that the dimension **A** is correct at 41 mm ($1\frac{5}{8}$ inch). Lubricate the rollers, hinge points and toothed sector of the regulator lightly with grease before refitting the parts.

FIG 13:9 Fitting Plasti-rivet clips

Rear door window:

The components and a sectioned view of the assembly are shown in **FIG 13:14** and the latch arrangement in **FIG 13:15**.

Half open the window and remove the latch securing screw. Take out the three screws and remove the frame trim 11. Take out the five screws and remove the latch slide 10 and then remove the glass run channel 7 which is secured by tags. Remove the lower moulding 10 and take out the sliding window 9. The wiper strip, secured by the two 'Plasti-rivets' 8, must be removed before taking out the fixed window 3.

FIG 13:10 Fitting the trim to a Plasti-rivet clip

The parts are refitted in the reverse order of removal. The fixed window must be refitted using a cord in the slit of the rubber to lift the rubber over the flange of the aperture, as for refitting windscreen or backlight glass. Strips of RR.1 No. 6.078.257 sealing compound (available in strips 15 x 3 mm, $\frac{1}{2}$ x $\frac{1}{8}$ inch) should be fitted between the latch slide 10 and door body at **A**. A fillet of sealing compound 2300 should be applied at **B**.

13:5 Door locks

Various modifications have been carried out over the years. New locks can be fitted to old doors and vice-versa, though modifications must be carried out. Some of the modifications only involve drilling holes but as others require spot- or arc-welding, it is best to leave the work to an agent.

Early front door lock:

The parts are shown in **FIG 13:16**. Remove the trim panels and plastic sealing panel. Take out the two screws that secure the remote control handle 1 and push it

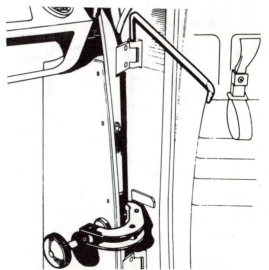

FIG 13:11 The correct method of removing a door

135

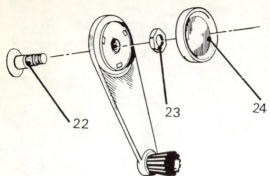

FIG 13:12   The later winder handle attachments

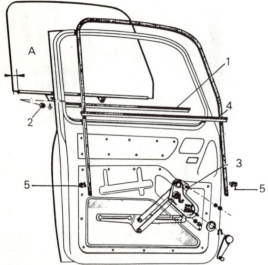

FIG 13:13   The glass and regulator attachments on a front door

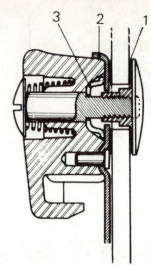

FIG 13:15   The latch on a rear door window

downwards to free the backplate 2. Note that screws have a pitch of .75mm up to car No. 28751 and after this they were changed to .8mm pitch. Lift the spring 3 from the rod 4.

Free the anti-rattle attachment 5 from the door and remove the link 4 from the lock in a downwards direction.

Take out the two screws that secure the outer handle, carefully collecting the spacer that is fitted between the handle and upright.

Take out the three bolts that secure the lock itself and free the lock-plunger button by swinging the lock around. The pull handle is secured by clips and a bridge-piece at the bottom, and the clips must be renewed after they have been removed.

The parts are refitted in the reverse order of removal, noting that the task will be easier if the window regulator

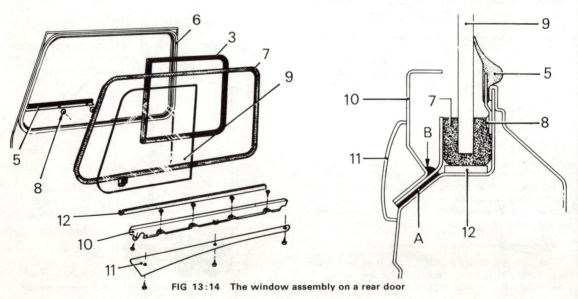

FIG 13:14   The window assembly on a rear door

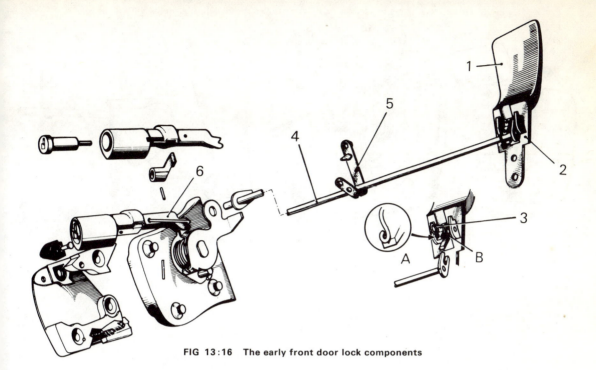

FIG 13:16   The early front door lock components

mechanism is out. When refitting the remote control handle place the connecting spring on the centre notch of the plate at **A**, fit the handle and its backplate and then engage the link tab into the handle, as shown at **B** and finally push down the connecting spring 3.

Later front door lock:

The parts are shown in **FIG 13:17**. The removal and refitting of the parts is very similar to the earlier models. Note the different attachment of the remote control link to the lock and also note the anti-rattle clips 6 and 7.

Early rear door lock:

The parts are shown in **FIG 13:18**. The removal and refitting of the lock mechanism is the same as for the

front lock, with the addition of the removal of the door latch 6 which is pressed over the clip 7. The lock will have to be turned through a complete turn to free the lock plunger button from the door pillar. The fitting on the remote control link 4 is pressed over the ball joint 8.

Note that the lock is fitted with a child-proof catch, only accessible when the door is open, which isolates the interior remote control handle.

Later rear door lock:

The parts are shown in **FIG 13:19** and the main difference is in the design of the remote control link and its anti-rattle clips. The sleeve 14 on the end of the rod can be cut from any electrical cable insulation or plastic tubing that fits snugly over the end of the rod.

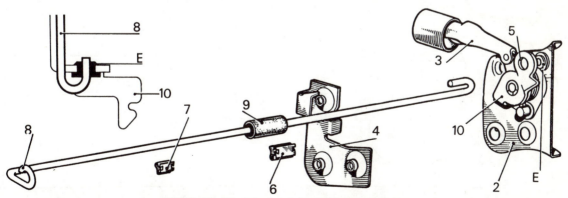

FIG 13:17   The later front door lock components

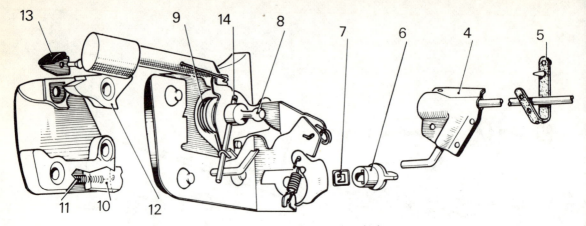

FIG 13:18   The earlier rear door lock

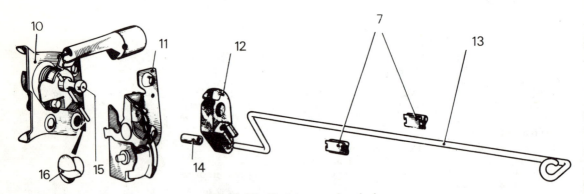

FIG 13:19   The later rear door lock

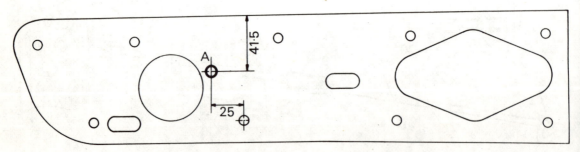

FIG 13:20   Modifying a later door to take an earlier lock assembly

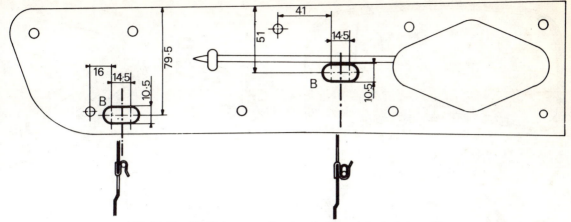

FIG 13:21   Modifying an earlier door to take a later lock assembly

Modifications:

The holes that need to be cut in the door panels when changing from one lock to the other are shown in **FIGS 13:20, 13:21** and **13:22**. All the dimensions are given in millimetres.

Striker plate:

A typical plate is shown in **FIG 13:18**. The unit is secured to the frame by three screws and a small amount of adjustment is allowed for. Slacken the screws sufficiently to allow the striker to move under pressure and then adjust it until the door shuts satisfactorily. **Tighten the screws very hard using a spanner and suitable fitting to tighten them.**

13:6 The windscreen and backlight glass

The windscreen is Luxrit B which becomes granular when broken. It is designed to break into larger granules in the centre so that there is still some forward view when the glass shatters. When removing a broken windscreen the task will be much easier if sheets of paper are stuck on both sides of the glass, as they will hold the granules and prevent them from dropping out. Make sure that all particles are removed from the car and if necessary partially dismantle the ventilation system to remove any particles that have fallen into the vents.

The embellisher strip is made of sections, clipped into a slot in the rubber weatherseal, and the ends are covered by sliding clips. To remove the embellishers, slide the clips to one side so as to expose the gap and then carefully lever out the embellisher, without twisting or distorting it.

If the glass has to be removed in an unbroken state, use a wooden wedge to free the inside lip of the surround. Apply pressure on the inside of the glass with the palm of the hand or the sole of the foot, wrapped with rags to prevent injury if the glass breaks. Start at the corners and have an assistant outside the car to take the glass as it comes free. Note that if sealant has been used around the rubber surround it is unlikely that the surround will be removed in an undamaged state. For this reason a new

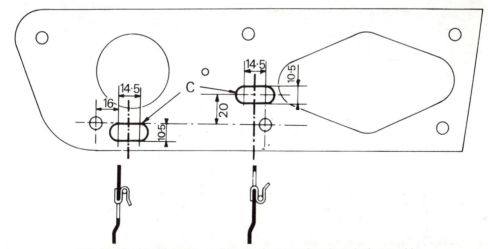

FIG 13:22   Modifying an earlier rear door to take a later lock assembly

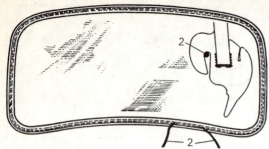

FIG 13:23   Refitting the windscreen or backlight

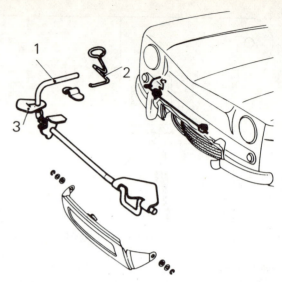

FIG 13:26   The spare wheel compartment door

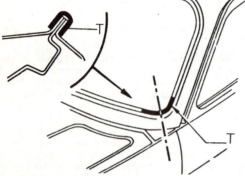

FIG 13:24   Adhesive tape fitted in the lower corners on models fitted with non-sealed windscreen rubber surrounds

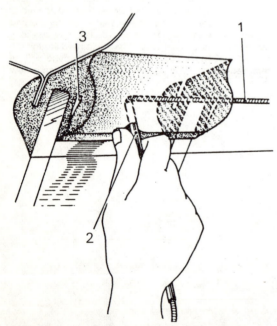

FIG 13:25   Positioning the cord ready for refitting the screen embellisher

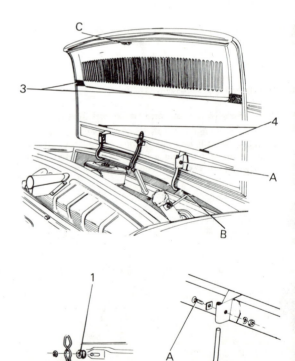

FIG 13:27   The engine compartment lid

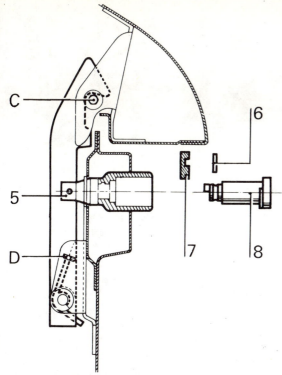

FIG 13:28 The latch for the engine compartment lid

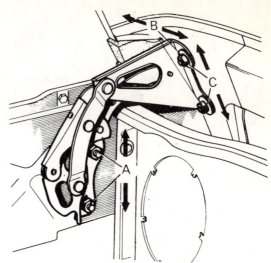

FIG 13:29 The luggage compartment lid hinge on R1130 models

rubber surround should then be used when refitting the glass, otherwise there is a possibility of water leaking in during rain.

Once the glass has been removed, check the flange in the aperture for damage or distortion. Dress out dents with a block and hammer and file down protrusions. **If this is not done then stress points can be set up in the glass causing it to fail in use.** Clean around the aperture to remove any old sealing compound.

Lay the windscreen onto a padded bench and fit the rubber surround to it. Insert a length of cord into the groove 2, shown in the inset in **FIG 13:23**, so that it encircles the surround, and so that the ends cross, with enough cord left hanging out to obtain a firm grip on.

On the R.1190 models the surround is not sealed with compound and there are two slots in the surround at the bottom corners to allow water to drain out. On these models fit two strips of adhesive tape **T**, 200mm (8 inches) long, into the bottom corners as shown in **FIG 13:24**.

Pass the ends of the cord through the windscreen aperture and have an assistant firmly and accurately press the glass and surround assembly into the aperture. From inside the car grip the ends of the cord and by pulling gently on either end lift the rubber over the body aperture flange. Carry on until all the surround is correctly in place and then seat the screen with a few careful blows of a rubber mallet.

On the R.1130 models use a sealant gun to inject sealant between the surround and rubber, wiping away surplus sealant with a piece of cloth **moistened, not**

soaked, in fuel or methylated spirits. On the other models fit the rubber spacers (No. 6.078.895) between the surround and bodywork so that gaps are made for the water to drain out through the slots in the surround.

If after fitting there are leaks around the surround, then sealant should be injected between glass and rubber as well as rubber and body to cure the leaks, but on the later normally non-sealed versions take care not to block the water drain holes with sealant.

Once the glass is in place lay a length of cord around the surround in the slot into which the embellisher fits. The best method is shown in **FIG 13:25**. The cord 1 is passed through a suitable length of tube 2 and the tube used to open the slot and lay the cord and apply firm pressure to the embellisher while drawing out the cord towards the centre of the window (parallel to the glass). The cord coming out will open the slot and allow the embellisher to enter. Water, soap solution or glycerine may be used as a lubricant on the rubber if the fitting is difficult.

FIG 13:30 Adjusting the position of the luggage compartment lid on R1130 models

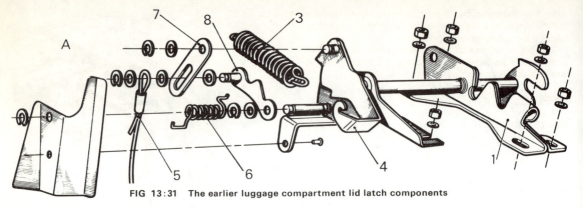

FIG 13:31   The earlier luggage compartment lid latch components

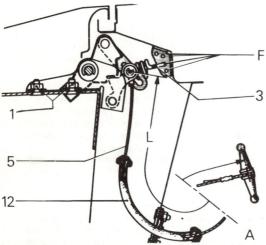

FIG 13:32   Sectioned view of the earlier luggage compartment lid latch

13:7 The spare wheel compartment door

The components of the door are shown in **FIG 13:26**. The door hinges about the spare wheel carrier and is secured by means of cup washers and clips. The rod 1 engages with the hook 2 to lock the door closed. The rubber cup 3 fits around the rod and seals it to prevent dirt or water entering.

13:8 The engine compartment lid

The attachments are shown in **FIG 13:27**. On later models (post 1967) the design of the lefthand bracket **A** has been altered in that it is now 270mm from the edge of the panel, instead of 305mm as all other brackets are. If a new lid is fitted to an old model then the lefthand hinge rod must be changed for a rod No. 77.00.502.432.

Sealing pads 3, bonded to the lid, seal the radiator compartment and anti-rattle pads 4 are fitted between the front cross-rail and panel.

To remove the lid first free the stop spring 1 from the body by pinching its ends together and then take out the

FIG 13:33   The luggage compartment lid hinge on R1190 models

roller 1 by removing the clip. Slacken the nuts and bolts on the hinges **A** and then slide the lid off the hinge rods, taking care not to damage paintwork.

The lid is refitted in the reverse order of removal. Longitudinal adjustments are made at the hinge points **A** and lateral adjustments at the hinge points **B**.

Latch:

A sectioned view of the latch mechanism is shown in **FIG 13:28**. The plunger can be removed after pushing out the lockpin 5. Push out the lockpin 6 to free the bolt 7 and tumbler 8.

The parts are reassembled in the reverse order of dismantling, but make sure that the end of the spring is in the slot **D**. The latch is adjusted by moving the pivot pin at **C**

13:9 The luggage compartment lid

The design of the lid varies not only with model but also with year of car.

R.1130:

The hinge point is shown in **FIG 13:29**. It will be necessary to remove the headlamps and the battery to gain access to the hinges. All the holes are elongated so that the lid can be accurately aligned with the bodywork. To adjust the lid lay six blocks of wood 8mm ($\frac{5}{16}$ inch) thick around between lid and car, as shown in **FIG 13:30**. Tighten the hinge securing screws until the lid is held in position but can be moved with pressure. Close the lid, making sure that the catch aligns centrally and adjust the position of the lid until it is in line with the body and in contact with the spacers. Tighten the securing screws fully and refit trim and headlamps.

The earlier latch parts are shown in **FIG 13:31** and a sectioned view in **FIG 13:32**. To remove the cable, disconnect the return spring 3 and then disconnect the cable

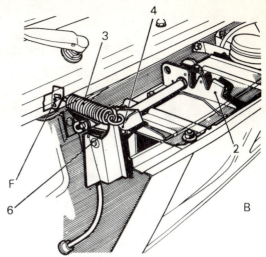

FIG 13:34   The later luggage compartment lid latch

5 by removing its clip. Take out the three nuts that secure the guide to the scuttle 12 and remove the assembly from inside the car. The cable is refitted in the reverse order of removal, but if a new cable is fitted it should be looped and crimped so that the dimension **L** is correct at 390mm ($21\frac{7}{16}$ inch) long.

The complete assembly can be removed, after disconnecting the operating cable, by taking out the nuts that secure the plate 1, removing the return spring 6 and link 7 and the lever 8 which is secured to the shaft by circlips.

Refit the parts in the reverse order of removal. If adjustment is necessary replace the latch pin on the lid with a dummy pin Car.56 (which allows access to the

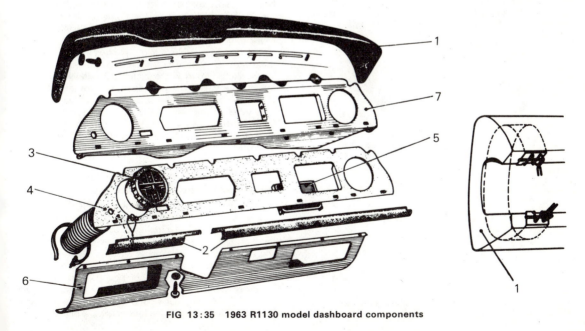

FIG 13:35   1963 R1130 model dashboard components

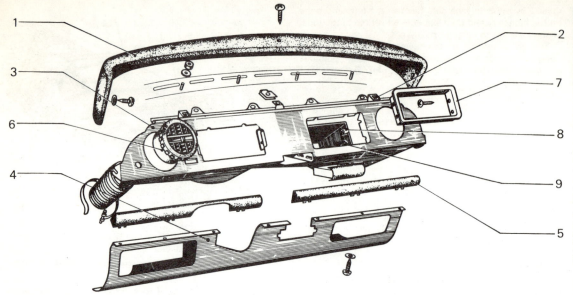

FIG 13:36   The later R1130 models dashboard components

nuts 1) and close the lid. Adjust the position of the plate 1 until the dummy pin fits accurately into the latch and then tighten the nuts that secure the plate. Open the lid and refit the correct latching pin and adjust it in its slots until the lid line is flush with the body line before fully tightening its nuts.

Make sure that the operating cable 5 slides freely and that the attachment point 4 for the spring 3 is not distorted or damaged. Fit the return spring 3 to the scuttle, using the alternative attachment points, until the spring tension is sufficient to allow the lid to partially open as soon as the control is pulled with sufficient tension to prevent the lid from closing under its own weight.

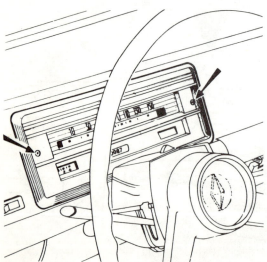

FIG 13:37   Removing the instrument panel on later R1130 models

R.1190 models:

The attachments of the lid are shown in **FIG 13:33.** At car No. 240.482 (28th December 1966) the shape of the panels was slightly altered, to ensure better sealing into the luggage compartment. It is possible to interchange parts but it is advisable to consult an agent and under all circumstances make sure that the front edge of the lid aligns with the upper edges of the front panel.

To remove the lid, first take off the circlip 4 that secures the locking roller 5, on both sides of the lid. Support the lid and remove the nuts 6 from the hinges and then lift off the lid. Refit the lid in the reverse order of removal, noting that lateral and longitudinal adjustment is available at the four slotted holes 7.

The latch assembly is slightly modified and the parts fitted are shown in **FIG 13:34.** Adjustment is available at the slotted holes in the plate 2. Generally adjustment follows the directions given for the earlier latch fitted to R.1130, and it should be noted that this type of latch is also fitted to later models of the R.1130 models. The control cable slides in an outer cover and the end of the cover is secured to a bracket inside the car. The later type of latch can be fitted in place of the earlier type.

13:10 The dashboard and instrument panel
1963 R.1130 models:

The dashboard parts are shown in **FIG 13:35.** The facia visor 1 is secured by three clips at the front, five at the back and four self-tapping screws to the windscreen framing. The padding strip 2 is clipped to the dashboard and the adjustable vent nozzle 3 is also secured by clips, but the joint between it and the scuttle should be sealed with a little 275 sealing compound. The dashboard embellisher panel 4 is secured to the dashboard with fillets of 275 sealing compound. The radio aperture cover is secured to the dash by four screws while the glove

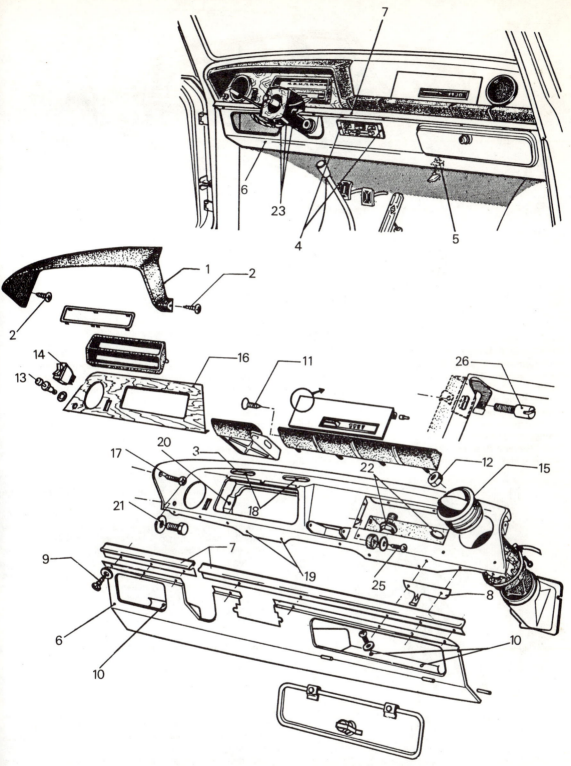

FIG 13:38   The dashboard components on R1190 models

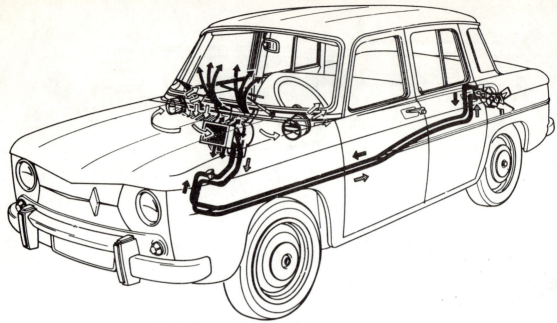

FIG 13:39   The heater and ventilation system layout

compartment tray panel 6 is secured by four self-tapping screws to the dashboard and by four screws to the scuttle.

The parts should be removed in the order given and refitted in the reverse order.

To remove the instrument panel first disconnect the battery as a safety precaution. Remove the dashboard visor, padding strip and tray panel. Take off the ventilation nozzle grilles, air inlet ducts, windscreen washer control

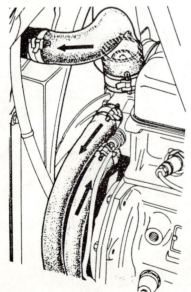

FIG 13:40   The flow through the heater pipes

and wiper switch. Remove the dash panel and disconnect the speedometer drive cable from the back of the instrument. Take out the two bolts that secure the instrument panel, now exposed, and partially pull out the instrument panel so that the leads can be disconnected and the panel completely removed. The parts are refitted in the reverse order of removal but note that the dash panel must be stuck back into place.

Later R.1130 models:

The dash parts are shown in **FIG 13:36**. The parts are similar to the earlier models but the attachments differ. The facia visor 1 is secured by two screws to the windscreen pillars and two more screws which go into the lugs 2. The dashboard 3 is finished in crackle paint and secured to the lower windscreen rail by four screws and by two screws to the front door pillars. The glove compartment tray panel is secured to the scuttle by three screws and to the dashboard by seven screws. The padding 5 is no longer clipped but secured by seven screws while the glove compartment is secured by four screws, acting in the 'rapid' anchor nuts 8 and the clip 9.

Removal of the instrument panel is much easier and the bolts that secure it are accessible after removing the embellisher which is secured by the two screws shown in **FIG 13:37**, without having to remove other parts.

R.1190 models:

The parts of the dashboard are shown in **FIG 13:38**. Removal of parts is easiest if they are taken off in numerical order, following the numbers in the figure. The figure shows the steering wheel removed and the task will be easier if this is done but it is not essential. Once the parts have been removed, the two bolts that secure

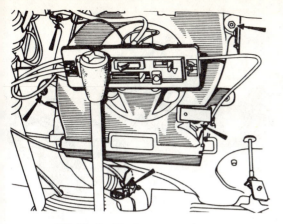

FIG 13:41   The heater attachments

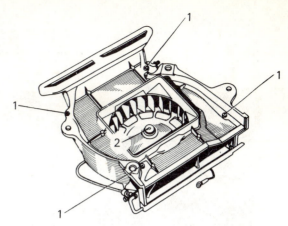

FIG 13:42   The heater motor attachments in the heater

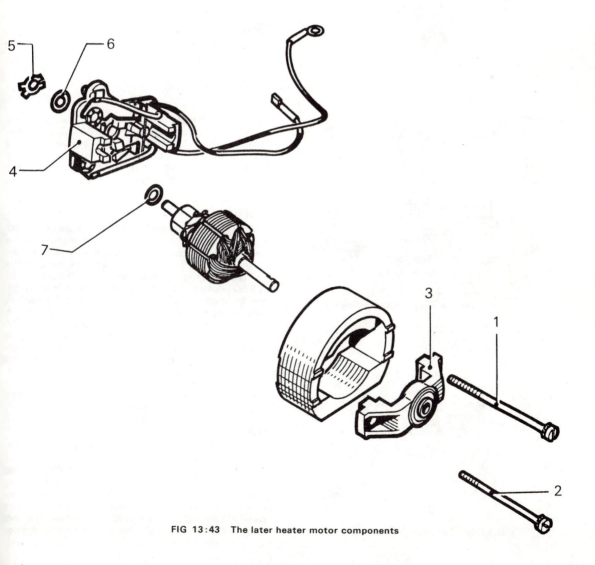

FIG 13:43   The later heater motor components

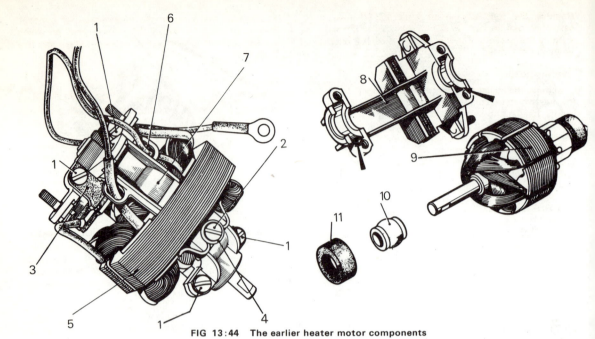

FIG 13:44   The earlier heater motor components

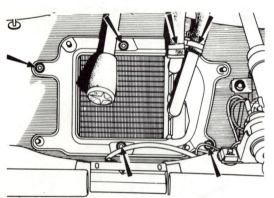

FIG 13:45   The heater radiator attachments

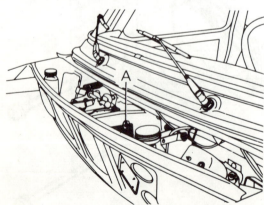

FIG 13:46   The heater bleed screw

the instrument panel can be taken out. Disconnect the speedometer drive cable and leads. Tilt the instrument panel so that the bottom edge comes out and then turn it so that the right end goes forward into the car as far as possible. The complete unit can then be drawn out through the aperture.

13:11 The heater

The layout of the ventilation system is shown in **FIG 13:39**. The heater can either supply hot or cold air and a fan is fitted to increase the airflow if desired. The controllable vents only pass cold air from the outside. The air from the heater is warmed by passing through a small radiator connected into the cooling system of the engine, and the coolant flow is controlled by a valve. The coolant flow to and from the engine, with the control open, is shown in **FIG 13:40**. The thermostat valve in the engine ensures that the coolant does not pass through the engine radiator when it is cold, but it is still allowed to pass through the heater to ensure rapid warming up in the car and demisting of the windscreen.

The heater was slightly altered in 1964, though the general instructions given in this section for later models will also cover the earlier models.

Heater removal:

The attachments of the heater are shown in **FIG 13:40**. Disconnect the battery and remove the two screws that secure the heater control unit in place. Remove the bracket that supports the luggage locker lid operating cable as well as the glove compartment and lower tray panel. Do not disconnect the leads but free the instrument panel. Disconnect the water control valve cable and also disconnect the electrical lead at the control casing

Remove the four attachment nuts and remove the assembly from the car.

Refit the assembly in the reverse order of removal, renewing any defective sealing rubbers.

Heater motor:

Remove the heater assembly as just described. Remove the nuts which secure the backplate to the casing, shown in **FIG 13:42**, and with the backplate removed take out the bolt 2, using an Allen key, and remove the fan. Unscrew the three nuts that secure the motor and remove the motor, carefully collecting the spacers and washers and guiding the leads through the hole in the casing.

Two different types of motor are fitted. The components of the later motor are shown in **FIG 13:43**. To check the brushes the supply leads must first be un-soldered and if any part of the brushgear is worn or damaged the complete rear part of light alloy motor bearing housing must be renewed. If the armature shaft bushes are worn the complete bearing carriers must be renewed as individual bushes are not available. When dismantling the motor, mark the parts so that they will be reassembled in the original alignment.

The parts of the earlier motor are shown in **FIG 13:44**. When removing the brushes, unsolder the field coil wires from the brush holders. To dismantle the motor, remove the screws 1 and 2, laying aside the brush carrier guides 3 and collecting the springs and washers 4. Pull the brush carriers apart and remove the body 5 complete with field coils, easing the wires through their guide 6. Separate the half-bearing carriers 7 and 8 and remove the armature 9.

Reassemble the motor in the reverse order of removal, making sure that the area of the armature shaft on which the self-lubricating bearings 10 operate is clean and free from burrs.

Heater radiator:

The attachments are shown in **FIG 13:44**. Before removing the heater radiator drain the cooling system, collecting the coolant in clean containers. Disconnect the hoses to the heater radiator and then remove the radiator after taking out the attachment nuts arrowed.

Refit the heater radiator in the reverse order of removal. Fill and bleed the cooling system as described in **Chapter 4**. The bleed screw for the heater is shown in **FIG 13:45**.

Heater control:

On all models the control is secured by two screws, accessible from the front. From 1964 onwards the unit is also secured to the heater by two nuts. To remove the unit, disconnect the battery and take off the dashboard tray panel. Disconnect the leads and electrical cables and remove the unit.

The connections on the earlier units are directly accessible but on later units the parts are held together by three nuts. When separating the parts of the later unit take great care not to lose the rubber spacers which secure the cables to the levers as the levers and control cables are not held in position once the nuts have been removed.

APPENDIX

TECHNICAL DATA

        Engine   Fuel system   Ignition system   Cooling system
        Clutch   Synchromesh transmission   Steering   Suspension
        Brakes   Electrical equipment   Capacities   Dimensions
        Torque wrench settings

WIRING DIAGRAMS

        FIG 14:1   R1130, 1963 model
        FIG 14:2   R1130, 1964 model
        FIG 14:3   R1190, early
        FIG 14:4   R1190, later
        FIG 14:5   R1192 model

CONVERSION TABLES

HINTS ON MAINTENANCE AND OVERHAUL

GLOSSARY OF TERMS

INDEX

TECHNICAL DATA

*Unless otherwise stated dimensions are given in millimetres
and the dimension in brackets is in inches*

ENGINE

Type	4 cylinder in-line, rear mounted. Water-cooled. OHV using camshaft in crankcase with pushrods and rockers. Extensive use of light-alloy
Capacities:	
R1130	956 cc (58.4 cu in) — 689 type
R1190	1108 cc (67.6 cu in) — 688 type
R1192	1289 cc (78.7 cu in) — 810 type
Compression ratio:	
R1130 and R1190	8.5:1
R1192	8.0:1
Firing order	1−3−4−2
Bore:	
956 cc	65 (2.559)
1108 cc	70 (2.756)
1289 cc	73 (2.874)
Stroke:	
956 cc	72 (2.835)
1108 cc	72 (2.835)
1289 cc	77 (3.031)
Crankshaft	5 bearing
Main journal diameter	46 (1.811)
Bearing shells	Steel-backed, renewable
Undersizes	.25 to .50 (.0098 to .0196)
Crankpin diameter	43.98 (1.731)
Undersizes	.25 to .50 (.0098 to .0196)
End float	.45 to .19 (.002 to .0075)
Cylinder head:	
Material	Light alloy with inserts
Standard height:	
956 cc	70.05 (2.758)
1108 cc	71.86 (2.829)
1289 cc	74.25 (2.923)
Minimum height:	
956 cc	69.75 (2.746)
1108 cc	71.56 (2.817)
1289 cc	73.95 (2.912)
Maximum permissible bow	.05 (.002)
Valve seat width:	
Inlet	1.6 ($\frac{1}{16}$)
Exhaust	2 ($\frac{3}{32}$)
Valve seat angle	45 deg.
Combustion chamber volume:	
956 cc	27.08 cc (1.652 cu in)
1108 cc	31.17 cc (1.963 cu in)
1289 cc	40.88 cc (2.495 cu in)
Camshaft end float	.06 to .11 (.002 to .005)

Pistons:

Type	Aluminium-alloy, solid skirt
Top ring	'Firing' section square chrome-plated
Second ring	Non-phosphated taper compression ring
Oil control ring	U-flex
Ring gaps	Gap adjusted in manufacture
Gudgeon pins	Floating in piston, interference fit in connecting rod

Valve guides:

Internal diameter	7.00 (.276) after reaming
External diameter:	
Standard	11 (.433)
First oversize	11.10 (.437)—one groove
Second oversize	11.25 (.433)—two groove

Valve springs:

	956 and 1108 cc	*1289 cc*
Free length (all)	39.8 ($1\frac{9}{16}$)	42 ($1\frac{21}{32}$)
Test length	32 mm at 13.5 kg ($1\frac{1}{4}$ inch at 30 lb)	25 mm at 36 kg ($\frac{63}{64}$ inch at 80 lb)
Colour	—	Light green
Wire diameter	3 (.118)	3.4 (.134)

FUEL SYSTEM

Type	Single carburetter with mechanically operated fuel pump

Idling speeds:

Emission control models — **Accurate tachometer must be used**
Speed given in rev/min

	Manual trans	*Automatic trans*
Idling speed	675	750
Fast-idle speed:		
New	1350±50	1350±50
Run-in	1490±40	1500±50
Standard model	600 to 650 rev/min	

Jet sizes:

Solex standard carburetters: *32.PDIST*   *32.DITA.3*

	956 cc	*1108 cc*	*1289 cc*
Choke tube	23	23	24
Main jet	117	122	135
Air compensator	120	140	150
Idling jet	45	45	47.5
Needle valve	1.5 mm (.059 inch)	1.5 mm (.059 inch)	1.5 mm (.059 inch)
Accelerator pump	85	80	47.5

Solex emission control carburetters:

26-32.DIDTA.5:	*1st barrel*	*2nd barrel*
Choke tube	20.5	22
Main jet	115	125
Air compensator	115	160
Idling jet	60	42.5
Float weight	7.3 grammes	7.3 grammes

26-32.DIDSA.2:		
Choke tube	22	26
Main jet	120	117.5
Air compensator	100	110
Idling jet	65	75

26-32.DIDSA.10:

Choke tube	..	..	..	22	22
Main jet	..	..	..	122.5	130
Air compensator	..	..	..	110	120
Idling jet	..	..	..	65	70

IGNITION SYSTEM

Sparking plugs:
Gap	..	..	..	.6 (.025)
Type	..	..	..	Champion L-87Y
				AC 44F
				Marchal 36
				Autolite AE.32

Ignition static setting	..	..	..	0 deg., as per timing marks
Firing order	..	..	..	1−3−4−2
Distributor rotation	..	..	..	Clockwise when viewed from above
Points gap ..	..	..	..	.4 to .5 (.017 to .020)

COOLING SYSTEM

Type	..	..	..	Sealed system, using expansion bottle. Filled with mixture of distilled water and antifreeze in all climates
Normal operating temperature ..	..	..		84°C (183°F)

Thermostat:
Valve starts to open	..	..	..	84°C
Valve fully open ..	..	..	..	94°C (201.2°F)
Valve opening	..	..	..	6.5 to 8.0 ($\frac{1}{4}$ to $\frac{5}{16}$)

CLUTCH

Type	..	..	..	Single dry plate, operated by cable

Withdrawal pad:
956 cc	..	..	..	Graphite bearing
Early 1108 cc	..	..	..	Needle bearing
Later 1108 cc and 1289 cc	..	..	Guided ball*

Yellow spot for normal cars, Red spot for 'poor road' and special versions

Adjustment	..	..	..	At clutch release lever, 2 to 3 mm ($\frac{3}{32}$ inch) free play

SYNCHROMESH TRANSMISSION

Type 318:
Number of forward gears..	..	..	..	Four
Synchromesh	..	..	..	Second, third and fourth gear

Ratio:
Top	..	..	..	1.03:1
Third ..	..	..	..	1.52:1
Second	..	..	..	2.27:1
First ..	..	..	..	3.70:1
Reverse	..	..	..	3.70:1
Speedometer drive	..	..	..	5 start worm and 12-tooth pinion
Crownwheel	..	..	..	35 teeth
Pinion	..	..	..	8 teeth

Type 325:

Number of forward gears	Three
Synchromesh	All forward gears
Ratio:	
Top	1.03:1
Second	1.81:1
First	3.54:1
Reverse	3.60:1
Speedometer drive	5 start worm and 12-tooth pinion
Crownwheel	35 teeth
Pinion	8 teeth

Type 330:

Number of forward gears	Four
Synchromesh	All forward gears
Ratio:	
Top	1.03:1
Third	1.48:1
Second	2.25:1
First	3.61:1
Reverse	3.07:1
Speedometer drive	6 start worm and 14-tooth pinion
Crownwheel	35 teeth
Pinion	8 teeth

STEERING

	R1190	R1130
Type	Rack and pinion	
Steering wheel turns	3.6 turns	
Reduction ratio	20:1	
Steering wheel diameter	$15\frac{3}{4}$ inch (400 mm)	
Turning circle diameter (between kerbs)	30 ft 4 in (9.25 m)	30 ft 3 in (9.25 m)
Turning circle diameter (between walls)	36 ft 1 in (11 m)	33 ft 7 in (10.25 m)

SUSPENSION

	R1132	R1190
Front road spring:		
Free length	260 ($10\frac{1}{4}$)	265 ($10\frac{7}{16}$)
Test length	196 mm at 268 kg	201 mm at 280 kg
	($7\frac{11}{16}$ in at 590 lb)	($7\frac{15}{16}$ in at 610 lb)
Number of coils	8	6
Wire diameter	12.5 (.492)	12.5 (.492)
Outside diameter	112 ($4\frac{7}{16}$)	112 ($4\frac{7}{16}$)
Rear road spring:		
Free length	294 ($11\frac{9}{16}$)	307 ($12\frac{1}{16}$) *
Test length	214 mm at 300 kg	227 mm at 300 kg*
	($8\frac{7}{16}$ in at 660 lb)	($8\frac{15}{16}$ in at 660 lb)
Wire diameter	12.3 (.484)	12.3 (.484)
External diameter	101 (4)	101 (4)

*After car number 159.601 free length changed to 302 ($11\frac{7}{8}$) and test length 222 ($8\frac{3}{4}$) at 300 kg (660 lb)

Kingpin angle	9 deg. 30 min. ±30 min.
Castor angle	9 ±2 deg.
Camber angle	1 deg. 40 min. ±30 min.
Front wheel alignment	2 mm toe-in—1 mm toe-out

BRAKES

Type	Disc brakes on all four wheels. Hydraulically operated from brake pedal. Rear brakes only mechanically operated by handbrake
Hydraulic fluid	SAE.70.R.1 on earlier models, SAE.70.R.3 on later models. Indicated on reservoir cap. Do not intermix fluids
Hydraulic system:	
Standard	Single system with pressure limiter valve to rear brakes
USA	Tandem master cylinder with dual-circuit hydraulics. Pressure drop indicator fitted

ELECTRICAL EQUIPMENT

Battery:	
Type	Fulmen or Tudor
Capacity	40 amp/hr
Capacity (R1192)	45 amp/hr
Voltage regulator:	
Type	Ducellier 8311A, Paris/Rhone YD216 or Bosch 3 element non-adjustable RS U/UA 240/12/42
Details	Two section, 12 volt, 22 amp
Generator:	
Type	Ducellier 7267 or Paris/Rhone G10C14
Field	Positive
Nominal power	290 watts
Maximum speed for current flow of 22 amps at 12 volts (Ducellier)	2800 rev/min
Maximum speed for current flow of 22 amps at 12 volts (Paris/Rhone)	2400 rev/min
Cutting-in speed (Ducellier)	1800 to 1900 rev/min
Cutting-in speed (Paris/Rhone)	1500 rev/min
Field coil resistance	5.6 ohms at 13.2 volts
Length of new brushes (Ducellier) ..	.866 inch (22 mm)
Length of new brushes (Paris/Rhone) ..	.591 inch (15 mm)
Minimum brush length (Ducellier) ..	.433 inch (11 mm)
Minimum brush length (Paris/Rhone) ..	.315 inch (8 mm)
Commutator diameter (Ducellier) ..	1.473 inch (37 mm)
Commutator diameter (Paris/Rhone) ..	1.453 inch (36.5 mm)
Minimum commutator diameter (Ducellier)	1.413 inch (35.5 mm)
Minimum commutator diameter (Paris/Rhone)	1.354 inch (34 mm)
Type	Bosch LJ/GG 240/12/2400 AR21
Maximum output	30 amps at 3100 rev/min
Cutting-in speed	1800 rev/min
Field coil resistance	4.8 ohms
Minimum commutator diameter	1.378 inch (35 mm)
Type (R1192)	Ducellier 7348 or Paris/Rhone G.10.C.58
Starter motor:	
Type	Paris/Rhone D8.E41 or Ducellier 6128A
Lock torque (Ducellier)	6 lb ft (.8 kg m)
Lock torque (Paris/Rhone)	8 lb ft (1.05 kg m)
Current flow with pinion locked (Ducellier)	330 amps
Current flow with pinion locked (Paris/Rhone)	400 amps
Brush length (Ducellier)	.590 inch (15 mm)

Brush length (Paris/Rhone) .. .. $\frac{35}{64}$ inch (14 mm)
Minimum brush length (Ducellier) .. .295 inch (7.5 mm)
Minimum brush length (Paris/Rhone) .. $\frac{7}{16}$ inch (8 mm)
Commutator diameter (Ducellier) .. 1.532 inch (33.5 mm)
Commutator diameter (Paris/Rhone) .. $1\frac{7}{16}$ inch (36.5 mm)
Minimum commutator diameter (Ducellier) 1.511 inch (33 mm)
Minimum commutator diameter (Paris/Rhone) $1\frac{11}{32}$ inch (34 mm)
Commutator insulation undercut .. .. .002 inch (.5 mm)
Clearance between front stop and pinion
   when operating (Ducellier) .. .. .002 to .059 inch (.05 to 1.5 mm)
Clearance between front stop and pinion
   when operating (Paris/Rhone) .. .. .020 to .099 inch (.5 to 2.5 mm)
Type (R1192) .. .. Ducellier 6187
Lock torque .. .. 7 lb ft (.95 kg m)
Current flow with pinion locked .. .. 330 amps

Auxiliaries:
Stop switch operating pressure .. .. 85 lb/sq in (6 kg/sq cm)
Wiper motor type.. .. .. .. S.E.V.
Flasher unit type .. .. Klaxon 2L 40–45W
Fuses .. .. Two 25 amp
Fuel gauge .. .. Jaeger rheostat and graduated scale
Temperature gauge type .. .. .. Jaeger
Temperature switch closing temperature .. 231±9°F (111±5°C)
Headlights .. .. Assymetric beam CIBIE recessed
                              European code, reference E2

CAPACITIES

Fuel tank (R1130, 1963) .. .. $6\frac{1}{2}$ gallons (30 litres)
Fuel tank (R1130, 1964) .. .. $8\frac{1}{4}$ gallons (37 litres)
Fuel tank .. .. $8\frac{1}{2}$ gallons (38 litres)
Engine maximum (R1130) .. .. $4\frac{1}{2}$ pints (2.5 litres)
Engine minimum (R1130) .. .. $2\frac{3}{4}$ pints (1.6 litres)
Engine maximum (R1190) .. .. 4 pints (2.5 litres)
Engine minimum (R1190) .. .. $2\frac{1}{2}$ pints (1.5 litres)
Engine maximum (R1192) .. .. $5\frac{1}{4}$ pints (3 litres)
Engine minimum (R1192) .. .. $3\frac{1}{2}$ pints (2 litres)
Gearbox type 318 .. .. $2\frac{3}{4}$ pints (1.6 litres)
Gearbox type 325 .. .. $2\frac{3}{4}$ pints (1.6 litres)
Gearbox type 330 .. .. $3\frac{1}{4}$ pints (1.9 litres)
Cooling system R1130 .. .. 14 pints (7.6 litres)
Cooling system R1190 .. .. $12\frac{1}{2}$ pints (7.1 litres)
Braking system .. .. $\frac{1}{2}$ pint (.27 litres)

DIMENSIONS

Overall length R1130 .. .. 157$\frac{3}{32}$ inch (3.99 m)
Overall length R1190 .. .. 165$\frac{1}{4}$ inch (4.197 m)
Overall width R1130 .. .. 58$\frac{21}{32}$ inch (1.49 m)
Overall width R1190 .. .. 60$\frac{1}{16}$ inch (1.526 m)
Overall height R1130 .. .. 53$\frac{19}{32}$ inch (1.361 m)
Overall height R1190 .. .. 55$\frac{5}{16}$ inch (1.405 m)
Wheelbase R1130 .. .. 89$\frac{3}{8}$ inch (2.27 m)
Wheelbase R1190 .. .. 89$\frac{3}{8}$ inch (2.27 m)
Ground clearance R1130 .. .. 5$\frac{11}{16}$ inch (.145 m)
Ground clearance R1190 .. .. 4$\frac{3}{4}$ inch (.120 m)
Front track R1130 .. .. 49$\frac{7}{32}$ inch (1.25 m)
Front track R1190 .. .. 49$\frac{7}{32}$ inch (1.25 m)
Rear track R1130 .. .. 48$\frac{1}{32}$ inch (1.22 m)
Rear track R1190 .. .. 48$\frac{1}{4}$ inch (1.226 m)

TORQUE WRENCH SETTINGS

Engine:

Camshaft flange	15 lb ft (2 kg m)
Main bearing caps	45 lb ft (6 kg m)
Flywheel securing bolts	35 lb ft (5 kg m)
Big-end bearing caps	25 lb ft (3.5 kg m)
Camshaft sprocket bolt	15 lb ft (2 kg m)
Cylinder head bolts	45 lb ft (6 kg m)
Oil filter coverplate	15 lb ft (2 kg m)
Rear crossmember bolt	45 lb ft (6 kg m)

Transmission:

318 type:

Crownwheel securing bolts	45 lb ft (6 kg m)
Speedometer drive worm	85 lb ft (12 kg m)
Half-shell securing nuts	35 lb ft (5 kg m)

325 type:

Crownwheel securing bolts	45 lb ft (6 kg m)
Speedometer drive worm	85 lb ft (12 kg m)
Half-shell securing nuts	35 lb ft (5 kg m)

330 type:

Crownwheel securing bolts	45 lb ft (6 kg m)
Speedometer drive worm	85 lb ft (12 kg m)
Half-shell securing nuts	35 lb ft (5 kg m)

Steering:

Flexible coupling flange nuts	10 lb ft (1.5 kg m)
Steering bush pin	25 lb ft (3 kg m)
Steering ball joint nut	30 lb ft (4 kg m)
Steering wheel securing nut	45 lb ft (6 kg m)

Front suspension:

Lower suspension arm hinge pin nut	70 lb ft (10 kg m)
Upper suspension arm hinge pin nut	55 lb ft (7.5 kg m)
Suspension arm lower bearing securing point	25 lb ft (3.2 kg m)
Steering linkpin	30 lb ft (4 kg m)
Damper lower attachment point	20 lb ft (2.5 kg m)
Anti-roll bar bearing on sidemembers	25 lb ft (3 kg m)
Anti-roll bar bearing on lower suspension arm ..	5 lb ft (.8 kg m)
Front stub axle carrier ball joint nut	50 lb ft (7 kg m)
Wheel nut	60 lb ft (8 kg m)
Brake flange securing nut	15 lb ft (2.2 kg m)
Damper lower securing lug	20 lb ft (3 kg m)
Brake hose on caliper	15 lb ft (2 kg m)
Hub nut	145 lb ft (20 kg m)
Hub securing bolt	40 lb ft (5.5 kg m)

Rear suspension:

Pad/bracket assembly nuts	35 lb ft (5 kg m)
Tie bar nut	70 lb ft (9.5 kg m)
Hub nut	145 lb ft (20 kg m)

Brakes:

Stop switch tightening torque	20 lb ft (2.5 kg m)
Locknut on caliper guide pin	10 lb ft (1.5 kg m)
Caliper bracket securing nuts	15 lb ft (2 kg m)

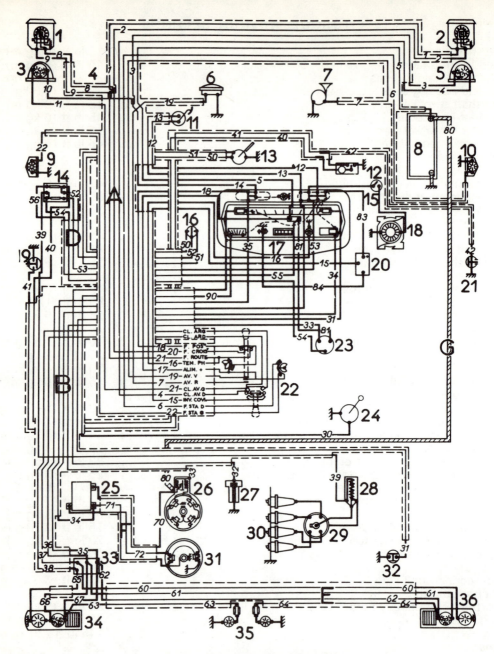

FIG 14:1   Renault R1130, 1963 model

Key to Fig 14:1

List of components: 1 N/S headlight   2 O/S headlight   3 N/S/F side and direction indicator light   4 Branch leads
5 O/S/F side and direction indicator light   6 Road horn   7 Town horn   8 Battery   9 N/S parking or direction indicator light
10 O/S parking or direction indicator light   11 Stop switch   12 Interior light   13 Windscreen wiper   14 Fusebox
15 Heater switch   16 Windscreen wiper switch   17 Instrument panel   18 Heater   19 N/S door switch   20 Flasher unit
21 O/S door switch   22 Horn, lighting and direction indicator switch   23 Ignition and starter switch   24 Fuel contents rheostat
25 Voltage regulator   26 Starter   27 Temperature switch   28 Ignition coil   29 Distributor   30 Sparking plugs
31 Generator   32 Oil pressure switch   33 Rear terminal plate   34 N/S/R light, stoplight, and direction indicator
35 Number plate light   36 O/S/R light, stoplight, and direction indicator

Wiring harnesses: A Front harness   B N/S harness   C Interior light harness   D Fuse harness   E Rear harness
F Charging circuit   G Positive system feed lead

List of wires:

Reference		Sleeve and wire colour	Wire connected		Conductor diameter	
Harness	Wire		from	to	in mm	conversion in AWG
A	1	Green wire	4	2	12/10	16
	2	Salmon pink wire	4	2	12/10	16
	3	Black wire	4	2	9/10	18
	4	Brown	22	5	12/10	16
	5	Blue	8	17	25/10	10
	6	Red wire	22	10	9/10	18
	7	Violet	22	7	12/10	16
	8	Salmon pink wire	4	1	12/10	16
	9	Green wire	4	1	12/10	16
	10	Black wire	4	3	9/10	18
	11	Violet	22	3	12/10	16
	12	Red	17	11	12/10	16
	13	Pink	11	17	12/10	16
	14	Yellow	17	4	9/10	18
	15	Blue	22	20	12/10	16
	16	Blue	22	17	9/10	18
	17	Blue	17	22	20/10	12
	18	Yellow	22	17	16/10	14
	19	White	22	6	12/10	16
	20	Pink	22	4	16/10	14
	21	Blue wire	22	4	16/10	14
	22	Violet	22	9	9/10	18
B	30	Yellow	17	24	9/10	18
	31	Black	17	32	12/10	16
	32	Brown	17	27	12/10	16
	33	Aluminium	23	26	20/10	12
	34	Blue	17	25	9/10	18
	35	Yellow	17	33	12/10	16
	36	Pink	17	33	12/10	16
	37	Brown	22	33	9/10	18
	38	Violet	22	33	9/10	18
	39	Red	14	28	12/10	16
	40	Blue	14	12	9/10	18
	41	Black wire	19	12	9/10	18
	42	Black wire	21	12	9/10	18
C	45	Aluminium wire	12 connecting			
	46	Aluminium wire	12 to harness B			
C	50	Green	16	13	12/10	16
	51	Blue	16	13	12/10	16
	52	White and blue to 16, blue to 14 ..	14	16	12/10	16
	53	Red	14	17	16/10	14
	54	Red	23	14	20/10	12
	55	Blue	17	14	12/10	16
E	60	Brown	33	36	9/10	18
	61	Pink	33	26	9/10	18
	62	Yellow	33	36	9/10	18
	63	Yellow	34	35	9/10	18
	64	Yellow	36	35	9/10	18
	65	Violet	33	34	9/10	18
	66	Pink	33	34	9/10	18
	67	Yellow	33	34	9/10	18
F	70	White	25	26	25/10	10
	71	Blue	25	31	25/10	10
	72	Green	25	31	12/10	16
Single wires	81	Blue/white	17 (blue)	23 (white)	20/10	12
	82	Red	17	15	16/10	14
	83	Red	17	20	12/10	16
	84	Black wire	17	20	9/10	18

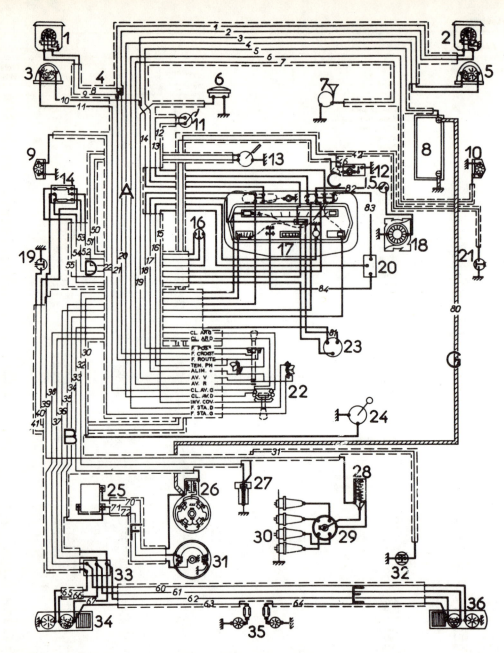

FIG 14:2   Renault R1130, 1964 model

Key to Fig 14:2

List of components: 1 N/S headlight   2 O/S headlight   3 N/S/F side and direction indicator light   4 Branch leads
5 O/S/F side and direction indicator light   6 Road horn   7 Town horn   8 Battery   9 N/S parking or direction indicator light
10 O/S parking or direction indicator light   11 Stop switch   12 Interior light   13 Windscreen wiper   14 Fusebox
15 Heater switch   16 Windscreen wiper switch   17 Instrument panel   18 Heater   19 N/S door switch
20 Flasher unit   21 O/S door switch   22 Horn, lighting and direction indicator switch   23 Ignition and starter switch
24 Fuel contents rheostat   25 Voltage regulator   26 Starter   27 Temperature switch   28 Ignition coil
29 Distributor   30 Sparking plugs   31 Generator   32 Oil pressure switch   33 Rear terminal plate
34 N/S/R light, stoplight, and direction indicator   35 Number plate light   36 O/S/R light, stoplight and direction indicator

Wiring harnesses: A Front harness   B N/S harness   C Interior light harness   D Fuse harness   E Rear harness
F Charging circuit   G Positive system feed lead

162

List of wires:

Harness	Wire	Sleeve and wire colour	Wire connected from	Wire connected to	Conductor diameter in mm	Conductor diameter conversion in AWG
A	1	Green wire	4	2	12/10	16
	2	Salmon pink wire	4	2	12/10	16
	3	Black wire	4	2	9/10	18
	4	Brown on red wire	22	5	12/10	16
	5	Blue	8	17	25/10	10
	6	Brown on red wire	22	10	9/10	18
	7	Violet	22	7	12/10	16
	8	Salmon pink wire	4	1	12/10	16
	9	Green wire	4	1	12/10	16
	10	Black wire	4	3	9/10	18
	11	Violet on red wire	22	3	12/10	16
	12	Red	17	11	12/10	16
	13	Pink	11	17	12/10	16
	14	Yellow	17	4	9/10	18
	15	Blue	22	20	12/10	16
	16	Green	22	17	9/10	18
	17	Blue	17	22	20/10	12
	18	Yellow	22	17	16/10	14
	19	White	22	6	12/10	16
	20	Pink	22	4	16/10	14
	21	Green	22	4	16/10	14
	22	Violet on black wire	22	9	9/10	18
B	30	Yellow	17	24	9/10	18
	31	Black	27	32	12/10	16
	32	Brown	17	27	12/10	16
	33	Aluminium	23	26	20/10	12
	34	Blue	17	25	9/10	18
	35	Yellow	17	33	12/10	16
	36	Pink	17	33	12/10	16
	37	Brown	22	33	9/10	18
	38	Violet	22	33	9/10	18
	39	Red	14	28	12/10	16
	40	Blue	14	12	9/10	18
	41	Black wire	19	12	9/10	18
	42	Black wire	21	12	9/10	18
C	45	Aluminium wire	12 connecting			
	46	Aluminium wire	12 to harness B			
D	50	Green	16	13	12/10	16
	51	Blue	16	13	12/10	16
	52	White and blue	14 blue	16 white/blue	12/10	16
	53	Red	14	17	16/10	14
	54	Red	23	14	20/10	12
	55	Blue	17	14	12/10	16
E	60	Brown	33	36	9/10	18
	61	Pink	33	36	9/10	18
	62	Yellow	33	36	9/10	18
	63	Yellow	34	35	9/10	18
	64	Yellow	34	35	9/10	18
	65	Violet	33	34	9/10	18
	66	Pink	33	34	9/10	18
	67	Yellow	33	34	9/10	18
F	70	White	25	26	25/10	10
	71	Blue	25	31	25/10	10
	72	Green	25	31	12/10	16
G	80		8	26		
Single wires	81	Blue and white	17 blue	23 white	20/10	12
	82	Red	17	15	16/10	14
	83	Red	17	20	12/10	16
	84	Black wire	17	20	9/10	18

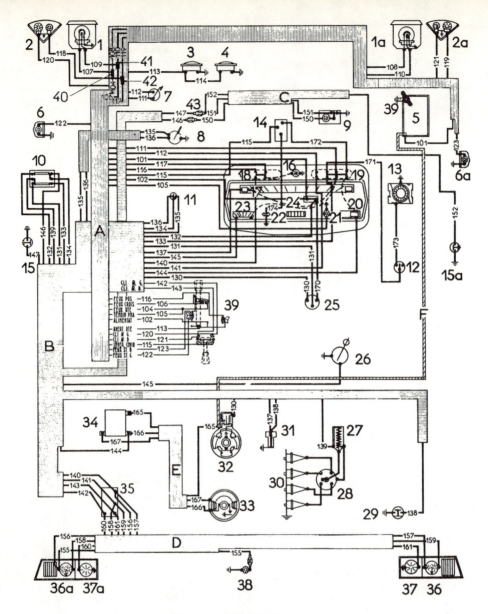

FIG 14:3   Renault R1190 model

Key to Fig 14:3

List of components: 1 N/S headlight   1a O/S headlight   2 N/S/F side and direction indicator light
2a O/S/F side and direction indicator light   3 Road horn   4 Town horn   5 Battery   6 N/S wing light
7 O/S wing light   7 Stop switch   8 Windscreen wiper   9 Interior light   10 Fuse box   11 Windscreen wiper switch
12 Heater switch   13 Heater   14 Flasher unit   15 N/S/F door switch   15a O/S/F door switch
16 Instrument panel light   17 Oil pressure and water temperature switch   18 N/S connection plate on instrument panel
19 O/S connection plate on instrument panel   20 Charge discharge warning light   21 Headlight warning light
22 Direction indicator tell-tale   23 Fuel contents indicator   24 Main feed two terminal connection plate
25 Ignition and starter switch   26 Fuel contents rheostat   27 Ignition coil   28 Distributor   29 Oil pressure switch
30 Sparking plugs   31 Temperature switch   32 Starter   33 Generator   34 Voltage regulator
35 Rear connection plate   36 OS rear and stoplight   36a NS rear and stoplight   37 OS direction indicator light
37a NS direction indicator light   38 Number plate light   39 Horn, lighting and direction indicator switch
40 Front wiring harness connection (headlight)   41 Front wiring harness connection (dipped headlight)
42 Front wiring harness connection (side light)   43 B and C wiring harness connection
List of wiring harnesses: A Front harness   B N/S harness   C Interior light harness   D Rear harness
E Charging circuit harness   F Positive starter cable

List of wires (1966 model):

Reference		Sleeve and wire colour	Wire connected		Conductor diameter	
Harness	Wire		from	to	in mm	conversion in AWG
A	101	Blue on black wire	5	24	25/10	10
	102	Blue on grey wire	24	39	20/10	12
	104	Green on blue wire	39	40	16/10	14
	105	Green on black wire	39	21	9/10	19
	106	Pink on red wire	39	41	16/10	14
	107	Green wire (green connection) ..	40	1	12/10	16
	108	Green wire (green connection) ..	40	1a	12/10	16
	109	Salmon wire (pink connection) ..	41	1	12/10	16
	110	Salmon wire (pink connection) ..	41	1a	12/10	16
	111	Red on grey wire	19	7	12/10	16
	112	Pink on salmon wire	7	19	12/10	16
	113	White on green wire	39	3	12/10	16
	114	Violet on grey wire	3	4	12/10	16
	115	Blue on grey wire	14	39	12/10	16
	116	Yellow on yellow wire ..	18	39	12/10	16
	117	Yellow on black wire ..	18	42	9/10	19
	118	Black wire	42	2	9/10	19
	119	Black wire	42	2a	9/10	19
	120	Violet on red wire	39	2	9/10	19
	121	Brown on red wire	39	2a	9/10	19
	122	Violet on black wire	39	6	9/10	19
	123	Brown on black wire	39	6a	9/10	19
B	130	Aluminium on grey wire	25	32	20/10	12
	131	Red on beige wire	25	10	20/10	12
	132	Blue on grey wire	24	10	12/10	16
	133	Red on red wire	10	19	16/10	14
	134	Blue on salmon wire	10	11	12/10	16
	135	Blue on grey wire	11	8	12/10	16
	136	Green on green wire	11	8	12/10	16
	137	Brown on green wire ..:	17	31	12/10	16
	138	Black wire	31	29	12/10	16
	139	Red on grey wire	10	27	12/10	16
	140	Yellow on yellow wire ..	18	35	12/10	16
	141	Pink on salmon wire	19	35	12/10	16
	142	Violet on white wire	39	35	9/10	19
	143	Brown on red wire	39	35	9/10	19
	144	Blue on black wire	34	20	9/10	19
	145	Yellow on white wire ..	23	26	9/10	19
	146	Blue on blue wire	10	43	9/10	19
	147	Black wire	43	15	9/10	19
C	150	Blue wire	43	9	9/10	19
	151	Black wire	9	43	9/10	19
	152	Black wire	43	15a	9/10	19
D	155	Yellow on white wire ..	36a	38	9/10	19
	156	Yellow on white wire ..	35	36a	9/10	19
	157	Yellow on white wire ..	35	36	9/10	19
	158	Pink on blue wire	35	36a	9/10	19
	159	Pink on blue wire	35	36	9/10	19
	160	Violet on red wire	35	37a	9/10	19
	161	Brown on red wire	35	37	9/10	19
E	165	White on black wire	32	34	25/10	10
	166	Blue on black wire	33	34	25/10	10
	167	Green on green wire	34	33	12/10	16
Single wires	170	White on grey wire	24	25	20/10	12
	171	Red on red wire	19	12	16/10	14
	172	Red on grey wire	19	14	12/10	16
	173	Black wire	12	13	12/10	16
	174	Black wire	14	22	9/10	19

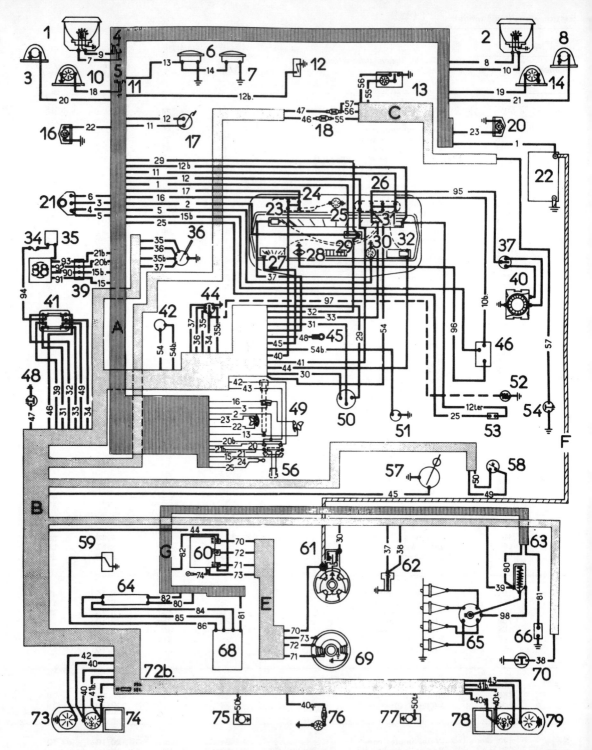

FIG 14:4   Renault R1190 model (later)

List of wires (1967 model):

Harness	Wire	Sleeve and wire colour	from	to	in mm	conversion in AWG
			Wire connected		**Conductor diameter**	
A	101	Clear on white wire	5	24	25/10	10
	102	Grey wire	24	39	20/10	12
	104	Clear on blue wire	39	40	16/10	14
	105	Clear on black wire	39	21	9/10	19
	106	Red wire, clip protector ..	39	41	16/10	14
	107	Green wire (green connection) ..	40	1	12/10	16
	108	Green wire (green connection) ..	40	1a	12/10	16
	109	Salmon wire (pink connection) ..	41	1	12/10	16
	110	Salmon wire (pink connection) ..	41	1a	12/10	16
	111	Grey wire	19	7	12/10	16
	112	Salmon wire	7	19	12/10	16
	113	Green wire	39	3	12/10	16
	114	Grey wire	3	4	12/10	16
	115	Green wire	14	39	12/10	16
	116	Yellow wire	18	39	12/10	16
	117	White wire	18	42	9/10	19
	118	White wire (yellow connection) ..	42	2	9/10	19
	119	White wire (yellow connection) ..	42	2a	9/10	19
	120	Blue wire	39	2	9/10	19
	121	Red wire	39	2a	9/10	19
	122	Black wire	39	6	9/10	19
	123	Brown on black wire	39	6a	9/10	19
B	130	Grey wire	25	32	20/10	12
	131	Beige wire	25	10	20/10	12
	132	Salmon wire	24	10	12/10	16
	133	Red wire	10	19	16/10	14
	134	Salmon wire	10	11	12/10	16
	135	Grey wire	11	8	12/10	16
	136	Green wire	11	8	12/10	16
	137	Green wire	17	31	12/10	16
	138	Green wire	31	29	12/10	16
	139	Grey wire	10	27	12/10	16
	140	Yellow wire	18	35	12/10	16
	141	Salmon wire	19	35	12/10	16
	142	Blue wire	39	35	9/10	19
	143	Red wire	39	35	9/10	19
	144	Blue wire	34	20	9/10	19
	145	White wire	23	26	9/10	19
	146	Blue wire	10	43	9/10	19
	147	Clear on black wire	43	15	9/10	19
C	150	Blue wire	43	9	9/10	19
	151	Black wire	9	43	9/10	19
	152	Black wire	43	15a	9/10	19
D	155	Clear on white wire	36a	38	9/10	19
	156	Clear on white wire	35	36a	9/10	19
	157	Clear white wire	35	36	9/10	19
	158	Clear black wire	35	36a	9/10	19
	159	Clear black wire	35	36	9/10	19
	160	Clear blue wire	35	37a	9/10	19
	161	Clear red wire	35	37	9/10	19
E	165	Clear white wire	32	34	25/10	10
	166	Clear on black wire	33	34	25/10	10
	167	Clear on green wire	34	33	12/10	16
Single wires	170	Clear on grey wire	24	25	20/10	12
	171	Red wire	19	12	16/10	14
	172	Clear on grey wire	19	14	12/10	16
	173	Black wire	12	13	12/10	16
	174	Black wire	14	22	9/10	19

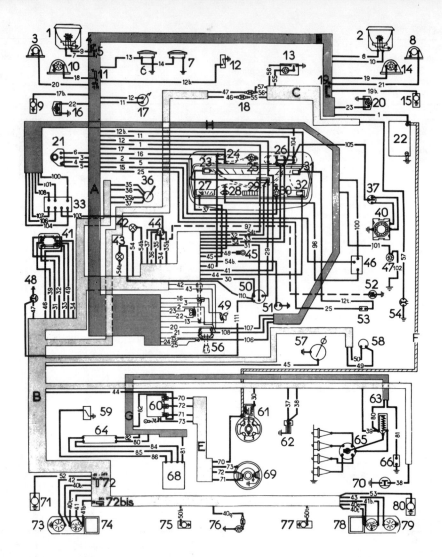

FIG 14:5   Renault R1192 model

List of components: 1 N/S headlight   2 O/S headlight   3 N/S front sidelight   4 Dipped beam junction
5 Headlight junction   6 Road horn   7 Town horn   8 O/S front sidelight   9 N/S illuminated cats' eyes (1970)
10 N/S front flasher   11 N/S front sidelight junction   12 Loss of brake pressure switch   13 Interior light rear view mirror
14 O/S front flasher   15 O/S illuminated cats' eyes (1970)   16 N/S parking light   17 Stoplight switch
18 Interior light wiring junction box   19 O/S front sidelight junction   20 O/S parking light   21 Foot dipswitch
22 Battery   23 Oil pressure and water temperature warning light   24 N/S junction box on instrument panel
25 Instrument panel lighting   26 O/S junction box on instrument panel   27 Fuel level indicator   28 Flasher warning light
29 Main feed   30 Headlight tell-tale   31 Brake pressure loss tell-tale   32 Charge-discharge warning light
33 Hazard warning switch (1970)   34 Flasher unit fuse   35 Flasher unit   36 Windscreen wiper motor
37 Heater switch   38 Hazard warning light switch   39 Junction box   40 Heater   41 Fuse box
42 Choke warning light   43 Neiman warning light (1970)   44 Windscreen wiper switch   45 Rear harness coupling point
46 Flasher unit   47 Hazard warning tell-tale (1970)   48 N/S door pillar switch   49 Combination lighting switch
50 Ignition-starter switch   51 Choke warning light switch   52 Cigar lighter   53 Switch for checking brake pressure loss bulb
54 O/S door pillar switch   55 Neutral switch   56 Front harness coupling point   57 Fuel gauge   58 Reversing light switch
59 Solenoid flap valve   60 Regulator   61 Starter   62 Temperature sender switch   63 Ignition coil
64 Anti-pollution fuse box (1970)   65 Distributor   66 Governor   67 Junction box   68 Anti-pollution system relay
69 Dynamo   70 Oil pressure switch   71 N/S rear illuminated cats' eyes (1970)   72 Rear light junction
72bis Reversing light junction   73 N/S rear flasher   74 N/S rear light and stoplight   75 N/S reversing light
76 Licence plate light   77 O/S reversing light   78 O/S rear light and stoplight   79 O/S rear flasher
80 O/S rear illuminated cats' eyes (1970)

Wiring harnesses: A Front harness   B N/S harness   C Roof harness   D Rear harness   E Charging circuit harness
F Starter positive cable   G Anti-pollution harness   H Hazard warning light harness

List of wires:

No.	Description	Colour			Connecting			Cross section	
		1968	1969	1970	1968	1969	1970	Dia.	Gauge
1	Main feed		White (clear)			22 to 29		30/10	9
2	Feed to combination lighting switch		Grey			29 to 49		20/10	12
3	Feed to pedal dipswitch		White (black)			49 to 21		16/10	14
4	Feed to headlights		Blue (green)			21 to 5		16/10	14
5	Main beam tell-tale		Blue			21 to 30		9/10	19
6	Feed to dipped beam		Red			21 to 4		16/10	14
7	N/S headlight		Green			5 to 1		12/10	16
8	O/S headlight		Green			5 to 2		12/10	16
9	N/S dipped beam		Pink			4 to 1		12/10	16
10	O/S dipped beam		Pink			4 to 2		12/10	16
10bis	Feed to flasher unit	Grey			26 to 46			12/10	16
11	Feed to stoplight switch		Grey			26 to 17		12/10	16
12	Return from stoplight		Pink			17 to 26		12/10	16
12bis	Loss of pressure indicator		Black			12 to 31		9/10	19
12ter	Loss of pressure light switch		Black			53 to 31		9/10	19
13	Road horn		White			56 to 6		16/10	14
14	Road horn		Grey			6 to 7		12/10	16
15	Feed to flasher changeover switch (lighting switch to junction box)	Grey (blue)		Grey (green)	56 to 39		46 to 56	12/10	16
15bis	Flasher changeover switch (unit to plate)	Green (blue)			46 to 39			12/10	16
16	Feed to wing mounted lights		Yellow			56 to 24		12/10	16
17	Feed to front sidelights and cats' eyes		White			24 to 11			
17bis	N/S front cats' eyes			White			11 to 9	9/10	19
18	N/S front sidelight			White			11 to 10	9/10	19
18bis	Feed to O/S sidelight and cats' eyes			White			11 to 19		
19	O/S front sidelight			White			11 to 14 / 19 to 14	9/10	19
19bis	Front O/S cats' eyes			White			19 to 15	9/10	19
20	N/S front flasher			Blue			56 to 3	9/10	19
20bis	N/S flasher (combination lighting switch to junction box)		Blue			56 to 39		9/10	19
21	O/S front flasher			Red			56 to 8	9/10	19
21bis	O/S flasher (combination lighting switch to junction box)		Red			56 to 39		9/10	19
22	N/S parking light or N/S flasher			Black			56 to 16	9/10	19
23	O/S parking light or O/S flasher			Black (maroon)			56 to 20	9/10	19
24	Cable attachment			White			56 dead wire	16/10	14
25	Loss of pressure warning light switch earth (ground)			Black			56 to 53	9/10	19
29	Feed to ignition starter switch			Grey (clear)			25 to 50	12/10	16
30	Starter relay			Grey			50 to 61	20/10	12
31	Neiman to fuse			Beige			50 to 41	20/10	12
32	Direct feed to fuse			Pink			29 to 41	12/10	16
33	Feed to instrument panel		Red			41 to 26		12/10	16
34	Feed to windscreen wiper switch		Pink			41 to 44		12/10	16
35	Direct feed to w.w. motor		Pink (blue)			44 to 36		12/10	16
35bis	Windscreen wiper park		Grey (black)			44 to 36		12/10	16
36	W.w. slow speed		Green (green)			44 to 36		12/10	16
36bis	W.w. fast speed		Yellow (red)			44 to 36		12/10	16
37	Feed to water temperature switch and oil pressure switch			Green			62 to 23	12/10	16
38	Oil pressure switch			Grey			70 to 62	12/10	16
39	Ignition coil			Red			41 to 63	16/10	14
40	Feed to rear lights			Yellow	24 to 67	24 to 74	24 to 72	12/10	16
40bis	N/S rear lights			White			72 to 74		
40ter	O/S rear lights			White		74 to 78	72 to 78	9/10	19
40qu	Feed to licence plate light			White			78 to 76	9/10	19
41	Feed to stoplights		Pink		26 to 67	26 to 74		12/10	16
41bis	O/S stoplight			Black			74 to 78	9/10	19
42	N/S rear flasher		Blue		56 to 67	56 to 73		9/10	19
43	O/S rear flasher		Red		56 to 67	56 to 79		9/10	19
44	Charge-discharge warning light		Blue			60 to 32		9/10	19
45	Fuel gauge		White			57 to 27		9/10	19
46	Feed to interior light		Blue			41 to 18		9/10	19
47	N/S door pillar earth (ground)		Black			48 to 18		9/10	19
48	Cable fixing		White			45 dead wire		16/10	14
49	Feed to reverse light switch		Grey			41 to 58		12/10	16
50	Feed to reversing lights	Grey		Green		58 to 67		12/10	19
50bis	N/S reversing light			Green			72bis to 75	12/10	16

No.	Description	Colour			Connecting			Cross-section	
		1968	1969	1970	1968	1969	1970	Dia.	Gauge
50ter	O/S reversing light			Green			72bis to 77	12/10	16
52	N/S rear cats' eyes			White			72 to 71	9/10	19
53	O/S rear cats' eyes			White			72 to 80	9/10	19
54	Feed to choke warning light			Grey			26 to 42	12/10	16
54bis	Choke warning light earth (ground)			Black			51 to 42	9/10	19
54ter	Feed to anti-theft key warning light			Pink			29 to 43	12/10	16
55	Feed to interior light		Blue			18 to 13		9/10	19
56	N/S door pillar		Black			18 to 13		9/10	19
57	O/S door pillar		Black			54 to 13		9/10	19
60	Licence plate light	White			74 to 76			9/10	19
61	N/S rear light	White			67 to 74			9/10	19
62	O/S rear light	White			67 to 78			9/10	19
63	N/S stoplight	Black			67 to 74			9/10	19
64	O/S stoplight	Black			67 to 78			9/10	19
65	N/S rear flasher	Blue			67 to 73			9/10	19
66	O/S rear flasher	Red			67 to 79			9/10	19
67	N/S reversing light	Green			67 to 75			12/10	16
68	O/S reversing light	Green			67 to 77			12/10	16
70	Regulator to starter			Yellow			60 to 62	30/10	9
71	Dynamo +			Yellow			60 to 69	30/10	9
72	Field			Green			60 to 69	12/10	16
73	Regulator earth (ground) to dynamo			Grey			60 to 69	12/10	16
74	Regulator earth (ground)			Grey			60 to earth	12/10	16
80	Ignition coil to box +	Pink			63 to 68			12/10	16
81	Neutral switch +	Pink			55 to 68			12/10	16
82	Neutral switch to box	Grey			55 to 68			12/10	16
83	Solenoid flap valve +	Grey (terminal cover)			68 to 59			12/10	16
84	Contact points to box	Yellow			63 to 68			12/10	16
85	Box earth (ground)	Green			68 to earth (ground)			12/10	16
90	Switch		Yellow (blue)			39 to 38		12/10	16
91	Switch		Yellow (blue)			39 to 38		12/10	16
92	Switch		Red (violet)			39 to 38		12/10	16
93	Switch		Red (maroon)			39 to 38		12/10	16
94	Switch		Maroon (maroon)			41 to 34		12/10	16
95	Feed to heater switch		Red			26 to 37		16/10	14
96	Flasher tell-tale			Black			46 to 28	9/10	19
97	Feed to cigar lighter			Grey			44 to 52	12/10	16
100	Flasher unit +			Beige (red)			33 to 46	12/10	16
101	Hazard warning light tell-tale + (direct)			Black (black)			33 to 47	12/10	16
102	Hazard warning light tell-tale earth (ground)			Grey			102 to earth	12/10	16
103	Hazard warning light + (direct)			Pink (blue)			44 to 33	12/10	16
104	Hazard warning light + (after switch)			Yellow			33 to 26	12/10	16
105	Feed to heater switch			Red			26 to 37	16/10	14
106	Hazard warning light to flasher unit (switch)			Green (green)			33 to 56	12/10	16
107	N/S flasher			Grey (silver)			33 to 56	12/10	16
108	O/S flasher			Grey (silver)			33 to 56	12/10	16
110	Return from Neiman tell-tale			Grey			50 to 43	12/10	16
111	N/S door pillar switch to Neiman			Black			48 to 50	12/10	16

Inches	Decimals	Milli-metres	Inches to Millimetres		Millimetres to Inches	
			Inches	mm	mm	Inches
1/64	.015625	.3969	.001	.0254	.01	.00039
1/32	.03125	.7937	.002	.0508	.02	.00079
3/64	.046875	1.1906	.003	.0762	.03	.00118
1/16	.0625	1.5875	.004	.1016	.04	.00157
5/64	.078125	1.9844	.005	.1270	.05	.00197
3/32	.09375	2.3812	.006	.1524	.06	.00236
7/64	.109375	2.7781	.007	.1778	.07	.00276
1/8	.125	3.1750	.008	.2032	.08	.00315
9/64	.140625	3.5719	.009	.2286	.09	.00354
5/32	.15625	3.9687	.01	.254	.1	.00394
11/64	.171875	4.3656	.02	.508	.2	.00787
3/16	.1875	4.7625	.03	.762	.3	.01181
13/64	.203125	5·1594	.04	1.016	.4	.01575
7/32	.21875	5.5562	.05	1.270	.5	.01969
15/64	.234375	5.9531	.06	1.524	.6	.02362
1/4	.25	6.3500	.07	1.778	.7	.02756
17/64	.265625	6.7469	.08	2.032	.8	.03150
9/32	.28125	7.1437	.09	2.286	.9	.03543
19/64	.296875	7.5406	.1	2.54	1	.03937
5/16	.3125	7.9375	.2	5.08	2	.07874
21/64	.328125	8.3344	.3	7.62	3	.11811
11/32	.34375	8.7312	.4	10.16	4	.15748
23/64	.359375	9.1281	.5	12.70	5	.19685
3/8	.375	9.5250	.6	15.24	6	.23622
25/64	.390625	9.9219	.7	17.78	7	.27559
13/32	.40625	10.3187	.8	20.32	8	.31496
27/64	.421875	10.7156	.9	22.86	9	.35433
7/16	.4375	11.1125	1	25.4	10	.39370
29/64	.453125	11.5094	2	50.8	11	.43307
15/32	.46875	11.9062	3	76.2	12	.47244
31/64	.484375	12.3031	4	101.6	13	.51181
1/2	.5	12.7000	5	127.0	14	.55118
33/64	.515625	13.0969	6	152.4	15	.59055
17/32	.53125	13.4937	7	177.8	16	.62992
35/64	.546875	13.8906	8	203.2	17	.66929
9/16	.5625	14.2875	9	228.6	18	.70866
37/64	.578125	14.6844	10	254.0	19	.74803
19/32	.59375	15.0812	11	279.4	20	.78740
39/64	.609375	15.4781	12	304.8	21	.82677
5/8	.625	15.8750	13	330.2	22	.86614
41/64	.640625	16.2719	14	355.6	23	.90551
21/32	.65625	16.6687	15	381.0	24	.94488
43/64	.671875	17.0656	16	406.4	25	.98425
11/16	.6875	17.4625	17	431.8	26	1.02362
45/64	.703125	17.8594	18	457.2	27	1.06299
23/32	.71875	18.2562	19	482.6	28	1.10236
47/64	.734375	18.6531	20	508.0	29	1.14173
3/4	.75	19.0500	21	533.4	30	1.18110
49/64	.765625	19.4469	22	558.8	31	1.22047
25/32	.78125	19.8437	23	584.2	32	1.25984
51/64	.796875	20.2406	24	609.6	33	1.29921
13/16	.8125	20.6375	25	635.0	34	1.33858
53/64	.828125	21.0344	26	660.4	35	1.37795
27/32	.84375	21.4312	27	685.8	36	1.41732
55/64	.859375	21.8281	28	711.2	37	1.4567
7/8	.875	22.2250	29	736.6	38	1.4961
57/64	.890625	22.6219	30	762.0	39	1.5354
29/32	.90625	23.0187	31	787.4	40	1.5748
59/64	.921875	23.4156	32	812.8	41	1.6142
15/16	.9375	23.8125	33	838.2	42	1.6535
61/64	.953125	24.2094	34	863.6	43	1.6929
31/32	.96875	24.6062	35	889.0	44	1.7323
63/64	.984375	25.0031	36	914.4	45	1.7717

UNITS	Pints to Litres	Gallons to Litres	Litres to Pints	Litres to Gallons	Miles to Kilometres	Kilometres to Miles	Lbs. per sq. In. to Kg. per sq. Cm.	Kg. per sq. Cm. to Lbs. per sq. In.
1	.57	4.55	1.76	.22	1.61	.62	.07	14.22
2	1.14	9.09	3.52	.44	3.22	1.24	.14	28.50
3	1.70	13.64	5.28	.66	4.83	1.86	.21	42.67
4	2.27	18.18	7.04	.88	6.44	2.49	.28	56.89
5	2.84	22.73	8.80	1.10	8.05	3.11	.35	71.12
6	3.41	27.28	10.56	1.32	9.66	3.73	.42	85.34
7	3.98	31.82	12.32	1.54	11.27	4.35	.49	99.56
8	4.55	36.37	14.08	1.76	12.88	4.97	.56	113.79
9		40.91	15.84	1.98	14.48	5.59	.63	128.00
10		45.46	17.60	2.20	16.09	6.21	.70	142.23
20				4.40	32.19	12.43	1.41	284.47
30				6.60	48.28	18.64	2.11	426.70
40				8.80	64.37	24.85		
50					80.47	31.07		
60					96.56	37.28		
70					112.65	43.50		
80					128.75	49.71		
90					144.84	55.92		
100					160.93	62.14		

UNITS	Lb ft to kgm	Kgm to lb ft	UNITS	Lb ft to kgm	Kgm to lb ft
1	.138	7.233	7	.967	50.631
2	.276	14.466	8	1.106	57.864
3	.414	21.699	9	1.244	65.097
4	.553	28.932	10	1.382	72.330
5	.691	36.165	20	2.765	144.660
6	.829	43.398	30	4.147	216.990

HINTS ON MAINTENANCE AND OVERHAUL

There are few things more rewarding than the restoration of a vehicle's original peak of efficiency and smooth performance.

The following notes are intended to help the owner to reach that state of perfection. Providing that he possesses the basic manual skills he should have no difficulty in performing most of the operations detailed in this manual. It must be stressed, however, that where recommended in the manual, highly-skilled operations ought to be entrusted to experts, who have the necessary equipment, to carry out the work satisfactorily.

Quality of workmanship:

The hazardous driving conditions on the roads to-day demand that vehicles should be as nearly perfect, mechanically, as possible. It is therefore most important that amateur work be carried out with care, bearing in mind the often inadequate working conditions, and also the inferior tools which may have to be used. It is easy to counsel perfection in all things, and we recognize that it may be setting an impossibly high standard. We do, however, suggest that every care should be taken to ensure that a vehicle is as safe to take on the road as it is humanly possible to make it.

Safe working conditions:

Even though a vehicle may be stationary, it is still potentially dangerous if certain sensible precautions are not taken when working on it while it is supported on jacks or blocks. It is indeed preferable not to use jacks alone, but to supplement them with carefully placed blocks, so that there will be plenty of support if the car rolls off the jacks during a strenuous manoeuvre. Axle stands are an excellent way of providing a rigid base which is not readily disturbed. Piles of bricks are a dangerous substitute. Be careful not to get under heavy loads on lifting tackle, the load could fall. It is preferable not to work alone when lifting an engine, or when working underneath a vehicle which is supported well off the ground. To be trapped, particularly under the vehicle, may have unpleasant results if help is not quickly forthcoming. Make some provision, however humble, to deal with fires. Always disconnect a battery if there is a likelihood of electrical shorts. These may start a fire if there is leaking fuel about. This applies particularly to leads which can carry a heavy current, like those in the starter circuit. While on the subject of electricity, we must also stress the danger of using equipment which is run off the mains and which has no earth or has faulty wiring or connections. So many workshops have damp floors, and electrical shocks are of such a nature that it is sometimes impossible to let go of a live lead or piece of equipment due to the muscular spasms which take place.

Work demanding special care:

This involves the servicing of braking, steering and suspension systems. On the road, failure of the braking system may be disastrous. Make quite sure that there can be no possibility of failure through the bursting of rusty brake pipes or rotten hoses, nor to a sudden loss of pressure due to defective seals or valves.

Problems:

The chief problems which may face an operator are:
1. External dirt.
2. Difficulty in undoing tight fixings.
3. Dismantling unfamiliar mechanisms.
4. Deciding in what respect parts are defective.
5. Confusion about the correct order for reassembly.
6. Adjusting running clearance.
7. Road testing.
8. Final tuning.

Practical suggestions to solve the problems:

1. Preliminary cleaning of large parts—engines, transmissions, steering, suspensions, etc.,—should be carried out before removal from the car. Where road dirt and mud alone are present, wash clean with a high-pressure water jet, brushing to remove stubborn adhesions, and allow to drain and dry. Where oil or grease is also present, wash down with a proprietary compound (Gunk, Teepol etc.,) applying with a stiff brush—an old paint brush is suitable—into all crevices. Cover the distributor and ignition coils with a polythene bag and then apply a strong water jet to clear the loosened deposits. Allow to drain and dry. The assemblies will then be sufficiently clean to remove and transfer to the bench for the next stage.

   On the bench, further cleaning can be carried out, first wiping the parts as free as possible from grease with old newspaper. Avoid using rag or cotton waste which can leave clogging fibres behind. Any remaining grease can be removed with a brush dipped in paraffin. If necessary, traces of paraffin can be removed by carbon tetrachloride. Avoid using paraffin or petrol in large quantities for cleaning in enclosed areas, such as garages, on account of the high fire risk.

   When all exteriors have been cleaned, and not before, dismantling can be commenced. This ensures that dirt will not enter into interiors and orifices revealed by dismantling. In the next phases, where components have to be cleaned, use carbon tetrachloride in preference to petrol and keep the containers covered except when in use. After the components have been cleaned, plug small holes with tapered hard wood plugs cut to size and blank off larger orifices with grease-proof paper and masking tape. Do not use soft wood plugs or matchsticks as they may break.

2. It is not advisable to hammer on the end of a screw thread, but if it must be done, first screw on a nut to protect the thread, and use a lead hammer. This applies particularly to the removal of tapered cotters. Nuts and bolts seem to 'grow' together, especially in exhaust systems. If penetrating oil does not work, try the judicious application of heat, but be careful of starting a fire. Asbestos sheet or cloth is useful to isolate heat.

   Tight bushes or pieces of tail-pipe rusted into a silencer can be removed by splitting them with an open-ended hacksaw. Tight screws can sometimes be started by a tap from a hammer on the end of a suitable screwdriver. Many tight fittings will yield to the judicious use of a hammer, but it must be a soft-faced hammer if damage is to be avoided, use a heavy block on the opposite side to absorb shock. Any parts of the steering system which have been damaged should be renewed, as attempts to repair them may lead to cracking and subsequent failure, and steering ball joints should be disconnected using a recommended tool to prevent damage.

3 If often happens that an owner is baffled when trying to dismantle an unfamiliar piece of equipment. So many modern devices are pressed together or assembled by spinning-over flanges, that they must be sawn apart. The intention is that the whole assembly must be renewed. However, parts which appear to be in one piece to the naked eye, may reveal close-fitting joint lines when inspected with a magnifying glass, and, this may provide the necessary clue to dismantling. Left-handed screw threads are used where rotational forces would tend to unscrew a right-handed screw thread.

Be very careful when dismantling mechanisms which may come apart suddenly. Work in an enclosed space where the parts will be contained, and drape a piece of cloth over the device if springs are likely to fly in all directions. Mark everything which might be reassembled in the wrong position, scratched symbols may be used on unstressed parts, or a sequence of tiny dots from a centre punch can be useful. Stressed parts should never be scratched or centre-popped as this may lead to cracking under working conditions. Store parts which look alike in the correct order for reassembly. Never rely upon memory to assist in the assembly of complicated mechanisms, especially when they will be dismantled for a long time, but make notes, and drawings to supplement the diagrams in the manual, and put labels on detached wires. Rust stains may indicate unlubricated wear. This can sometimes be seen round the outside edge of a bearing cup in a universal joint. Look for bright rubbing marks on parts which normally should not make heavy contact. These might prove that something is bent or running out of true. For example, there might be bright marks on one side of a piston, at the top near the ring grooves, and others at the bottom of the skirt on the other side. This could well be the clue to a bent connecting rod. Suspected cracks can be proved by heating the component in a light oil to approximately 100°C, removing, drying off, and dusting with french chalk, if a crack is present the oil retained in the crack will stain the french chalk.

4 In determining wear, and the degree, against the permissible limits set in the manual, accurate measurement can only be achieved by the use of a micrometer. In many cases, the wear is given to the fourth place of decimals; that is in ten-thousandths of an inch. This can be read by the vernier scale on the barrel of a good micrometer. Bore diameters are more difficult to determine. If, however, the matching shaft is accurately measured, the degree of play in the bore can be felt as a guide to its suitability. In other cases, the shank of a twist drill of known diameter is a handy check.

Many methods have been devised for determining the clearance between bearing surfaces. To-day the best and simplest is by the use of Plastigage, obtainable from most garages. A thin plastic thread is laid between the two surfaces and the bearing is tightened, flattening the thread. On removal, the width of the thread is compared with a scale supplied with the thread and the clearance is read off directly. Sometimes joint faces leak persistently, even after gasket renewal. The fault will then be traceable to distortion, dirt or burrs. Studs which are screwed into soft metal frequently raise burrs at the point of entry. A quick cure for this is to chamfer the edge of the hole in the part which fits over the stud.

5 **Always check a replacement part with the original one before it is fitted.**

If parts are not marked, and the order for reassembly is not known, a little detective work will help. Look for marks which are due to wear to see if they can be mated. Joint faces may not be identical due to manufacturing errors, and parts which overlap may be stained, giving a clue to the correct position. Most fixings leave identifying marks especially if they were painted over on assembly. It is then easier to decide whether a nut, for instance, has a plain, a spring, or a shakeproof washer under it. All running surfaces become 'bedded' together after long spells of work and tiny imperfections on one part will be found to have left corresponding marks on the other. This is particularly true of shafts and bearings and even a score on a cylinder wall will show on the piston.

6 Checking end float or rocker clearances by feeler gauge may not always give accurate results because of wear. For instance, the rocker tip which bears on a valve stem may be deeply pitted, in which case the feeler will simply be bridging a depression. Thrust washers may also wear depressions in opposing faces to make accurate measurement difficult. End float is then easier to check by using a dial gauge. It is common practice to adjust end play in bearing assemblies, like front hubs with taper rollers, by doing up the axle nut until the hub becomes stiff to turn and then backing it off a little. Do not use this method with ballbearing hubs as the assembly is often preloaded by tightening the axle nut to its fullest extent. If the splitpin hole will not line up, file the base of the nut a little.

Steering assemblies often wear in the straight-ahead position. If any part is adjusted, make sure that it remains free when moved from lock to lock. Do not be surprised if an assembly like a steering gearbox, which is known to be carefully adjusted outside the car, becomes stiff when it is bolted in place. This will be due to distortion of the case by the pull of the mounting bolts, particularly if the mounting points are not all touching together. This problem may be met in other equipment and is cured by careful attention to the alignment of mounting points.

When a spanner is stamped with a size and A/F it means that the dimension is the width between the jaws and has no connection with ANF, which is the designation for the American National Fine thread. Coarse threads like Whitworth are rarely used on cars to-day except for studs which screw into soft aluminium or cast iron. For this reason it might be found that the top end of a cylinder head stud has a fine thread and the lower end a coarse thread to screw into the cylinder block. If the car has mainly UNF threads then it is likely that any coarse threads will be UNC, which are not the same as Whitworth. Small sizes have the same number of threads in Whitworth and UNC, but in the $\frac{1}{2}$ inch size for example, there are twelve threads to the inch in the former and thirteen in the latter.

7 After a major overhaul, particularly if a great deal of work has been done on the braking, steering and suspension systems, it is advisable to approach the problem of testing with care. If the braking system has been overhauled, apply heavy pressure to the brake pedal and get a second operator to check every possible source of leakage. The brakes may work extremely well, but a leak could cause complete failure after a few miles.

Do not fit the hub caps until every wheel nut has been checked for tightness, and make sure the tyre pressures are correct. Check the levels of coolant, lubricants and hydraulic fluids. Being satisfied that all is well, take the car on the road and test the brakes at once. Check the steering and the action of the handbrake. Do all this at moderate speeds on quiet roads, and make sure there is no other vehicle behind you when you try a rapid stop.

Finally, remember that many parts settle down after a time, so check for tightness of all fixings after the car has been on the road for a hundred miles or so.

8 It is useless to tune an engine which has not reached its normal running temperature. In the same way, the tune of an engine which is stiff after a rebore will be different when the engine is again running free. Remember too, that rocker clearances on pushrod operated valve gear will change when the cylinder head nuts are tightened after an initial period of running with a new head gasket.

Trouble may not always be due to what seems the obvious cause. Ignition, carburation and mechanical condition are interdependent and spitting back through the carburetter, which might be attributed to a weak mixture, can be caused by a sticking inlet valve.

For one final hint on tuning, never adjust more than one thing at a time or it will be impossible to tell which adjustment produced the desired result.

GLOSSARY OF TERMS

Allen key   Cranked wrench of hexagonal section for use with socket head screws.

Alternator   Electrical generator producing alternating current. Rectified to direct current for battery charging.

Ambient temperature   Surrounding atmospheric temperature.

Annulus   Used in engineering to indicate the outer ring gear of an epicyclic gear train.

Armature   The shaft carrying the windings, which rotates in the magnetic field of a generator or starter motor. That part of a solenoid or relay which is activated by the magnetic field.

Axial   In line with, or pertaining to, an axis.

Backlash   Play in meshing gears.

Balance lever   A bar where force applied at the centre is equally divided between connections at the ends.

Banjo axle   Axle casing with large diameter housing for the crownwheel and differential.

Bendix pinion   A self-engaging and self-disengaging drive on a starter motor shaft.

Bevel pinion   A conical shaped gearwheel, designed to mesh with a similar gear with an axis usually at 90 deg. to its own.

bhp   Brake horse power, measured on a dynamometer.

bmep   Brake mean effective pressure. Average pressure on a piston during the working stroke.

Brake cylinder   Cylinder with hydraulically operated piston(s) acting on brake shoes or pad(s).

Brake regulator   Control valve fitted in hydraulic braking system which limits brake pressure to rear brakes during heavy braking to prevent rear wheel locking.

Camber   Angle at which a wheel is tilted from the vertical.

Capacitor   Modern term for an electrical condenser. Part of distributor assembly, connected across contact breaker points, acts as an interference suppressor.

Castellated   Top face of a nut, slotted across the flats, to take a locking splitpin.

Castor   Angle at which the kingpin or swivel pin is tilted when viewed from the side.

cc   Cubic centimetres. Engine capacity is arrived at by multiplying the area of the bore in sq cm by the stroke in cm by the number of cylinders.

Clevis   U-shaped forked connector used with a clevis pin, usually at handbrake connections.

Collet   A type of collar, usually split and located in a groove in a shaft, and held in place by a retainer. The arrangement used to retain the spring(s) on a valve stem in most cases.

Commutator   Rotating segmented current distributor between armature windings and brushes in generator or motor.

Compression   The ratio, or quantitative relation, of the total volume (piston at bottom of stroke) to the unswept volume (piston at top of stroke) in an engine cylinder.

Condenser   See capacitor.

Core plug   Plug for blanking off a manufacturing hole in a casting.

Crownwheel   Large bevel gear in rear axle, driven by a bevel pinion attached to the propeller shaft. Sometimes called a 'ring wheel'.

'C'-spanner   Like a 'C' with a handle. For use on screwed collars without flats, but with slots or holes.

Damper   Modern term for shock-absorber, used in vehicle suspension systems to damp out spring oscillations.

Depression   The lowering of atmospheric pressure as in the inlet manifold and carburetter.

Dowel   Close tolerance pin, peg, tube, or bolt, which accurately locates mating parts.

Drag link   Rod connecting steering box drop arm (pitman arm) to nearest front wheel steering arm in certain types of steering systems.

Dry liner   Thinwall tube pressed into cylinder bore.

Dry sump   Lubrication system where all oil is scavenged from the sump, and returned to a separate tank.

Dynamo   See Generator.

Electrode   Terminal, part of an electrical component, such as the points or 'Electrodes' of a sparking plug.

Electrolyte   In lead-acid car batteries a solution of sulphuric acid and distilled water.

End float   The axial movement between associated parts, end play.

EP   Extreme pressure. In lubricants, special grades for heavily loaded bearing surfaces, such as gear teeth in a gearbox, or crownwheel and pinion in a rear axle.

Fade Of brakes. Reduced efficiency due to overheating.

Field coils Windings on the polepieces of motors and generators.

Fillets Narrow finishing strips usually applied to interior bodywork.

First motion shaft Input shaft from clutch to gearbox.

Fullflow filter Filters in which all the oil is pumped to the engine. If the element becomes clogged, a bypass valve operates to pass unfiltered oil to the engine.

FWD Front wheel drive.

Gear pump Two meshing gears in a close fitting casing. Oil is carried from the inlet round the outside of both gears in the spaces between the gear teeth and casing to the outlet, the meshing gear teeth prevent oil passing back to the inlet, and the oil is forced through the outlet port.

Generator Modern term for 'Dynamo . When rotated produces electrical current.

Grommet A ring of protective or sealing material. Can be used to protect pipes or leads passing through bulkheads.

Grubscrew Fully threaded headless screw with screwdriver slot. Used for locking, or alignment purposes.

Gudgeon pin Shaft which connects a piston to its connecting rod. Sometimes called 'wrist pin', or 'piston pin'.

Halfshaft One of a pair transmitting drive from the differential.

Helical In spiral form. The teeth of helical gears are cut at a spiral angle to the side faces of the gearwheel.

Hot spot Hot area that assists vapourisation of fuel on its way to cylinders. Often provided by close contact between inlet and exhaust manifolds.

HT High Tension. Applied to electrical current produced by the ignition coil for the sparking plugs.

Hydrometer A device for checking specific gravity of liquids. Used to check specific gravity of electrolyte.

Hypoid bevel gears A form of bevel gear used in the rear axle drive gears. The bevel pinion meshes below the centre line of the crownwheel, giving a lower propeller shaft line.

Idler A device for passing on movement. A free running gear between driving and driven gears. A lever transmitting track rod movement to a side rod in steering gear.

Impeller A centrifugal pumping element. Used in water pumps to stimulate flow.

Journals Those parts of a shaft that are in contact with the bearings.

Kingpin The main vertical pin which carries the front wheel spindle, and permits steering movement. May be called 'steering pin' or 'swivel pin'.

Layshaft The shaft which carries the laygear in the gearbox. The laygear is driven by the first motion shaft and drives the third motion shaft according to the gear selected. Sometimes called the 'countershaft' or 'second motion shaft.'

lb ft A measure of twist or torque. A pull of 10 lb at a radius of 1 ft is a torque of 10 lb ft.

lb/sq in Pounds per square inch.

Little-end The small, or piston end of a connecting rod. Sometimes called the 'small-end'.

LT Low Tension. The current output from the battery.

Mandrel Accurately manufactured bar or rod used for test or centring purposes.

Manifold A pipe, duct, or chamber, with several branches.

Needle rollers Bearing rollers with a length many times their diameter.

Oil bath Reservoir which lubricates parts by immersion. In air filters, a separate oil supply for wetting a wire mesh element to hold the dust.

Oil wetted In air filters, a wire mesh element lightly oiled to trap and hold airborne dust.

Overlap Period during which inlet and exhaust valves are open together.

Panhard rod Bar connected between fixed point on chassis and another on axle to control sideways movement.

Pawl Pivoted catch which engages in the teeth of a ratchet to permit movement in one direction only.

Peg spanner Tool with pegs, or pins, to engage in holes or slots in the part to be turned.

Pendant pedals Pedals with levers that are pivoted at the top end.

Phillips screwdriver A cross-point screwdriver for use with the cross-slotted heads of Phillips screws.

Pinion A small gear, usually in relation to another gear.

Piston-type damper Shock absorber in which damping is controlled by a piston working in a closed oil-filled cylinder.

Preloading Preset static pressure on ball or roller bearings not due to working loads.

Radial Radiating from a centre, like the spokes of a wheel.

Radius rod	Pivoted arm confining movement of a part to an arc of fixed radius.
Ratchet	Toothed wheel or rack which can move in one direction only, movement in the other being prevented by a pawl.
Ring gear	A gear tooth ring attached to outer periphery of flywheel. Starter pinion engages with it during starting.
Runout	Amount by which rotating part is out of true.
Semi-floating axle	Outer end of rear axle halfshaft is carried on bearing inside axle casing. Wheel hub is secured to end of shaft.
Servo	A hydraulic or pneumatic system for assisting, or, augmenting a physical effort. See 'Vacuum Servo'.
Setscrew	One which is threaded for the full length of the shank.
Shackle	A coupling link, used in the form of two parallel pins connected by side plates to secure the end of the master suspension spring and absorb the effects of deflection.
Shell bearing	Thinwalled steel shell lined with anti-friction metal. Usually semi-circular and used in pairs for main and big-end bearings.
Shock absorber	See 'Damper'.
Silentbloc	Rubber bush bonded to inner and outer metal sleeves.
Socket-head screw	Screw with hexagonal socket for an Allen key.
Solenoid	A coil of wire creating a magnetic field when electric current passes through it. Used with a soft iron core to operate contacts or a mechanical device.
Spur gear	A gear with teeth cut axially across the periphery.
Stub axle	Short axle fixed at one end only.
Tachometer	An instrument for accurate measurement of rotating speed. Usually indicates in revolutions per minute.
TDC	Top Dead Centre. The highest point reached by a piston in a cylinder, with the crank and connecting rod in line.
Thermostat	Automatic device for regulating temperature. Used in vehicle coolant systems to open a valve which restricts circulation at low temperature.
Third motion shaft	Output shaft of gearbox.
Threequarter floating axle	Outer end of rear axle halfshaft flanged and bolted to wheel hub, which runs on bearing mounted on outside of axle casing. Vehicle weight is not carried by the axle shaft.
Thrust bearing or washer	Used to reduce friction in rotating parts subject to axial loads.
Torque	Turning or twisting effort. See 'lb ft'.
Track rod	The bar(s) across the vehicle which connect the steering arms and maintain the front wheels in their correct alignment.
UJ	Universal joint. A coupling between shafts which permits angular movement.
UNF	Unified National Fine screw thread.
Vacuum servo	Device used in brake system, using difference between atmospheric pressure and inlet manifold depression to operate a piston which acts to augment brake pressure as required. See 'Servo'.
Venturi	A restriction or 'choke' in a tube, as in a carburetter, used to increase velocity to obtain a reduction in pressure.
Vernier	A sliding scale for obtaining fractional readings of the graduations of an adjacent scale.
Welch plug	A domed thin metal disc which is partially flattened to lock in a recess. Used to plug core holes in castings.
Wet liner	Removable cylinder barrel, sealed against coolant leakage, where the coolant is in direct contact with the outer surface.
Wet sump	A reservoir attached to the crankcase to hold the lubricating oil.

INDEX

Make	Author	Title

ALFA ROMEO

Model				Author	Title
1600 Giulia TI 1961–67	..	..	..	Ball	Alfa Romeo Giulia 1962–71 Autobook
1600 Giulia Sprint 1962–68	..	..	..	Ball	Alfa Romeo Giulia 1962–71 Autobook
1600 Giulia Spider 1962–68	..	..	..	Ball	Alfa Romeo Giulia 1962–71 Autobook
1600 Giulia Super 1965–70	..	..	..	Ball	Alfa Romeo Giulia 1962–71 Autobook
1750 Giulia Saloon 1968–71	..	..	..	Ball	Alfa Romeo Giulia 1962–71 Autobook
1750 Giulia Spider 1968–71	..	..	..	Ball	Alfa Romeo Giulia 1962–71 Autobook
1750 Giulia Coupé 1968–71	..	..	..	Ball	Alfa Romeo Giulia 1962–71 Autobook

ASTON MARTIN

Model				Author	Title
All models 1921–58	..	..	..	Coram	Aston Martin 1921–58 Autobook

AUDI

Model				Author	Title
Auto Union Audi 100 ..	..	..	..	Ball	Audi 100 1969–71 Autobook
Audi 100 1969–71	..	..	..	Ball	Audi 100 1969–71 Autobook
Audi 100 S 1969–71	..	..	..	Ball	Audi 100 1969–71 Autobook
Audi 100 LS 1969–71 ..	..	..	..	Ball	Audi 100 1969–71 Autobook

AUSTIN

Model				Author	Title
A30 1951–56 ..	..	..	..	Ball	Austin A30, A35, A40 Autobook
A35 1956–62 ..	..	..	..	Ball	Austin A30, A35, A40 Autobook
A40 Farina 1957–67	..	..	..	Ball	Austin A30, A35, A40 Autobook
A40 Cambridge 1954–57	..	..	..	Ball	BMC Autobook Three
A50 Cambridge 1954–57	..	..	..	Ball	BMC Autobook Three
A55 Cambridge Mk 1 1957–58	..	..	..	Ball	BMC Autobook Three
A55 Cambridge Mk 2 1958–61	..	..	..	Ball	Austin A55 Mk 2, A60 1958–69 Autobook
A60 Cambridge 1961–69	..	..	..	Ball	Austin A55 Mk 2, A60 1958–69 Autobook
A99 1959–61 ..	..	..	..	Ball	Austin A99, A110 1959–68 Autobook
A110 1961–68	..	..	..	Ball	Austin A99, A110 1959–68 Autobook
Mini 1959–71 ..	..	..	..	Ball	Mini 1959–71 Autobook
Mini Clubman 1969–71	..	..	..	Ball	Mini 1959–71 Autobook
Mini Cooper 1961–70 ..	..	..	..	Ball	Mini Cooper 1961–70 Autobook
Mini Cooper S 1963–70	..	..	..	Ball	Mini Cooper 1961–70 Autobook
1100 Mk 1 1963–67 ..	..	..	..	Ball	1100 Mk 1 1962–67 Autobook
1100 Mk 2 1968–70 ..	..	..	..	Ball	1100 Mk 2, 1300 Mk 1, 2, America 1968–71 Autobook
1300 Mk 1, 2 1968–71	..	..	..	Ball	1100 Mk 2, 1300 Mk 1, 2, America 1968–71 Autobook
America 1968–71	..	..	..	Ball	1100 Mk 2, 1300 Mk 1, 2, America 1968–71 Autobook
1800 Mk 1, 2 1964–71	..	..	..	Ball	1800 1964–71 Autobook
1800 S 1969–71	..	..	..	Ball	1800 1964–71 Autobook
Maxi 1500 1969–71	..	..	..	Ball	Austin Maxi 1969–71 Autobook
Maxi 1750 1970–71	..	..	..	Ball	Austin Maxi 1969–71 Autobook

AUSTIN HEALEY

Model				Author	Title
100/6 1955–59	..	..	..	Ball	Austin Healey 100/6, 3000 1956–68 Autobook
Sprite 1958–71	..	..	..	Ball	Sprite, Midget 1958–71 Autobook
3000 Mk 1, 2, 3 1959–68	..	..	..	Ball	Austin Healey 100/6, 3000 1956–68 Autobook

BEDFORD

Model				Author	Title
CA Mk 1 and 2 1957–64	..	..	..	Ball	Vauxhall Victor 1, 2 FB 1957–64 Autobook
Beagle HA 1964–66 ..	..	..	..	Ball	Vauxhall Viva HA 1964–66 Autobook

BMW

Model				Author	Title
1600 1966–70	..	..	..	Ball	BMW 1600 1966–70 Autobook
1600–2 1966–70	..	..	..	Ball	BMW 1600 1966–70 Autobook
1600TI 1966–70	..	..	..	Ball	BMW 1600 1966–70 Autobook
1800 1964–70	..	..	..	Ball	BMW 1800 1964–70 Autobook
1800TI 1964–67	..	..	..	Ball	BMW 1800 1964–70 Autobook
2000 1966–70	..	..	..	Ball	BMW 2000, 2002 1966–70 Autobook

Make					Author	Title
2000A 1966–70	..	..	..	..	Ball	BMW 2000, 2002 1966–70 Autobook
2000TI 1966–70	..	..	..	..	Ball	BMW 2000, 2002 1966–70 Autobook
2000CS 1967–70	.:	..	..	..	Ball	BMW 2000, 2002 1966–70 Autobook
2000CA 1967–70	..	..	..	..	Ball	BMW 2000, 2002 1966–70 Autobook
2002 1968–70	..	..	..	..	Ball	BMW 2000, 2002 1966–70 Autobook

CITROEN

Make					Author	Title
DS19 1955–65	..	..	..	..	Ball	Citroen DS19, ID19 1955–66 Autobook
ID19 1956–66	..	..	..	..	Ball	Citroen DS19, ID19 1955–66 Autobook

COMMER

Make				Author	Title
Cob Series 1, 2, 3 1956–65	..	..	..	Ball	Hillman Minx 1 to 5 1956–65 Autobook
Imp Vans 1963–68	..	..	..	Smith	Hillman Imp 1963–68 Autobook
Imp Vans 1969–71	..	..	..	Ball	Hillman Imp 1969–71 Autobook

DAIMLER

Make		Author	Title
Daimler Sovereign 2.8, 4.2 litre 1970–72	..	Ball	Jaguar XJ6 1968–72 Autobook

DE DION BOUTON

Make				Author	Title
One-cylinder 1899–1907	..	..	..	Mercredy	De Dion Bouton Autobook One
Two-cylinder 1903–1907	..	..	..	Mercredy	De Dion Bouton Autobook One
Four-cylinder 1905–1907	..	..	..	Mercredy	De Dion Bouton Autobook One

DATSUN

Make					Author	Title
1200 B 110 1970–72	..	..	..	..	Ball	Datsun 1200 1970–72 Autobook
1200 KB 110 1970–72	..	..	..	..	Ball	Datsun 1200 1970–72 Autobook
1300 1968–70	..	..	..	..	Ball	Datsun 1300, 1600 1968–70 Autobook
1600 1968–70	..	..	..	..	Ball	Datsun 1300, 1600 1968–70 Autobook
240Z HLS 1970–71	..	..	..	..	Ball	Datsun 240Z Sport 1970–71 Autobook
240Z HS 1970–71	..	..	..	..	Ball	Datsun 240Z Sport 1970–71 Autobook

FIAT

Make					Author	Title
500 1957–61	..	..	..	..	Ball	Fiat 500 1957–69 Autobook
500D 1960–65	..	..	..	..	Ball	Fiat 500 1957–69 Autobook
500F 1965–69	..	..	..	..	Ball	Fiat 500 1957–69 Autobook
500L 1968–69	..	..	..	..	Ball	Fiat 500 1957–69 Autobook
600 633 cc 1955–61	..	..	..	..	Ball	Fiat 600, 600D 1955–69 Autobook
600D 767 cc 1960–69	..	..	..	..	Ball	Fiat 600, 600D 1955–69 Autobook
850 1964–71	..	..	..	..	Ball	Fiat 850 1964–71 Autobook
850S 1964–71	..	..	..	..	Ball	Fiat 850 1964–71 Autobook
850S Coupé 1965–68	..	..	..	..	Ball	Fiat 850 1964–71 Autobook
850S Special 1968–71	..	..	..	..	Ball	Fiat 850 1964–71 Autobook
850S Spyder 1965–68	..	..	..	..	Ball	Fiat 850 1964–71 Autobook
850 Sport 903 cc 1968–71	..	..	..	..	Ball	Fiat 850 1964–71 Autobook
1300 1961–66	..	..	..	..	Ball	Fiat 1300, 1500 1961–67 Autobook
1500 1961–67	..	..	..	..	Ball	Fiat 1300, 1500 1961–67 Autobook
124A 1966–71	..	..	..	..	Ball	Fiat 124 1966–71 Autobook
124AF 1967–71	..	..	..	..	Ball	Fiat 124 1966–71 Autobook
124 Special 1969–71	..	..	..	..	Ball	Fiat 124 1966–71 Autobook
124 Spyder 1966–70	..	..	..	..	Ball	Fiat 124 Sport 1966–70 Autobook
124 Coupé 1967–69	..	..	..	..	Ball	Fiat 124 Sport 1966–70 Autobook

FORD

Make					Author	Title
Anglia 100E 1953–59	..	..	..	..	Ball	Ford Anglia Prefect 100E Autobook
Anglia 105E 1959–67	..	..	..	..	Smith	Ford Anglia 105E, Prefect 107E 1959–67 Autobook
Anglia Super 123E 1962–67	..	..	..	..	Smith	Ford Anglia 105E, Prefect 107E 1959–67 Autobook
Capri 109E 1962	..	..	..	..	Smith	Ford Classic, Capri 1961–64 Autobook
Capri 116E 1962–64	..	..	..	..	Smith	Ford Classic, Capri 1961–64 Autobook
Capri 1300, 1300GT 1968–71	..	..	..	Ball	Ford Capri 1300, 1600 1968–71 Autobook
Capri 1600, 1600GT 1968–71	..	..	..	Ball	Ford Capri 1300, 1600 1968–71 Autobook
Capri 2000 GT 1969–71	..	..	Ball	Ford Capri 2000 GT, 3000 GT 1969–71 Autobook

Make				Author	Title
Capri 3000 GT 1969–71	..	..	..	Ball	Ford Capri 2000 GT, 3000 GT 1969–71 Autobook
Capri 3000 E 1969–71	..	..	..	Ball	Ford Capri 2000 GT, 3000 GT 1969–71 Autobook
Classic 109E 1961–62	..	..	..	Smith	Ford Classic, Capri 1961–64 Autobook
Classic 116E 1962–63	..	..	..	Smith	Ford Classic, Capri 1961–64 Autobook
Consul Mk 1 1950–56	..	..	..	Ball	Ford Consul, Zephyr, Zodiac 1, 2 1950–62 Autobook
Consul Mk 2 1956–62	..	..	..	Ball	Ford Consul, Zephyr, Zodiac 1, 2 1950–62 Autobook
Corsair Straight Four 1963–65	..	..	..	Ball	Ford Corsair Straight Four 1963–65 Autobook
Corsair Straight Four GT 1963–65	..	..	..	Ball	Ford Corsair Straight Four 1963–65 Autobook
Corsair V4 3004E 1965–68	..	..	..	Smith	Ford Corsair V4 1965–68 Autobook
Corsair V4 GT 1965–66	..	..	..	Smith	Ford Corsair V4 1965–68 Autobook
Corsair V4 1663 cc 1969–70	..	..	..	Ball	Ford Corsair V4 1969–70 Autobook
Corsair 2000, 2000E 1966–68	..	..	..	Smith	Ford Corsair V4 1965–68 Autobook
Corsair 2000, 2000E 1969–70	..	..	..	Ball	Ford Corsair V4 1969–70 Autobook
Cortina 113E 1962–66	..	..	..	Smith	Ford Cortina 1962–66 Autobook
Cortina Super 118E 1963–66	..	..	..	Smith	Ford Cortina 1962–66 Autobook
Cortina Lotus 125E 1963–66	..	..	..	Smith	Ford Cortina 1962–66 Autobook
Cortina GT 118E 1963–66	..	..	..	Smith	Ford Cortina 1962–66 Autobook
Cortina 1300 1967–68	..	..	..	Smith	Ford Cortina 1967–68 Autobook
Cortina 1300 1969–70	..	..	..	Ball	Ford Cortina 1969–70 Autobook
Cortina 1500 1967–68	..	..	..	Smith	Ford Cortina 1967–68 Autobook
Cortina 1600 (including Lotus) 1967–68	..	..		Smith	Ford Cortina 1967–68 Autobook
Cortina 1600 1969–70	..	..	..	Ball	Ford Cortina 1969–70 Autobook
Cortina 1600 OHC Mk 3, GT 1971–72	..			Ball	Ford Cortina 1600 GT, 2000, OHC, Mk 3 1971–72 Autobook
Cortina 2000 OHC HC Mk 3 1971–72		..		Ball	Ford Cortina 1600 GT, 2000, OHC, Mk 3 1971–72 Autobook
Escort 100E 1955–59	..	..	..	Ball	Ford Anglia Prefect 100E Autobook
Escort 1100 1967–71	..	..	..	Ball	Ford Escort 1967–71 Autobook
Escort 1300 1967–71	..	..	..	Ball	Ford Escort 1967–71 Autobook
Executive 1966–71	..	..	..	Ball	Ford Zephyr V4, V6, Zodiac 1966–71 Autobook
Prefect 100E 1954–59	..	..	..	Ball	Ford Anglia Prefect 100E Autobook
Prefect 107E 1959–61	..	..	..	Smith	Ford Anglia 105E, Prefect 107E 1959–67 Autobook
Popular 100E 1959–62	..	..	..	Ball	Ford Anglia Prefect 100E Autobook
Squire 100E 1955–59	..	..	..	Ball	Ford Anglia Prefect 100E Autobook
Taunus 1300 OHC LC and HC 1971–72	..			Ball	Ford Cortina 1600 GT, 2000, OHC, Mk 3, 1971–72 Autobook
Taunus 1600 OHC GT 1971–72	..			Ball	Ford Cortina 1600 GT, 2000, OHC, Mk 3 1971–72 Autobook
Zephyr Mk 1 1950–56	..	..	..	Ball	Ford Consul, Zephyr, Zodiac 1, 2 1950–62 Autobook
Zephyr Mk 2 1956–62	..	..	..	Ball	Ford Consul, Zephyr, Zodiac 1, 2 1950–62 Autobook
Zephyr 4 Mk 3 1962–66	..	..	..	Ball	Ford Zephyr, Zodiac Mk 3 1962–66 Autobook
Zephyr 6 Mk 3 1962–66	..	..	..	Ball	Ford Zephyr, Zodiac Mk 3 1962–66 Autobook
Zodiac Mk 3 1962–66	..	..	..	Ball	Ford Zephyr, Zodiac Mk 3 1962–66 Autobook
Zodiac Mk 1 1953–56	..	..	..	Ball	Ford Consul, Zephyr, Zodiac 1, 2 1950–62 Autobook
Zodiac Mk 2 1956–62	..	..	..	Ball	Ford Consul, Zephyr, Zodiac 1, 2 1950–62 Autobook
Zephyr V4 2 litre 1966–71	..	..	..	Ball	Ford Zephyr V4, V6, Zodiac 1966–71 Autobook
Zephyr V6 2.5 litre 1966–71	..	..	..	Ball	Ford Zephyr V4, V6, Zodiac 1966–71 Autobook
Zodiac V6 3 litre 1966–71	..	..	..	Ball	Ford Zephyr V4, V6, Zodiac 1966–71 Autobook

HILLMAN

Make				Author	Title
Avenger, 1970–71	..	..	..	Ball	Hillman Avenger 1970–71 Autobook
Avenger, GT 1970–71	..			Ball	Hillman Avenger 1970–71 Autobook
Hunter, GT 1966–71	..	..	..	Ball	Hillman Hunter 1966–71 Autobook
Minx series 1, 2, 3 1956–59	..			Ball	Hillman Minx 1 to 5 1956–65 Autobook
Minx series 3A, 3B, 3C 1959–63		..		Ball	Hillman Minx 1 to 5 1956–65 Autobook
Minx series 5 1963–65	..	..		Ball	Hillman Minx 1 to 5 1956–65 Autobook
Minx series 6 1965–67	..	..		Ball	Hillman Minx 1965–67 Autobook
New Minx 1500, 1725 1966–70	..		..	Ball	Hillman Minx 1966–70 Autobook
Imp 1963–68	..	..	..	Smith	Hillman Imp 1963–68 Autobook
Imp 1969–71	..	..	..	Ball	Hillman Imp 1969–71 Autobook

Make				Author	Title
Husky series 1, 2, 3 1958–65	..	..	..	Ball	Hillman Minx 1 to 5 1956–65 Autobook
Husky Estate 1969–71	..	..	..	Ball	Hillman Imp 1969–71 Autobook
Super Minx Mk 1, 2, 3 1961–65	..	..	..	Ball	Hillman Super Minx 1961–65 Autobook
Super Minx Mk 4 1965–67	..	..	..	Ball	Hillman Minx 1965–67 Autobook

HUMBER

Sceptre Mk 1 1963–65				Ball	Hillman Super Minx 1961–65 Autobook
Sceptre Mk 2 1965–67				Ball	Hillman Minx 1965–67 Autobook
Sceptre 1967–71	..	..	..	Ball	Hillman Hunter 1966–71 Autobook

JAGUAR

XK 120 1948–54	..	..	..	Ball	Jaguar XK 120, 140, 150 Mk 7, 8, 9 1948–61 Autobook
XK 140 1954–57	..	..	..	Ball	Jaguar XK 120, 140, 150 Mk 7, 8, 9 1948–61 Autobook
XK 150 1957–61	..	..	..	Ball	Jaguar XK 120, 140, 150 Mk 7, 8, 9 1948–61 Autobook
XK 150S 1959–61	..	..	..	Ball	Jaguar XK 120, 140, 150 Mk 7, 8, 9 1948–61 Autobook
Mk 7, 7M, 8, 9 1950–61	..	..	..	Ball	Jaguar XK 120, 140, 150 Mk 7, 8, 9 1948–61 Autobook
2.4 Mk 1, 2 1955–67	..	..	..	Ball	Jaguar 2.4, 3.4, 3.8 Mk 1, 2 1955–69 Autobook
3.4 Mk 1, 2 1957–67	..	..	..	Ball	Jaguar 2.4, 3.4, 3.8 Mk 1, 2 1955–69 Autobook
3.8 Mk 2 1959–67	..	..	..	Ball	Jaguar 2.4, 3.4, 3.8 Mk 1, 2 1955–69 Autobook
240 1967–69	..	..	..	Ball	Jaguar 2.4, 3.4, 3.8 Mk 1, 2 1955–69 Autobook
340 1967–69	..	..	..	Ball	Jaguar 2.4, 3.4, 3.8 Mk 1, 2 1955–69 Autobook
E Type 3.8 1961–65	..	..	..	Ball	Jaguar E Type 1961–70 Autobook
E Type 4.2 1964–69	..	..	..	Ball	Jaguar E Type 1961–70 Autobook
E Type 4.2 2+2 1966–70	..	..	..	Ball	Jaguar E Type 1961–70 Autobook
E Type 4.2 Series 2 1969–70	..	..	..	Ball	Jaguar E Type 1961–70 Autobook
S Type 3.4 1963–68	..	..	..	Ball	Jaguar S Type and 420 1963–68 Autobook
S Type 3.8 1963–68	..	..	..	Ball	Jaguar S Type and 420 1963–68 Autobook
420 1963–68	..	..	..	Ball	Jaguar S Type and 420 1963–68 Autobook
XJ6 2.8 litre 1968–72	..			Ball	Jaguar XJ6 1968–72 Autobook
XJ6 4.2 litre 1968–72	..			Ball	Jaguar XJ6 1968–72 Autobook

JOWETT

Javelin PA 1947–49	..	..	..	Mitchell	Jowett Javelin Jupiter 1947–53 Autobook
Javelin PB 1949–50	..	..	..	Mitchell	Jowett Javelin Jupiter 1947–53 Autobook
Javelin PC 1950–51	..	..	..	Mitchell	Jowett Javelin Jupiter 1947–53 Autobook
Javelin PD 1951–52	..	..	..	Mitchell	Jowett Javelin Jupiter 1947–53 Autobook
Javelin PE 1952–53	..	..	..	Mitchell	Jowett Javelin Jupiter 1947–53 Autobook
Jupiter Mk 1 SA 1949–52	..	..	..	Mitchell	Jowett Javelin Jupiter 1947–53 Autobook
Jupiter Mk 1A SC 1952–53	..	..	..	Mitchell	Jowett Javelin Jupiter 1947–53 Autobook

LANDROVER

Series 1 1948–58	..	..	..	Ball	Landrover 1, 2 1948–61 Autobook
Series 2 1997cc 1959–61	..	..	..	Ball	Landrover 1, 2 1948–61 Autobook
Series 2 2052cc 1959–61	..	..	..	Ball	Landrover 1, 2 1948–61 Autobook
Series 2 2286cc 1959–61	..	..	..	Ball	Landrover 2, 2A 1959–71 Autobook
Series 2A 2286cc 1961–71	..	..	..	Ball	Landrover 2, 2A 1959–71 Autobook
Series 2A 2625cc 1967–71	..	..	..	Ball	Landrover 2, 2A 1959–71 Autobook

MG

TA 1936–39	..	..	..	..	Ball	MG TA to TF 1936–55 Autobook
TB 1939	..	..	..	..	Ball	MG TA to TF 1936–55 Autobook
TC 1945–49	..	..	..	..	Ball	MG TA to TF 1936–55 Autobook
TD 1950–53	..	..	..	..	Ball	MG TA to TF 1936–55 Autobook
TF 1953–54	..	..	..	..	Ball	MG TA to TF 1936–55 Autobook
TF 1500 1954–55	..	..	..	..	Ball	MG TA to TF 1936–55 Autobook
Midget 1961–71	..	..	..	..	Ball	Sprite, Midget 1958–71 Autobook
Magnette ZA, ZB 1955–59	..	..	..	..	Ball	BMC Autobook Three
MGA 1500, 1600 1955–62	..	..	..	..	Ball	MGA, MGB 1955–68 Autobook
MGA Twin Cam 1958–60	..	..	..	..	Ball	MGA, MGB 1955–68 Autobook

Make					Author	Title
MGB 1962–68	..	..	..	..	Ball	MGA, MGB 1955–68 Autobook
MGB 1969–71	..	..	..	..	Ball	MG MGB 1969–71 Autobook
1100 Mk 1 1962–67	..	..	..	..	Ball	1100 Mk 1 1962–67 Autobook
1100 Mk 2 1968	..	..	..	..	Ball	1100 Mk 2, 1300 Mk 1, 2, America 1968–71 Autobook
1300 Mk 1, 2 1968–71	..	..	..	..	Ball	1100 Mk 2, 1300 Mk 1, 2, America 1968–71 Autobook

MERCEDES-BENZ

190B 1959–61	..	..	..	..	Ball	Mercedes-Benz 190 B, C, 200 1959–68 Autobook
190C 1961–65	..	..	..	..	Ball	Mercedes-Benz 190 B, C, 200 1959–68 Autobook
200 1965–68	..	..	..	..	Ball	Mercedes-Benz 190 B, C, 200 1959–68 Autobook
220B 1959–65	..	..	..	..	Ball	Mercedes-Benz 220 1959–65 Autobook
220SB 1959–65	..	..	..	..	Ball	Mercedes-Benz 220 1959–65 Autobook
220SEB 1959–65	..	..	..	..	Ball	Mercedes-Benz 220 1959–65 Autobook
220SEBC 1961–65	..	..	..	..	Ball	Mercedes-Benz 220 1959–65 Autobook
230 1965–67	..	..	..	..	Ball	Mercedes-Benz 230 1963–68 Autobook
230 S 1965–68	..	..	..	..	Ball	Mercedes-Benz 230 1963–68 Autobook
230 SL 1963–67	..	..	..	..	Ball	Mercedes-Benz 230 1963–68 Autobook
250 S 1965–68	..	..	..	..	Ball	Mercedes-Benz 250 1965–67 Autobook
250 SE 1965–67	..	..	..	..	Ball	Mercedes-Benz 250 1965–67 Autobook
250 SE BC 1965–67	..	..	..	..	Ball	Mercedes-Benz 250 1965–67 Autobook
250 SL 1967	..	..	..	..	Ball	Mercedes-Benz 250 1965–67 Autobook

MORGAN

Four wheelers 1936–69	..	..	..	Clarke	Morgan 1936–69 Autobook	

MORRIS

Oxford 2. 3 1954–59	..	..	..	..	Ball	BMC Autobook Three
Oxford 5, 6 1959–70	..	..	..	..	Ball	Morris Oxford 5, 6 1959–70 Autobook
Marina 1.3, 1.3 TC 1971–72	..	..	..		Ball	Morris Marina 1971–72 Autobook
Marina 1.8, 1.8 TC 1971–72	..	..	..		Ball	Morris Marina 1971–72 Autobook
Minor series 2 1952–56	..	..	..		Ball	Morris Minor 1952–71 Autobook
Minor 1000 1957–71	..	..	..		Ball	Morris Minor 1952–71 Autobook
Mini 1959–71	..	..	..	..	Ball	Mini 1959–71 Autobook
Mini Clubman 1969–71	..	..	..		Ball	Mini 1959–71 Autobook
Minor series 2 1952–56	..	..	..		Ball	Morris Minor 1952–71 Autobook
Minor 1000 1957–71	..	..	..		Ball	Morris Minor 1952–71 Autobook
Mini Cooper 1961–70	..	..	..	..	Ball	Mini Cooper 1961–70 Autobook
Mini Cooper S 1963–70	..	..	..		Ball	Mini Cooper 1961–70 Autobook
1100 Mk 1 1962–67	..	..	..		Ball	1100 Mk 1 1962–67 Autobook
1100 Mk 2 1968–70	..	..	..		Ball	1100 Mk 2, 1300 Mk 1, 2, America 1968–71 Autobook
1300 Mk 1, 2 1968–71	..	..	..		Ball	1100 Mk 2, 1300 Mk 1, 2, America 1968–71 Autobook
1800 Mk 1, 2 1966–71	..	..	..		Ball	1800 1964–71 Autobook
1800 S 1968–71	..	..	..	..	Ball	1800 1964–71 Autobook

NSU

Prinz 1000 L, LS 1963–67	..	..	..	Ball	NSU 1000 1963–70 Autobook	
Prinz TT, TTS 1965–70	..	..	..	Ball	NSU 1000 1963–70 Autobook	
1000 C 1967–70	..	..	..	Ball	NSU 1000 1963–70 Autobook	
TYP 110 1966–67	..	..	..	Ball	NSU 1000 1963–70 Autobook	
110 SC 1967	..	..	..	Ball	NSU 1000 1963–70 Autobook	
1200, C, TT 1967–70	..	..	..	Ball	NSU 1000 1963–70 Autobook	

OPEL

Kadett 993 cc 1962–65	..	..	Ball	Opel Kadett, Olympia 993 cc and 1078 cc 1962–71 Autobook	
Kadett 1078 cc 1965–71	..	..	Ball	Opel Kadett, Olympia 993 cc and 1078 cc 1962–71 Autobook	
Kadett 1492 cc 1967–71	..	..	Ball	Opel Kadett, Olympia 1492 cc, 1698 cc and 1897 cc 1967–71 Autobook	
Kadett 1698 cc 1967–70	..	..	Ball	Opel Kadett, Olympia 1492 cc, 1698 cc and 1897 cc 1967–71 Autobook	

Make	Author	Title
Kadett 1897cc 1967–71	Ball	Opel Kadett, Olympia 1492cc, 1698cc and 1897cc 1967–71 Autobook
Olympia 1078cc 1967–70	Ball	Opel Kadett, Olympia 993cc and 1078cc 1962–71 Autobook
Olympia 1492cc 1967–70	Ball	Opel Kadett, Olympia 1492cc, 1698cc and 1897cc 1967–71 Autobook
Olympia 1698cc 1967–70	Ball	Opel Kadett, Olympia 1492cc, 1698cc and 1897cc 1967–71 Autobook
Olympia 1897cc 1967–70	Ball	Opel Kadett, Olympia 1492cc, 1698cc and 1897cc 1967–71 Autobook
Rekord C 1.5, 1.7, 1.9 1966–70	Ball	Opel Rekord C 1966–70 Autobook

PEUGEOT

Make	Author	Title
404 1960–69	Ball	Peugeot 404 1960–69 Autobook
504 1968–70 (incl. fuel injection)	Ball	Peugeot 504 1968–70 Autobook

PLYMOUTH

Make	Author	Title
Cricket 1971	Ball	Hillman Avenger 1970–71 Autobook

PORSCHE

Make	Author	Title
356A 1957–59	Ball	Porsche 356A, 356B, 356C 1957–65 Autobook
356B 1959–63	Ball	Porsche 356A, 356B, 356C 1957–65 Autobook
356C 1963–65	Ball	Porsche 356A, 356B, 356C 1957–65 Autobook
911 1964–67	Ball	Porsche 911 1964–69 Autobook
911L 1967–68	Ball	Porsche 911 1964–69 Autobook
911S 1966–69	Ball	Porsche 911 1964–69 Autobook
911T 1967–69	Ball	Porsche 911 1964–69 Autobook
911E 1968–69	Ball	Porsche 911 1964–69 Autobook
912 1582cc 1965–69	Ball	Porsche 912 1965–69 Autobook

RELIANT

Make	Author	Title
Regal Coupé 1952–56	Ball	Reliant Regal 1952–70 Autobook
Regal Mk 3, 4, 5, 6 1957–62	Ball	Reliant Regal 1952–70 Autobook
Regal 3/25 1962–68	Ball	Reliant Regal 1952–70 Autobook
Regal 3/30 1968–70	Ball	Reliant Regal 1952–70 Autobook
5 cwt, Super, Supervan 1956–70	Ball	Reliant Regal 1952–70 Autobook

RENAULT

Make	Author	Title
R4L 748cc, 845cc 1961–65	Ball	Renault R4, R4L, 4 1961–70 Autobook
R4 845cc 1962–66	Ball	Renault R4, R4L, 4 1961–70 Autobook
4 845cc 1966–70	Ball	Renault R4, R4L, 4 1961–70 Autobook
6 1968–70	Ball	Renault 6 1968–70 Autobook
R8 956cc 1962–65	Ball	Renault 8, 10, 1100 1962–70 Autobook
8 956cc, 1108cc 1965–70	Ball	Renault 8, 10, 1100 1962–70 Autobook
8S 1108cc, 1968–70	Ball	Renault 8, 10, 1100 1962–70 Autobook
1100 1108cc 1964–69	Ball	Renault 8, 10, 1100 1962–70 Autobook
R10 1108cc 1967–69	Ball	Renault 8, 10, 1100 1962–70 Autobook
10 1289cc 1969–70	Ball	Renault 8, 10, 1100 1962–70 Autobook
Dauphine (R1090) 1957–64	Ball	Renault Dauphine Floride 1957–67 Autobook
Gordini Models (R1091 and R1095) 1959–67	Ball	Renault Dauphine Floride 1957–67 Autobook
Floride (R1092) 1959–63	Ball	Renault Dauphine Floride 1957–67 Autobook
16 1470cc 1965–71	Ball	Renault R16 1965–71 Autobook
16TS 1968–71	Ball	Renault R16 1965–71 Autobook
16TL 1970–71	Ball	Renault R16 1965–71 Autobook
12L 1969–71	Ball	Renault 12 1969–71 Autobook
12TL 1969–71	Ball	Renault 12 1969–71 Autobook

Make					Author	Title

RILEY

Make					Author	Title
1.5 1957–65	..	..	..	..	Ball	BMC Autobook Three
Elf Mk 1, 2, 3 1961–69		..	..	..	Ball	Mini 1959–71 Autobook
1100 Mk 1 1965–67	..	..	..	..	Ball	1100 Mk 1 1962–67 Autobook
1100 Mk 2 1968	..		..	..	Ball	1100 Mk 2, 1300 Mk 1, 2 America 1968–71 Autobook
1300 Mk 1, 2 1968–69	..		..	..	Ball	1100 Mk 2, 1300 Mk 1, 2 America 1968–71 Autobook

ROVER

Make					Author	Title
60 1953–59	..	..	..	..	Ball	Rover 60–110 1953–64 Autobook
75 1954–59	..	..	..	..	Ball	Rover 60–110 1953–64 Autobook
80 1959–62	..	..	..	..	Ball	Rover 60–110 1953–64 Autobook
90 1954–59	..	..	..	..	Ball	Rover 60–110 1953–64 Autobook
95 1962–64	..	..	..	..	Ball	Rover 60–110 1953–64 Autobook
100 1959–62	..	..	..	..	Ball	Rover 60–110 1953–64 Autobook
105R 1957–58	..	..	..	..	Ball	Rover 60–110 1953–64 Autobook
105S 1957–59	..	..	..	..	Ball	Rover 60–110 1953–64 Autobook
110 1962–64	..	..	..	..	Ball	Rover 60–110 1953–64 Autobook
2000 SC 1963–71	..	..	..	..	Ball	Rover 2000 1963–71 Autobook
2000 TC 1963–71	..	..	..	..	Ball	Rover 2000 1963–71 Autobook
3 litre Saloon Mk 1, 1A 1958–62		..	..	..	Ball	Rover 3 litre 1958–67 Autobook
3 litre Saloon Mk 2, 3 1962–67		..	..	..	Ball	Rover 3 litre 1958–67 Autobook
3 litre Coupé 1965–67		..	..	..	Ball	Rover 3 litre 1958–67 Autobook
3500, 3500S 1968–70		..	..	..	Ball	Rover 3500, 3500S 1968–70 Autobook

SAAB

Make					Author	Title
95, 96 1960–64	..	..	..	..	Ball	Saab 95, 96 Sport 1960–68 Autobook
95(5), 96(5) 1964–68		..	..	..	Ball	Saab 95, 96 Sport 1960–68 Autobook
Sport 1962–66	..	..	..	..	Ball	Saab 95, 96 Sport 1960–68 Autobook
Monte Carlo 1965–66	..	..	..	..	Ball	Saab 95, 96 Sport 1960–68 Autobook
99 1969–70	..	..	..	..	Ball	Saab 99 1969–70 Autobook

SIMCA

Make					Author	Title
1000 1961–65	..	..	..	..	Ball	Simca 1000 1961–71 Autobook
1000 Special 1962–63		..	..	..	Ball	Simca 1000 1961–71 Autobook
1000 GL 1964–71	..	..	..	..	Ball	Simca 1000 1961–71 Autobook
1000 GLS 1964–69	..	..	..	..	Ball	Simca 1000 1961–71 Autobook
1000 GLA 1965–69	..	..	..	..	Ball	Simca 1000 1961–71 Autobook
1000 LS 1965–71	..	..	..	..	Ball	Simca 1000 1961–71 Autobook
1000 L 1966–68	..	..	..	..	Ball	Simca 1000 1961–71 Autobook
1000 Special 1968–71		..	..	..	Ball	Simca 1000 1961–71 Autobook
1100 LS 1967–70	..	..	..	..	Ball	Simca 1100 1967–70 Autobook
1100 GL, GLS 1967–70		..	..	..	Ball	Simca 1100 1967–70 Autobook
1204 1970	..	..	..	..	Ball	Simca 1100 1967–70 Autobook
1300 GL 1963–65	..	..	..	..	Ball	Simca 1300, 1301, 1500, 1501 1963–71 Autobook
1300 LS 1965–66	..	..	..	..	Ball	Simca 1300, 1301, 1500, 1501 1963–71 Autobook
1301 GL 1966–71	..	..	..	..	Ball	Simca 1300, 1301, 1500, 1501 1963–71 Autobook
1301 LS 1966–68	..	..	..	..	Ball	Simca 1300, 1301, 1500, 1501 1963–71 Autobook
1500 L 1963–65	..	..	..	..	Ball	Simca 1300, 1301, 1500, 1501 1963–71 Autobook
1500 GL 1965–66	..	..	..	..	Ball	Simca 1300, 1301, 1500, 1501 1963–71 Autobook
1500 GLS 1965–66	..	..	..	..	Ball	Simca 1300, 1301, 1500, 1501 1963–71 Autobook
1501 GL 1966–70	..	..	..	..	Ball	Simca 1300, 1301, 1500, 1501 1963–71 Autobook
1501 GLS 1966–68	..	..	..	..	Ball	Simca 1300, 1301, 1500, 1501 1963–71 Autobook
1501 GLS 1970–71	..	..	..	..	Ball	Simca 1300, 1301, 1500, 1501 1963–71 Autobook
1501 Special 1968–71		..	..	..	Ball	Simca 1300, 1301, 1500, 1501 1963–71 Autobook

SINGER

Make					Author	Title
Chamois 1964–68	..	..	..	..	Smith	Hillman Imp 1963–68 Autobook
Chamois 1969–70	..	..	..	..	Ball	Hillman Imp 1969–71 Autobook
Chamois Sport 1964–68	..	..	..	..	Smith	Hillman Imp 1963–68 Autobook
Chamois Sport 1969–70	..	..	..	..	Ball	Hillman Imp 1969–71 Autobook
Gazelle series 2A 1958	..	..	..	..	Ball	Hillman Minx 1 to 5 1956–65 Autobook
Gazelle 3, 3A, 3B, 3C 1958–63		..	..	..	Ball	Hillman Minx 1 to 5 1956–65 Autobook

Make					Author	Title
Gazelle series 5 1963–65	..	..	..		Ball	Hillman Minx 1 to 5 1956–65 Autobook
Gazelle series 6 1965–67	..	..	..		Ball	Hillman Minx 1965–67 Autobook
New Gazelle 1500, 1725 1966–70	..	..			Ball	Hillman Minx 1966–70 Autobook
Vogue Mk 1 to 3 1961–65	..	..	..		Ball	Hillman Super Minx 1961–65 Autobook
Vogue series 4 1965–67	..	..	..		Ball	Hillman Minx 1965–67 Autobook
New Vogue 1966–70	..	..	..		Ball	Hillman Hunter 1966–71 Autobook

SKODA

440, 445, 450 1957–69	..	..	..		Skoda	Skoda Autobook One

SUNBEAM

Alpine series 1, 2, 3, 4 1959–65	..	..			Ball	Sunbeam Rapie Alpine 1955–65 Autobook
Alpine series 5 1965–67	..	..	..		Ball	Hillman Minx 1965–67 Autobook
Alpine 1969–71	..	..	..		Ball	Hillman Hunter 1966–71 Autobook
Arrow 1969–71	..	..	..		Ball	Hillman Hunter 1966–71 Autobook
Rapier series 1, 2, 3, 3A, 4 1955–65	..	..			Ball	Sunbeam Rapier Alpine 1955–65 Autobook
Rapier series 5 1965–67	..	..			Ball	Hillman Minx 1965–67 Autobook
Rapier H.120 1967–71	..	..			Ball	Hillman Hunter 1966–71 Autobook
Imp Sport 1963–68	..	..	..		Smith	Hillman Imp 1963–68 Autobook
Imp Sport 1969–71	..	..	..		Ball	Hillman Imp 1969–71 Autobook
Stilletto 1967–68	..	..	..		Smith	Hillman Imp 1963–68 Autobook
Stilletto 1969–71	..	..	..		Ball	Hillman Imp 1969–71 Autobook
1250 1970–71	..	..	..		Ball	Hillman Avenger 1970–71 Autobook
1500 1970–71	..	..	..		Ball	Hillman Avenger 1970–71 Autobook

TOYOTA

Corolla 1100 1967–70	..	..	..		Ball	Toyota Corolla 1100 1967–70 Autobook
Corolla 1100 De luxe 1967–70	..	..			Ball	Toyota Corolla 1100 1967–70 Autobook
Corolla 1100 Automatic 1968–69	..	..			Ball	Toyota Corolla 1100 1967–70 Autobook
Corona 1500 Mk 1 1965–70	..	..			Ball	Toyota Corolla 1500 Mk 1 1965–70 Autobook
Corona 1900 Mk 2 1969–71	..	..			Ball	Toyota Corona 1900 Mk 2 1969–71 Autobook

TRIUMPH

TR2 1952–55	..	..	..	..	Ball	Triumph TR2, TR3, TR3A 1952–62 Autobook
TR3, TR3A 1955–62	..	..	..		Ball	Triumph TR2, TR3, TR3A 1952–62 Autobook
TR4, TR4A 1961–67	..	..	..		Ball	Triumph TR4, TR4A 1961–67 Autobook
TR5 1967–69	..	..	..		Ball	Triumph TR5, TR250, TR6 1967–70 Autobook
TR6 1969–70	..	..	..		Ball	Triumph TR5, TR250, TR6 1967–70 Autobook
TR250 1967–69	..	..	..		Ball	Triumph TR5, TR250, TR6 1967–70 Autobook
1300 1965–71	..	..	..		Ball	Triumph 1300, 1500 1965–71 Autobook
1300TC 1967–71	..	..	..		Ball	Triumph 1300, 1500 1965–71 Autobook
1500 1970–71	..	..	..		Ball	Triumph 1300, 1500 1965–71 Autobook
2000 Mk 1 1963–69	..	..	..		Ball	Triumph 2000 Mk 1, 2.5 Pl Mk 1 1963–69 Autobook
2000 Mk 2 1969–71	..	..	..		Ball	Triumph 2000 Mk 2, 2.5 Pl Mk 2 1969–71 Autobook
2.5 Pl Mk 1 1963–69	..	..	..		Ball	Triumph 2000 Mk 1, 2.5 Pl Mk 1 1963–69 Autobook
2.5 Pl Mk 2 1969–71	..	..	..		Ball	Triumph 2000 Mk 2, 2.5 Pl Mk 2 1969–71 Autobook
Herald 948 1959–64	..	..	..		Smith	Triumph Herald 1959–68 Autobook
Herald 1200 1961–68	..	..	..		Smith	Triumph Herald 1959–68 Autobook
Herald 1200 1969–70	..	..	..		Ball	Triumph Herald 1969–71 Autobook
Herald 12/50 1963–67	..	..	..		Smith	Triumph Herald 1959–68 Autobook
Herald 13/60 1967–68	..	..	..		Smith	Triumph Herald 1959–68 Autobook
Herald 13/60 1969–71	..	..	..		Ball	Triumph Herald 1969–71 Autobook
Spitfire 1962–68	..	..	..		Smith	Triumph Spitfire Vitesse 1962–68 Autobook
Spitfire Mk 3 1969–70	..	..	..		Ball	Triumph Spitfire Mk 3 1969–70 Autobook
Vitesse 1600 and 2 litre 1962–68	..	..			Smith	Triumph Spitfire Vitesse 1962–68 Autobook
Vitesse 2 litre 1969–70	..	..	..		Ball	Triumph GT6, Vitesse 2 litre 1969–70 Autobook
GT Six 2 litre 1966–68	..	..	..		Smith	Triumph Spitfire Vitesse 1962–68 Autobook
GT Six 1969–70	..	..	..		Ball	Triumph GT6, Vitesse 2 litre 1969–70 Autobook

Make					Author	Title

VANDEN PLAS

3 litre 1959–64	..	..	..	..	Ball	Austin A99, A110 1959–68 Autobook
1100 Mk 1 1963–67	..	..	..	..	Ball	1100 Mk 1 1962–67 Autobook
1100 Mk 2 1968	..	..	..	..	Ball	1100 Mk 2, 1300 Mk 1, 2 America 1968–71 Autobook
1300 Mk 1, 2 1968–71		..	..	..	Ball	1100 Mk 2, 1300 Mk 1, 2 America 1968–71 Autobook

VAUXHALL

Victor 1 1957–59	..	..	..	..	Ball	Vauxhall Victor 1, 2 FB 1957–64 Autobook
Victor 2 1959–61	..	..	..	..	Ball	Vauxhall Victor 1, 2 FB 1957–64 Autobook
Victor FB 1961–64	..	..	..	..	Ball	Vauxhall Victor 1, 2 FB 1957–64 Autobook
VX4/90 FBH 1961–64		..	..	..	Ball	Vauxhall Victor 1, 2 FB 1957–64 Autobook
Victor FC 101 1964–67		..	..	..	Ball	Vauxhall Victor 101 1964–67 Autobook
VX 4/90 FCH 1964–67		..	..	..	Ball	Vauxhall Victor 101 1964–67 Autobook
Victor FD 1599 cc 1967–71		..	..	..	Ball	Vauxhall Victor FD 1600, 2000 1967–71 Autobook
Victor FD 1975 cc 1967–71		..	..	..	Ball	Vauxhall Victor FD 1600, 2000 1967–71 Autobook
VX 4/90 1969–71	..	..	..	..	Ball	Vauxhall Victor FD 1600, 2000 1967–71 Autobook
Velox, Cresta PA 1957–62	..	..	..	..	Ball	Vauxhall Velox Cresta 1957–70 Autobook
Velox, Cresta PB 1962–65	..	..	..	..	Ball	Vauxhall Velox Cresta 1957–70 Autobook
Cresta PC 1965–70	..	..	..	..	Ball	Vauxhall Velox Cresta 1957–70 Autobook
Viscount 1966–70	..	..	..	..	Ball	Vauxhall Velox Cresta 1957–70 Autobook
Viva HA (including 90) 1964–66		..			Ball	Vauxhall Viva HA 1964–66 Autobook
Viva HB (including 90 and SL90) 1966–70		..			Ball	Vauxhall Viva HB 1966–70 Autobook
Viva HC 1159 cc 1971		..	..	..	Ball	Vauxhall Viva HC, Firenza 1971 Autobook
Viva HC SL 1159 cc 1971		..	..	..	Ball	Vauxhall Viva HC, Firenza 1971 Autobook
Firenza 1159 cc 1971	..	..	..	..	Ball	Vauxhall Viva HC, Firenza 1971 Autobook
Firenza SL 1159 cc 1971		..	..	..	Ball	Vauxhall Viva HC, Firenza 1971 Autobook

VOLKSWAGEN

1200 Beetle 1954–67	..	..	..	..	Ball	Volkswagen Beetle 1954–67 Autobook
1200 Beetle 1968–71	..	..	..	..	Ball	Volkswagen Beetle 1968–71 Autobook
1200 Karmann Ghia 1955–65	..		..	..	Ball	Volkswagen Beetle 1954–67 Autobook
1200 Transporter 1954–64	..		..	..	Ball	Volkswagen Transporter 1954–67 Autobook
1300 Beetle 1965–67	..	..	..	..	Ball	Volkswagen Beetle 1954–67 Autobook
1300 Beetle 1968–71	..	..	..	..	Ball	Volkswagen Beetle 1968–71 Autobook
1300 Karmann Ghia 1965–66	..		..	..	Ball	Volkswagen Beetle 1954–67 Autobook
1500 Beetle 1966–67	..	..	..	..	Ball	Volkswagen Beetle 1954–67 Autobook
1500 Beetle 1968–70	..	..	..	..	Ball	Volkswagen Beetle 1968–71 Autobook
1500 1961–65	..	..	..	..	Ball	Volkswagen 1500 1961–66 Autobook
1500N 1963–65	..	..	..	..	Ball	Volkswagen 1500 1961–66 Autobook
1500S 1963–65	..	..	..	..	Ball	Volkswagen 1500 1961–66 Autobook
1500A 1965–66	..	..	..	..	Ball	Volkswagen 1500 1961–66 Autobook
1500 Karmann Ghia 1966–67	..		..	..	Ball	Volkswagen Beetle 1954–67 Autobook
1500 Transporter 1963–67	..		..	..	Ball	Volkswagen Transporter 1954–67 Autobook
1500 Karmann Ghia 1968–70	..		..	..	Ball	Volkswagen Beetle 1968–71 Autobook
1600 TL 1965–70	..	..	..	..	Ball	Volkswagen 1600 Fastback 1965–70 Autobook
1600 Variant 1965–66	..	..	..	..	Ball	Volkswagen 1600 Fastback 1965–70 Autobook
1600 L 1966–67	..	..	..	..	Ball	Volkswagen 1600 Fastback 1966–70 Autobook
1600 Variant L 1966–70	..	..	..	..	Ball	Volkswagen 1600 Fastback 1965–70 Autobook
1600 T 1968–70	..	..	..	..	Ball	Volkswagen 1600 Fastback 1965–70 Autobook
1600 TA 1969–70	..	..	..	..	Ball	Volkswagen 1600 Fastback 1965–70 Autobook
1600 Variant A, M	..	..	..	..	Ball	Volkswagen 1600 Fastback 1965–70 Autobook
1600 Karmann Ghia	..	..	..	..	Ball	Volkswagen 1600 Fastback 1965–70 Autobook
Delivery Van 1600 1968–71	..		..	..	Ball	Volkswagen Transporter 1968–71 Autobook
Pick-up 1600 1968–71	..	..	..	..	Ball	Volkswagen Transporter 1968–71 Autobook
Kombi 1600 1968–71	..	..	..	..	Ball	Volkswagen Transporter 1968–71 Autobook
Micro-Bus 1600 1968–71	..	..	..	Ball	Volkswagen Transporter 1968–71 Autobook

Make					Author	Title

VOLVO

121, 131, 221 1962–68	..	..	..	Ball	Volvo P120 1961–68 Autobook
122, 132, 222 1961–68	..	..	..	Ball	Volvo P120 1961–68 Autobook
123 GT 1967–68	..	..	..	Ball	Volvo P120 1961–68 Autobook
142, 142S 1967–69	..	..	..	Ball	Volvo 140 1966–70 Autobook
144, 144S 1966–70	..	..	..	Ball	Volvo 140 1966–70 Autobook
145, 145S 1968–70	..	..	..	Ball	Volvo 140 1966–70 Autobook
P 1800 1961–63	..	..	..	Ball	Volvo 1800 1961–71 Autobook
1800S 1963–69	..	..	..	Ball	Volvo 1800 1961–71 Autobook
1800E 1969–71	..	..	..	Ball	Volvo 1800 1961–71 Autobook

WOLSELEY

1500 1959–65	..	..	..	Ball	BMC Autobook Three
15/50 1956–58	..	..	..	Ball	BMC Autobook Three
6/99 1959–61	..	..	..	Ball	Austin A99, A110 1959–68 Autobook
6/110 1961–68	..	..	..	Ball	Austin A99, A110 1959–68 Autobook
Hornet Mk 1, 2, 3 1961–71	..	..	..	Ball	Mini 1959–71 Autobook
1100 Mk 1 1965–67	..	..	..	Ball	1100 Mk 1 1962–67 Autobook
1100 Mk 2 1968	..	..	..	Ball	1100 Mk 2, 1300 Mk 1, 2 America 1968–71 Autobook
1300 Mk 1, 2 1968–71	..	..	..	Ball	1100 Mk 2, 1300 Mk 1, 2 America 1968–71 Autobook
18/85 Mk 1, 2 1967–71	..	..	..	Ball	1800 1964–71 Autobook
18/85 S 1969–71	..	..	..	Ball	1800 1964–71 Autobook